The experts praise *Negotiating Love*

"What a book! If I had read this material years ago my life, not to mention my lover's, would have been much easier, less traumatic, and much more fun. A must read for anyone who wants a relationship handbook."

—John Lee
Author of *The Flying Boy, Facing the Fire,* and *At My Father's Wedding*

"A fabulous book . . . Down-to-earth, accessible, rich in relationships savvy, *Negotiating Love* is a 'must-have' for all men and women with ailing relationships . . . Dr. Jones gives us hope, and better yet a map, for findin[illegible]ough dozens of all-too-familiar relation-
[illegible]hat love is indeed a negotiable item."

[illegible]aphne Rose Kingma
[illegible]thor of *True Love:*
[illegible]w to Make Your Relationship Sweeter, [illegible]eeper, and More Passionate

"Riki Robbins Jones' *Negotiating Love* is warm, loving, and intelligent; more than intelligent—it is wise. It is the most sensible and powerful book on the subject of bringing men and women into intimate partnership I've read. Openly celebrative of heterosexual love, it affirms the uniqueness of each gender and yet shows men and women how they can bridge the gap between their often conflicting needs. *Negotiating Love* is courageous and joyful, and it marks the next stage of male/female negotiating that can result in a win-win scenario for both sexes."

—Douglas Gillette
Author of *King/Warrior/Magician/Lover*
Cofounder, The Institute for World Spirituality

"*Negotiating Love* is for anyone seeking lasting balance and integrity in their relationships."

—Aaron Kipnis, Ph.D., and Elizabeth Herron, M.A.
Authors of *Gender War, Gender Peace: The Quest for Love and Justice Between Women and Men*

"If you want love to last a lifetime, you *must* get this book. It's the perfect gift for every male and female on the planet."

—Jed Diamond
Author of *The Warrior's Journey Home: Healing Men, Healing the Planet*

"*Negotiating Love* is an invaluable and practical guide for resolving and also appreciating the rich differences and gifts found in the art and craft of relationships. This is an outstanding source for both men and women, and all forms of relationships."

—Angeles Arrien, Ph.D., Cultural Anthropologist
Author of *The Four-Fold Way* and *Signs of Life*

"A splendid book . . . [*Negotiating Love*] makes a vital contribution toward ending the battle of the sexes and is rich in practical advice."

—Mel Krantzler, Ph.D.
Author of *The Seven Marriages of Your Marriage*

"Gender wounds cut deeply into the souls of women and men. Dr. Jones' book is groundbreaking . . . born from the fires and tears of her own life experience . . . and offers ingredients of a healing balm to all persons eager to embark on the path of the open heart."

—Forrest Craver, J.D.
Founder, North American Confederation of Men's Councils

"You don't have to be afraid of love anymore. *Negotiating Love* will teach you how to trust yourself and your partner to create the relationship you want."

—Judith Sherven, Ph.D., and James Sniechowski, Ph.D.
Cofounders, The Magic of Differences

"Every relationship faces conflict, so every relationship will benefit from *Negotiating Love.* The book is straightforward, moving, honest, and practical. To couples who are troubled, it gives hope. To couples in the prime of their love it gives confirmation."

—Michael Gurian
Author of *Mothers, Sons and Lovers* and *The Prince and the King*

"If you have good intentions but can't get past your differences, *Negotiating Love* is just what the doctor ordered. *Negotiating Love* shows both men and women the gentle art of negotiating differences for their mutual benefit. What a system: Everyone's a winner."

—Norman S. Goldner, Ph.D., and Carol L. Rhodes, Ph.D.
Authors of *Why Women and Men Don't Get Along*

"Having moved from disempowerment to re-empowerment in her own life, Riki Robbins Jones knows other men and women can do it too. Astutely she points out the destructive habits of both genders, and with compassion, encouragement, and direction shows ways all of us may gain love and power through more conscious everyday relationships."

—Tom Daly, Ph.D., and Jude Blitz
Codirectors, The Living Arts Foundation

"Valuable . . . Accessible . . . One of the most thoughtful and practical books on building/re-building loving relationships that I have ever read. *Negotiating Love* clearly identifies the common areas where couples struggle to be good lovers, and then teaches skills to help couples succeed. An empowering book which can serve as a road map for couples as they journey toward being both better lovers and more powerful and confident individuals."

—Bill Nordling, Ph.D.
Executive Director,
The National Institute of Relationship Enhancement

"Compromise is one of those platitudes everyone endorses—and few people do graciously or often. But it is at the heart of all long-term relationships and a great key to relationship survival as well as to individual feelings of well-being and equity. *Negotiating Love* is a pragmatic, compassionate and intelligent guide to the art of give and take. It helps men and women understand their feelings and how to find an answer that strengthens the relationship as well as supports individual goals."

—Pepper Schwartz
Author of *Peer Marriage:*
How Love Between Equals Really Works

Negotiating Love

HOW WOMEN AND MEN CAN RESOLVE THEIR DIFFERENCES

Riki Robbins Jones, Ph.D.

Ballantine Books • New York

 Published in the United States by Ballantine Books, a division of Random House, Inc., New York, and simultaneously in Canada by Random House of Canada Limited, Toronto.

Library of Congress Catalog Card Number: 94-94564

ISBN: 0-345-39061-X

Text design by Holly Johnson
Cover design by Kristine Mills
Cover photos by George Kerrigan

Manufactured in the United States of America

First Edition: April 1995

10 9 8 7 6 5 4 3 2 1

This Book Is Dedicated to
My Three Sons:
John, who fills my life with joy and inspiration;
Mark, of whom I am very proud;
and
Bill, whose spirit is with me always.

Contents

Acknowledgments

This book could not have been written without the help of my "angels":

Phil, my beloved husband and the "birthfather" of the book, who read every word of the first draft, made countless invaluable suggestions, and kept me supplied with carrot juice and "roll-up" sandwiches so I had the energy to keep going;

Susan Crawford, not only my literary agent but also my guiding light, who steered me in the right direction by insisting, "Give people a *solution*, Riki";

Joëlle Delbourgo, my editor-in-chief, who had the vision and the courage to champion this book;

Elizabeth Zack, my editor, whose excellent taste and sensitivity radiate from every page;

Susan Jeffers, Ph.D., a charismatic woman ahead of her time, whose breakthrough book *Opening Our Hearts to Men* inspired me to begin this one;

Warren Farrell, Ph.D., my good friend and mentor, who

has trusted his inner voice, courageously stood up for his beliefs, and taught me to follow his example;

Jim Sniechowski, Ph.D., and Judith Sherven, Ph.D., my talented colleagues, who have convinced me that domestic violence will end when couples learn how to resolve their differences peacefully;

Irwin Zucker, my fabulous publicist, who jump-started my writing career;

Helen Schucman, M.D., and William Thetford, M.D., the coauthors of *A Course in Miracles*, which provided the spiritual foundation for my research;

Forrest Craver, a brilliant and dedicated social activist, who opened his heart and his phone book to me because he believed in this project;

Christopher Harding, Ph.D., editor of *Wingspan*, who, although we had never met, offered me his network of contacts without hesitation;

Robert Bly, poet, prophet, and men's movement leader, who enabled me to understand the difference between women's and men's wounds;

Donald Greenstein, Esq., mediator and dispute resolution expert, who shared both his thorough knowledge of the mediation process and his boundless enthusiasm for my work;

Jim Bridy, my loyal researcher, who not only kept me up-to-date on current developments in the relationships field but also spent countless hours with me discussing them;

Chris Ketcham, M.Ed., my editorial assistant, whose consummate rewriting skills and unflagging support during the eleventh hour enabled me to bring the book to completion;

my "spirit sisters," Daphne Rose Kingma, Christina Hoopas, Susan Craver, Rhona Hume Konnelly, and Renée DeVigne, who nurtured me as I wrote each chapter;

my chiropractor, Dr. David C. Lewis, who showed me how to protect my body while I worked long hours at the computer;

my longtime confidant, Rona Mendelsohn, and my mother-in-law, Jean Jones, who were always there for me when I needed them;

my patient readers, Corinne Alfeld, Brien Benson, Frank DuVal, Jo Johnson, Larry Lima, Judy MacLeod, Bracken Polk, and Douglas Weinfield, who offered their helpful suggestions and comments;

the experts I interviewed who freely and generously shared their wisdom, their insights, and often their personal experiences: Angeles Arrien, Ph.D.; Asa Baber; Martha Baldwin, M.S.S.W.; Onaje Benjamin; Brad Blanton, Ph.D.; Shepherd Bliss, D. Min.; Robert Bly; Ivan Burnell, Ph.D.; Neil Chethik; Gordon Clay; Forrest Craver; Tom Daly, Ph.D.; Lawrence Diggs; David Ebaugh, M.A., C.P.C.; Warren Farrell, Ph.D.; Alice Forrester; Irene Gad, Ph.D.; Mark Gerzon; Douglas Gilmore; Donald Greenstein, Esq.; John Guarnaschelli, Ph.D.; Michael Gurian; Fredric Hayward; Daniel Henderson, M.Div., D.P.C.; Liz Herron, M.A.; Jean Houston, Ph.D.; Laurie Ingraham, M.S.W.; Susan Jeffers, Ph.D.; Bill Kauth, M.S.; Daphne Rose Kingma, M.A.; Aaron Kipnis, Ph.D.; John Lee; Joseph Mancini, Ph.D., L.C.S.W.; Patricia McCallum; Robert Moore, Ph.D.; Julio Olalla, M.A.; Joseph Palmour, Ph.D.; Nancy Richardson, L.C.S.W.; Roy Schenk, Ph.D.; Judith Sherven, Ph.D.; Amy Silverman; Jim Sniechowski, Ph.D.; Tamiko; Karen Kahn Wilson, Ed.D.; and Marion Woodman;

the women and men from all walks of life, who spent hours of their precious time being interviewed for this book;

and Mitsy, my dear chihuahua, who patiently sat by my computer hour after hour while I wrote.

Thank you all!

Introduction

Ten years ago I began to negotiate love. My first and second marriages had both ended in divorce and I was a single parent with three children. On a snowy January evening, I had met the man of my dreams. Phil and I were two extremely different people who nonetheless were irresistibly attracted to each other. How could we ever resolve our innumerable differences? I certainly didn't want a third trip to the divorce court.

At this point I felt very foolish: "I'm an intelligent person; I have a Ph.D. from Harvard, and I'm *supposed* to know what to do." But there I was with this wonderful, lovable human being and we couldn't get along with each other. There must be a way. But *how*? I was determined to find out the answer to my question. By trial and error (with an emphasis on error!) we taught each other the lessons that are in this book.

But could I be sure that our difficulty in getting along and resolving our disagreements was typical of other couples' situations? No, and I wanted to find out. So I embarked on a quest to find and learn from the best experts on the important, difficult topic of how a woman and a man can resolve conflicts. I located these experts by networking: one interview led to another which led to another and another. What a thrill it was to talk to some of the greatest authorities on women's issues, men's issues, and conflict resolution! Whenever possible I met my interviewees (whose names are listed in the acknowledgments) in person; otherwise, we spoke on the phone. Their interviews ranged from thirty to ninety minutes in length. Altogether I spoke to forty-five experts.

I also interviewed 205 "average" women and men who were willing to speak frankly to me about the difficulties they experienced in their relationships. Several couples (bless their hearts) even fought in front of me. My sample included people of all ages and ethnic groups, single and married, from throughout the United States as well as Canada. Some of our conversations lasted half an hour; other times we went on for three hours or more, well into the night.

Unbeknownst to me, my academic background had prepared me well to write this book. When I was studying political science, I used to be frustrated with the amount of time my professors spent teaching us about relationships between countries. Now I applied my background to individual people: Didn't they need to balance power and negotiate their disagreements too? A year after I met Phil I began devouring psychology books. Building upon the courses I had taken in college and graduate school, I ended up reading myself another Ph.D. in this field. Eventually I combined the two disciplines I knew best: political science (the study of power) and psychology (the study of human behavior). I also became an expert on gender issues. The subject of how women and men can resolve their differences has continued to fascinate me.

INTRODUCTION

During recent years I have become uncomfortable with the views of many spokespersons for women. As you will soon discern, I am not a man-hater. Rather, I am a leader of the new women's movement dedicated to reconciling our differences with men. I believe that while the women's movement has helped women politically and economically, that is not enough. It is now time to focus on another urgent concern: our relationships with the other sex. The organization I have founded, the Network for Empowering Women, offers a "new" path for women and men who are tired of bashing each other and instead seek cooperation, friendship, clear communication, and the opportunity to negotiate love.

Consequently I am writing about female–male relationships, not about lesbian and gay ones. Inherently, homosexual relationships deal with issues that heterosexuals do not face. Social prejudice, rejection by friends and family members, and coming out are three of them.

By and large, however, the issues of interpersonal growth and learning to resolve conflicts are common to *all* intimate relationships. In this sense, *all* couples seeking to understand and appreciate each other better can benefit from *Negotiating Love*. The eleven secrets of negotiating love were developed and tested in the laboratory of our living room. We did not go to the "negotiating table," as businesspersons and lawyers do; we talked in the car, in bed, at the dining-room table while we ate dinner, and most often, on the living-room couch. That's how we learned the ten ways to create the right mindset for negotiating. You can too. Your relationship doesn't have to be a life sentence of endless arguments and physical violence; in fact, it shouldn't be.

The methods presented in this book work. Between its covers are the guidelines you need to reach agreement with your lover so that your relationship can and will last. Chapters 1 through 8 contain the solution to the problem "How can a woman and a man resolve their differences peacefully?" At the beginning of Chapter 9, you will notice a definite change in tone. To avoid being overly optimistic, the last four chapters offer a realistic view of the difficulties women and men still face.

Negotiating Love was conceived in pain, nurtured by determination, and birthed with hope. Do not read it as an intellectual exercise; it is written from the heart. May it save you the frustration I've been through and enable you to form a lasting, loving bond with your partner.

CHAPTER 1

Can Lovers Negotiate?

"Negotiating love." At first glance these two words seem to go together like oil and wine. They just don't mix. When people negotiate, they try to get the best of each other; when people are in love, they want the best for each other.

But think about it for a minute. The purpose of negotiating is to resolve differences. Isn't this what lovers must do every day? After the initial glow of romance wears off, we're left face-to-face with someone who says, "I *always* squeeze the toothpaste tube in the middle," or "I don't want to make love with the light on." While we can buy a toothpaste pump or install a dimmer switch in the light fixture, sooner or later the two of us are going to collide. The next issue very well may be:

"I'm ready to have a baby."

"Well, I'm not. I want to wait at least two more years."

If we can learn to use some elements of negotiating in our romantic relationships, we will take a quantum leap. Negotiating love won't be the last step before we go to divorce court, but the *first* step after infatuation dims.

There's another reason that negotiating love is a major breakthrough. A common complaint of some women in love runs something like this: "My lover or husband doesn't listen, and he hardly ever talks to me. When I start a conversation he hides behind the newspaper or turns up the volume on the television. I guess men just don't know how to communicate."

Not true. Men *do* communicate all the time—*when they negotiate*. They talk and listen carefully during business negotiations to arrive at the right price to buy or sell. They participate in legal negotiations either by themselves or through their attorneys. They also carry on businesslike negotiations with one another whenever they get together socially. To take an ordinary example:

JACK: Let's watch *Star Trek*.
JIM: No, I'd rather see the end of the football game.
JACK: Well, why don't we flip between the two channels during commercials and time-outs? When the game is over, we can stay with *Star Trek*.

We *can* start a fruitful dialogue between women and men through negotiation, a kind of communication that most men—and many women—already know. To resolve our differences, we share information back and forth, dealing and bargaining, with the intention of reaching agreement: that's the most basic definition of negotiation.[1] But there are different types of negotiation, which depend on our approach.

In win–lose negotiations, either I get what I want or you get what you want. We struggle with each other until one of us wins and one of us loses. That's not loving. If you are a "hard" negotiator, your goal is to overpower your opponent. If you are a "soft" negotiator, your goal is to keep the relationship going no matter what. So you surrender in order to please the other person. Codependent people are especially skilled at this kind of negotiating. But neither "hard" nor "soft" negotiators are very effective when it comes to love relationships.

Negotiating love is none of the above. It is neither steamrolling nor surrendering, neither hard nor soft. Love relationships require a special kind of win–win negotiation that is based on the concept of problem-solving.

In win–win negotiations, your goal is *to solve the problem*. And when you separate the problem from the personalities involved, you win and so does the other person.[2] I give you what you want, and you give me what I want. We are two different people with two different positions, and our task is to figure out how we *both* can find a way to win.

Negotiating love uses the principles of win–win negotiating but extends them *much further*. While lovers' interests may at first seem different, actually they are the same. I want you to have what you need because I love you. You want me to have what I need because you love me. What benefits you benefits me; what benefits me benefits you. Our conversation is about how we can work together and support each other. We are lovers, not buddies, professional associates, or adversaries. Our approach is neither "hard" nor "soft" nor a combination of the two but flexible instead. We don't bargain; we brainstorm a solution together. And any solution is acceptable as long as you and I both are satisfied with it.

Loving negotiations don't have to last for a long-drawn-out time. In fact, they can be very brief. For example:

HE: The eleven o'clock news is on now. I can't wait to watch it.
SHE: I'm feeling down right now. I need to snuggle.
HE: So let's snuggle while we watch the news together.
SHE: (*smiling*) Okay.

This negotiation took only twenty seconds.

Loving negotiations don't even have to be in words. They can be in grunts, gestures, and glances—the whole range of our nonverbal communication. For example:

You're lying in bed next to each other. He reaches out his arm. ("I feel lonely; I need a hug.")

He nudges you gently. ("Will you?")

You hesitate a few seconds. ("I'm exhausted. I don't want to. . . . But then again, hugging feels so good, and if it'll make you happy. . . .")

You move over and put your arms around him. ("Yes.")

That negotiation took less than five seconds.

Of course, loving negotiations can take much more time, especially if the issue is more involved:

SHE: I'd like to start going out to dinner twice a week. I'm so burned out from taking care of the baby; I need a break from the routine.

HE: We don't have the money for restaurants and baby-sitters. We still owe a thousand to the obstetrician, and several thousand to the hospital. I've been up all night worrying about how we're going to manage to pay these bills.

SHE: How about inviting my mother over to cook? She could come over on Mondays and leave us leftovers for another meal later in the week.

HE: You know that I don't get along well with your mother. And I don't like her cooking. Besides, she would probably think that we were imposing on her.

SHE: What about going out to fast-food restaurants? We could take the baby with us and all go for a walk afterward.

HE: That sounds a lot more reasonable. Once the bills are paid, we can get a baby-sitter and eat out in a nicer restaurant once a month.

Loving negotiations like these require more time and patience. But if you both strive to find a solution that will benefit the two of you, ultimately you will feel satisfied with the result.

How a Loving Negotiation Differs from a Business Negotiation

Businesspersons' and lovers' negotiations do have the same purpose: to resolve a dispute between two people with different points of view. They do use the same method to reach that resolution: communication. But the spirit and communication style of lovers is unique. Negotiating love is a combination of male *and* female communication styles. It is *both* about achieving goals in the traditional male style *and* about expressing feelings in the traditional female style. Furthermore, lovers make a decision to trust each other; businesspeople generally don't, especially when they represent different interests. Altogether there are ten major differences in communication style and in spirit between businesslike negotiations and loving ones.

1. It is difficult for lovers to separate their emotions from the issues. During loving negotiations, feelings play a major role. In business and legal negotiations, feelings play a minor one.

Negotiators in business attire tend to be logical. They analyze facts and figure out solutions that are "right," never mind how the parties feel. They are consistent and should not contradict themselves. If they want something, they often have good reasons to justify it.

In negotiating love, feelings are *the* most important consideration. When you say to your lover, "I really need you to be here with me; I'm so sad about the death of my dad," you don't need any other rationale. You don't need to be logical, and you don't need to be consistent. Never mind that an hour ago you said, "Go away and leave me alone." You're in pain, and you're reaching out now. Perhaps when your mother had died, no one was there for you. Your new grief and your old wound are combined into one huge ache. You need your lover *now*.

Or perhaps you and your lover have discussed your relationship and decided, "We're better off spending more time apart. There are just too many differences we can't work out." But here you are in your own bed at three in the morning, dialing her number.

"I'm so lonely. I need you next to me. Tonight. And every night."

"Okay. I'll be right over."

What is this craziness? It's your emotions. And they're an essential part of negotiating love.

2. Lovers *share* their lives. They have much more in common than parties to a businesslike negotiation.

Lawyers and businessmen meet for an hour, for an afternoon, or for a day or two. After that they're gone. Lovers know that the person they negotiated with today will be with them tomorrow—and the day after that. You can't afford to casually insult the person with whom you're sharing a bed. *Nor should you want to.* This common bond between loving partners makes their communication much deeper.

3. Lovers negotiate as equals, not as unequals. They are interested in supporting each other, not in competing to be the best negotiator.

Loving negotiations will not work unless both people perceive their own power to be *equal*. It doesn't matter how powerful we really are; it's how we *perceive* our relative power. If I feel intimidated by you, I will not be able to negotiate love. I will constantly be worrying that you'll take advantage of me, overpower me, or hurt me. No matter how hard I try, I will not be able to hold my own during our conversation. Lovers who feel powerless don't make good negotiators. Conversely, lovers who hold the upper hand don't have any reason to negotiate at all.

In businesslike negotiations, what each party is doing is striving to be more powerful than the other. Win–win negotiations are no exception; your first priority is still to consolidate your own power. If one side or the other has better negotiators or a stronger bargaining position, it uses these superior resources to gain leverage. No wonder we have power politics, power lawyers, and power lunches.

4. People in love are caring friends. Their relationship is neither adversarial nor competitive, like that of lawyers, businesspersons, and diplomats.

Professionals meet in offices. They go to the "negotiating table," which is usually rectangular or square. Sitting across from each other, each side works to get the best deal they can for themselves or for their clients. Even if they are not fundamentally opposed, they certainly don't care deeply for each other. Lovers *do*. They have a common bond of friendship and shared goals. Friends have a common history and a vision for the future. So they sit side by side on a couch, on the floor, or at a table. And when they have the opportunity to select a table, they favor one that is either round or oval.

5. Lovers trust each other. Businesspersons don't.

It is absolutely necessary to trust each other before you negotiate love. What is trust? The dictionary tells us that trust is faith or confidence; a feeling that a person or thing will not fail in performance.[3]

But trust between lovers has a much deeper meaning. Lovers who trust each other share these beliefs:

We will keep our word. Except in an emergency, we will not break our agreements with each other. If you promise to fly home from your business trip in the event one of the kids gets sick, you will. If I tell you that I will meet you at the airport, I will be there.

We will be there for each other. I will not cut you off when you need me nor will you shut down when I need you. If it's five A.M. and I've just awakened from a terrible nightmare, you will hold me. If I've just left the doctor's office with bad news, I can call you—even if you're in a meeting at the office.

We will tell each other the truth. Neither of us will deliberately lie or withhold important information. If I ask you, "Did you kiss her?" you will give me an honest answer. If, unbeknownst to me, you did fool around with her, you will let me know.

We will be open with each other. Each of us will share our real selves instead of hiding important parts of us. When we are together, we will not be "plastic people" pretending to be someone we are not. If I feel embarrassed about my small breasts, I will confide this to you. If my fondest dream is to be a musician, even though I can't play a note, I will share it. If your deepest fantasy is to make love on the beach in the middle of the night, you will reveal it. If you are afraid of thunderstorms or feel bad about the day you had at work, you will tell me. This kind of self-disclosure is voluntary, however. I can choose to remove my own façade, but there is no way I can penetrate yours unless you allow me.

We will be kind to each other. We will not deliberately hurt each other, use each other, abuse each other, overcontrol each other, judge each other, humiliate each other, or take advantage of each other. Together we will create a comfortable, safe, secure emotional climate where we can both be ourselves. Both of us will feel that we can reveal our faults and show our wounds without fear of ridicule or reprisal.

What each of us needs is to be able to come out and say, "Yes, I screwed up. It was wrong to screw up. I don't always screw up, but I'm probably going to screw up again. I'm not perfect; I am not a prince or princess in a fairy tale. If you're going to show your anger with harsh words or the silent treatment every time I make a mistake, I have to leave. I can't stay in this relationship if I have to pretend to be perfect. *I need you to accept me as I am.*"

Kindness begets openness. If you are kind, then I will be open. The more kind you are, the more open I will be. We prepare ourselves for negotiating love by testing each other on simple matters first:

HE: Why don't you ever wear that blouse I gave you?
SHE: To be honest, I didn't like it. It didn't look good on me. I exchanged it for the blue one that goes with my new suit. I hope you don't mind. I knew you'd want me to have something I really liked.
HE: (*thoughtfully*) No, I guess that's all right. Come to think of it, I like the blue one better. Just make sure you think of me every time you wear it!

Or:

SHE: Why didn't you call me?
HE: I'm sorry; it's because I forgot. I went bowling with the guys and it slipped my mind.
SHE: Okay. Next time I'll tie a string around your finger.

Now, *that's* kindness.

What about when we work our way up to more difficult issues?

SHE: I need thirty dollars.
HE: We got one hundred out of the cash machine on Sunday. It was supposed to last you all week. What did you spend it on? I want to know exactly where every single dollar went.

SHE: (*after some thought*) Well, I spent $22.50 on subway tokens, $57.00 on lunches because I took my accountant out, then I picked up some extra panty hose because mine had runs in them. I bought three pairs for seven dollars.

HE: We still have $13.50 unaccounted for. What happened to the $13.50?

SHE: Actually, it's really bothering me that you're asking me to account for every penny that I spend. I feel like a stupid, powerless child when you interrogate me. If you don't trust me financially, we'll get separate bank accounts. I'll put the money I earn in my account, and you'll put the money you earn in yours.

HE: My primary concern isn't that you're spending too much. I'm concerned that we're not *saving* enough. What if I lose my job? Or you lose yours?

SHE: How about if we take a hundred a month and deposit it in a savings account? That way we won't have to be so concerned about the possibility of one of us losing a job. And we can spend the rest of our money without having to account for every single penny.

Or:

SHE: Why were you so friendly to that woman at the party?

HE: It felt great to see her. She's an attractive lady who likes my company. I enjoyed being with her and talking to her. Now, you can take my words and hold them against me for eternity, but I'm praying you won't.

SHE: I feel like it, but I'll try not to. Don't you know how much it hurts me when you flirt with another woman in public? I was so embarrassed in front of my friends. Were you trying to make me jealous?

HE: No. I just liked being with her. It was fun. But it's you that I *love.*

SHE: Are you going to call her?

HE: Yes. I'll probably meet her for lunch.

SHE: Well, I can't stop you, so I hope you enjoy it. But don't forget: It's okay for you to be friends with her, but I draw the line at sex. If you sleep with her, then you say bye-bye to me.

No one can be perfectly trustworthy. Only a saint always keeps her/his word, never lies, is completely open, is forever kind, and manages to be there one hundred percent of the time. Lovers aren't saints, but human beings who care enough to do their best to be worthy of each other's trust.

The opposite of trust is fear. If we don't have confidence in each other, I'm continually afraid of what you might say; you're always worried about what I might do. How, then, can we take off our masks and talk about what really matters to us? Before we can negotiate love we have to trust each other.

6. The language of lovers is about emotions, needs, and possibilities; the language of businesspersons and lawyers focuses on bargains and tricks.

When you read books or listen to tapes on businesslike negotiation, what you learn about are tactics, strategies, and tricks. They teach you how to ask for more than you really want, make false promises, and deliver fake ultimatums.[4] For example, one popular strategy is to ascertain your "BATNA" (Best Alternative to a Negotiated Settlement).[5] In other words, figure out your fall-back position if the negotiation fails. The stronger it is, the easier you can walk away from the negotiating table.

This is not the language of loving negotiations. As lovers we talk about what we feel, what we need, and how we can get what we need. For example:

SHE: I need a new mattress by the weekend.
HE: Why?
SHE: My back has been hurting a lot recently. My chiropractor told me it would help a lot if I slept on an extra-firm mattress.
HE: Could we still use our old bed frame?
SHE: I don't know. We can try to.
HE: Why do you need to have a new mattress right now?
SHE: I hurt whenever I stand up. The pain is making me irritable. I don't want my attitude to affect my relationship with you or others, so I'd like to get rid of the pain right away.
HE: Would you like to get a water bed? I've always fantasized about having one.
SHE: No, I really need an extra-firm mattress to sleep on. Next year when we have more money, we can buy a water bed for the guest room—and use it sometimes.
HE: Let's go shopping tonight. I hear there's a sale at Snoozy's.

Is this how you would negotiate this issue with your lover? Or would you use one of these tricks:

- Make your lover think it's her/his idea when it's really yours: "Take a look at these ads for furniture sales. The mattresses are half price."
- Ask for much more than you really want: "I want a whole new bedroom set."
- Make a false promise: "We'll have better sex more often on a new mattress."

• Insist that informed sources agree with you: "Yesterday I read in a health magazine that a soft mattress is bad for your back."

• Distract your lover with an irrelevant issue, while you push for what you're really after (this trick is called a red herring): "I'm sick and tired of your keeping me up at night. I haven't had a decent night's sleep in weeks."

• Have a hidden agenda: "We ought to add a new master bedroom onto the house."

• Pretend you're weak: "I can't possibly afford to buy a new mattress on my salary."

• Offer a mixed message: "I want a new mattress, but it'll be a waste of money because the cat will shed all over it."

• Give a fake ultimatum: "No more snuggling until we buy a new mattress."

How would your lover respond? Would s/he play a trick of her/his own, such as telling you s/he can't make the decision until s/he checks with someone else (this trick is known as "higher authority"): "I hate to keep you waiting, honey, but my stockbroker's out of town for a week. Before we buy the mattress I have to ask him how our investments are doing."

Some tricks can be extremely destructive if used in negotiating other issues lovers face:

Having a hidden agenda: "I don't want to have children" (when I really do).

Giving a fake ultimatum: "Marry me, or else I'll break up with you" (when I really love you and I don't want to date anyone else).

Neither women nor men have a monopoly on playing tricks. For every woman who says, "I can't sleep with you unless you tell me you love me," there's a man who insists, "I'll fix that leaky faucet tomorrow," when he knows full well that he'll never get around to doing it. Long ago, when women were powerless, we resorted to tricks frequently. Recently, men who have felt powerless have done the same thing. Now that the scales of power are balanced, it is possible for women and men to negotiate love instead.

Lovers don't bargain either. Loving negotiations are not business transactions where you exchange one item for another. "If I get to spend three hundred dollars on a new mattress, you will get to spend the same amount on new golf clubs." Lovers cooperate with each other. It is fair to make promises only if you fully intend to keep them: "If I get a new mattress, I will make the bed every day," or "If I get a new mattress, I will never smoke in bed again."

"Split the difference" is the only business negotiation tactic I know about that is sometimes appropriate for lovers. "If the mattress is three hundred dollars and you're willing to contribute one hundred, let's split the difference. You contribute two and I'll put up one hundred," can be a useful exchange. But this depends on the *spirit* in which the bargain is made. We had better be thinking, "How can we raise the money to buy the mattress you need?" rather than plotting, "How can I get the other to pay for most of it?" Lovers are generous; they do not haggle.

7. Negotiating love is about getting what you need, which often you do not recognize or understand. Business and legal negotiations are about getting what you want, which you already know.

In every loving negotiation there are two conversations: the words we use and what we really mean. What we say we *want* may not be what we really *need*. For example, I may tell you, "I want you to take me out to dinner on my birthday," but what I really mean is, "I need to feel loved and special. If you've tuned in carefully, you can call me three times that day and buy me the new dress I've been longing for instead of taking me out to eat. Doing this will ensure that I have a very happy birthday even though you may be five hundred miles away on a business trip."

Negotiating love is about getting our needs met. Each of us has an agenda of deepest needs that we hope our lover will figure out. Women's and men's agendas are different. As a woman, what I need most is to feel valued; as a man, my most profound need is to feel unconditionally nurtured. (In Chapters 9 and 10 we explore these needs—and how they can be met—in detail.) Besides our "gender" agenda, we also have our own personal agendas. While our gender agenda is similar to other men's or other women's, our personal agenda is unique and constantly changing. Right now your primary personal need may be security; mine may be adventure. Until we trust each other fully we will not share this precious information with each other. Moreover, even if the trust between us is strong, we may not be aware of what we need. Neither of us is deliberately deceiving the other; we just aren't aware.

Until we know what we need we cannot negotiate love. Our apparent conversation is not our real conversation. If I need adventure but don't know it, I may criticize you for wearing the same outfit three days in a row. "You always look the same." "Well, what's wrong with that?" you snap back. Now I've picked a fight with you, but it's not about what's really bothering me. Had I been more in touch with my own need for adventure, I might have said, "I'm bored. I need a change of scenery. How about we jump in the car this weekend and head for the mountains?"

It's a lot more simple when lawyers or businesspersons get together. In businesslike negotiations there are fewer non-conversations. Each party knows what it wants and states it up front, even though it may employ maneuvering and trickery to achieve these goals.

8. Lovers' issues are numerous and complex. Unlike business or law, there is no single, specific issue being negotiated.

Lovers are negotiating the fabric of their lives. Thus, there are a dozen major-issue areas that committed lovers must resolve in order to form a strong relationship bond. These are: money, careers, housework, neatness, time, religion and spirituality, family backgrounds, substance abuse, sex, sexual jealousy, children, and outsiders (relatives, friends, and business associates). I call these twelve critical issue areas "hotspots." In Chapter 8 you learn how lovers can successfully negotiate them. But before lovers can tackle these relationship hotspots, they must work out traditional dating dilemmas: initiatives, exclusivity, and commitment. I discuss negotiating these in Chapter 7.

By comparison, businesslike negotiations are simple. Issues like "How much money are you willing to settle for?" are a lot less complex than "Will we raise our kids in the Catholic or Jewish faith?"

When negotiating love, you cannot separate the issues from the personalities of the negotiators. Our emotions, our minds, and our spirits are all involved when we sit down to discuss a hotspot. We bring with us our past experiences with our families of origin (that, more often than not, are dysfunctional) and all the wounds we carry around as a result. "How often are we going to invite your father over to dinner?" can quickly escalate to "You hate my dad." "Are we going to buy a new mattress?" can become "We managed to come up with the money for your new stereo, didn't we? You're the only one who gets her/his needs met in this relationship." This type of wounding doesn't happen in the legal or the business world.

9. Unlike businesspersons and lawyers, lovers have no standards for fair agreement. What seems fair to one couple may seem grossly unfair to another.

Knowledgeable businesspersons and lawyers know what's reasonable. They can find out prices for similar items, or read previous cases that were decided on that particular subject. How do lovers know what's fair? They don't. Even if we survey our friends and family to get a consensus ("He wants his high school buddy to live with us for six months! Is that reasonable?"), we've got a very limited sample of responses. (Four yeses, three nos, and one maybe.) Besides, what your friends and family think is irrelevant. In the last analysis, *a workable agreement is whatever fits your and your lover's needs.* If s/he feels cheated or resentful, s/he will probably not do what s/he agreed to anyway. Neither will you. Not having the security of knowing what's fair puts the responsibility for deciding squarely on both of you—where it belongs.

10. Lovers usually negotiate for themselves; parties to a business or legal negotiation are often represented by someone else.

There are two versions to a negotiation: yours and mine. In order to reach agreement or solve the problem, we need to get these to coincide. Someone has to take what I hear, perceive, assume, and say and what you hear, perceive, assume, and say and make sense out of it all. And in loving negotiations there is an important additional ingredient: *what we both feel*. A good business or legal negotiator can avoid getting confused and feeling deeply by detaching him- or herself from the situation. Lovers *can't*. Not only do they usually speak for themselves but also their discussion rests on the quicksand of feelings. Lovers are emotionally involved with the issues; they care about each other and about each issue.

Negotiating love requires powerful communication skills that take a while to master; business and legal negotiation techniques can be learned more easily. Businesslike negotiating is like ice skating. It's difficult and a bit dangerous, but once you master the skills, "Off you go." Negotiating love is like skating on a partially melted pond. If you stop considering your lover's feelings, you can easily trip up, or worse. Once you know what spots to watch out for (your lover's feelings), you can skate (negotiate) more safely. The stakes when you negotiate love are a lot higher, the skills are more complex, and you have to be willing to practice a lot. But it gets easier once you know how.

In negotiating love you have one big advantage: *You already understand on a deep level how to do it*. Do you know how to negotiate? Probably. Do you know how to love? Probably. My purpose is to assist you in making the necessary connections between the two. With a little patience we can combine them in a way you never imagined possible. What an exciting project!

While negotiating love may seem at first to be a paradox, actually it is not. Instead, loving negotiations are the key to resolving our differences—after we deal with our anger.

CHAPTER 2

Getting Past Your Anger So You Can Sit Down and Talk

Taped on the mirror we look into every day should be a piece of paper with the words "Never negotiate love when you are angry." Why? Because when you are angry, your emotions take over. They blind you with their intensity so you can't focus on the issue at hand. You may be so overwhelmed by your angry feelings that you don't listen to what your lover—or perhaps even to what you yourself—is saying.

Angry Lovers Can't Negotiate

Your anger is a filter that distorts your lover's message. You may hear her/his words but not grasp the meaning behind them. Or you may hear a few words but not all of them. I remember one evening when Phil came home and told me, "I want to take three months' vacation by myself in California. I'm really burned out from working seven years straight at the office, and I need some rest." I blew up. All I heard—or at least I *thought* all I heard—was "I want . . . three months . . . by myself." I was furious. Underneath my fury was the pain from my old wounds inflicted by all those men, both family members and lovers, who'd left me in the past. I wasn't seeing Phil as he really was; *I was seeing him as if he were just like all those others.*

After I cooled down, I listened carefully as Phil told me how pressured he felt by a network of obligations. We discussed how he had always enjoyed having time alone to write in his journal, read books, and have adventures—but that this type of leisure time had not been available to him in years. In this frame of mind I could negotiate love. Finally we agreed that a month away would be sufficient.

Anger confuses us because it covers up other, deeper emotions. As pastoral counselor Dr. Daniel Henderson puts it, our feelings are like a layer cake.[1] The icing on the cake is numbness, which keeps us from feeling anything at all. Anger is the cake's top layer. A creative emotion, it protects us from our other feelings, which are the lower layers in the cake: fear, envy, guilt, loneliness, sadness, self-doubt, or general pain. When we are consumed by anger we don't deal with these other emotions.

It's only when we get past our anger that we can understand what we are actually feeling. Once we ask ourselves "Why am I angry?" we discover the truth. It might be that I am afraid. Perhaps I feel threatened. I could even be envious of my lover, or just plain lonely. I may be feeling that I've been abandoned or am not good enough. We experience anger for a while, until we are ready to face the true feelings. Anger distorts our reality and hides our deeper emotions. To think rationally while you're angry is difficult; to negotiate love, impossible.

Often it's necessary to experience our anger fully before we can know what's underneath. For example, I may find myself shouting, "You're just like your father. You just aren't capable of having an intimate relationship," even while I'm thinking, "That's not what's really bothering me. It's something else." Only later am I able to say, "What I really need is to feel that you love me. When I don't see you for days at a time or your attention wanders when you're with me, I feel that you don't care about me." But I may have to get involved in an argument before I can get to this point. Hopefully, in the process, you and I haven't damaged each other.

Expressing anger *is* scary. When we were children we were taught not to get angry. If we did scream, we were scolded, punished, abandoned, beaten, or emotionally abused by our parents, who were much larger than we were. Only adults were allowed to show anger.[2] We learned, "Mom yells. You're the child. You don't yell back; that's not your place. You don't speak disrespectfully to your parents. As long as you're in *our* house, you live by *our* rules." We carry this "Shut up and take it" attitude with us as we grow up. We hesitate to express our anger to our lover; we are terrified of its depths, which we may not have plumbed before. What will happen if we open up the valves of our rage? Will the anger we encounter be limitless?

Both sexes have problems expressing anger. Women have an especially difficult time because of the way we were brought up. When we were little, our parents and teachers said, "A nice girl doesn't get angry. If you act that way, no one will love you." We still carry this message within us. If we blow up, we think, "What is the matter with me? I'd better smooth things over to keep the relationship going." Our lovers reinforce this message. How many men are willing to contend with strong female anger in order to reach the pain beneath? Crying is a more acceptable way for us to express our emotions; it's less threatening. However, while both women and men are uncomfortable with female anger, many are slowly learning to accept it.

Men also try to hide their anger, according to Onaje Benjamin and Forrest Craver, two experts on male issues. Some men internalize their feelings, only to act them out in self-destructive behavior. Others go to great lengths to avoid conflict, especially with their lovers. These men are worried that they might lose control; they are terrified that their lovers might shame them. Yet by avoiding arguments they tighten the lid on the pressure cooker. When their anger inevitably erupts, it is usually toxic rage. Their lovers respond in kind, so that the physical and emotional violence escalates. If men like these would value their aggressiveness and channel it properly, both they *and* their lovers would benefit.[3]

Both sexes not only fear their own anger; they also fear each other's—especially if we don't fully trust our lover. Might we get mistreated physically or emotionally? Might we be abandoned? Will s/he leave me? For many of us, anger is particularly terrifying because we associate it with past experiences of sexual or emotional abuse. Getting angry or experiencing our lover's anger can bring up memories of this terrible time, so we try to avoid it at all costs. There's no way we can be fearful *and* have a productive conversation. No wonder angry lovers can't negotiate!

Lovers' First Agreement: How to Express Healthy Anger

Only when we are calm can we discuss how we will express our anger. This is the first, most fundamental loving negotiation we have with each other. How will we communicate when our buttons are pushed? What are our rules of engagement? What are our limits? What forms of anger are acceptable to us? Which purposes do we consider to be reasonable?

Most women and men find this kind of negotiation difficult. Why? Because a lot of us don't even know what anger *is*. We confuse healthy anger with toxic rage.[4] Our confusion began during childhood. When our parents got furious, we were traumatized. Scared to retaliate, we lost the opportunity to learn to express our angry feelings in a constructive way. Some of us grew up in homes where there was only toxic rage, so we don't even know what healthy anger is. Now we're afraid to feel our own anger and to experience our lover's.

Toxic rage has given healthy anger a bad name. Actually the two are quite different. Toxic rage is violent, explosive, and overcontrolling. Healthy anger is nonviolent, flowing, and shared; it is a vital part of loving relationships. We use healthy anger to communicate powerfully with our lover about what we will and will not allow him/her to do. "No, you cannot take something out of my purse without my permission." Or, "I will not allow you to insult my friends. Don't ever do that again." We might say these admonitions gently, but the anger behind them strengthens their power.

A way of distinguishing toxic rage from healthy anger is to ask, "What is my purpose? Is it to dominate, manipulate, scare, or hurt my lover?" That's toxic rage, and it's cruel. But if it's to express my feelings, get rid of my negativity, and clear the air, that's healthy anger, and it's fundamentally compassionate. Healthy anger sounds something like this: "I have to admit it: I'm furious. This is the fifth night in a row I've cooked dinner and cleaned up afterward by myself. I have a full-time job now; I need you to pitch in. A week ago you promised you would start, and you haven't lifted a finger since. Why not? *(Pause)* Come on, now it's your turn to talk." In this case, I'm not using my anger to destroy; my purpose is to share my feelings, to bring the two of us closer together.

We learn about ourselves and each other by expressing our anger in a healthy way. Jude Blitz, who together with her husband, Dr. Tom Daly, gives couples workshops nationwide, gave me this illustration: "Tom's mother had died; all her furniture was due to arrive at our house. When it was delivered, I realized that I felt invaded—pushed out—by her furniture. I wanted it to go away. But Tom was still in his mourning period. He needed the furniture to be there for a while so he could eventually let go of his grief. We told each other how we felt, and I even suggested that we put it in the basement. I felt bad saying this; a little voice whispered to me what a selfish person I was. But if I hadn't actually honored my anger and realized that I was entitled to feel, 'I'm being invaded by these pieces of furniture,' I wouldn't have been able to feel Tom's grief and pain. Only if I accepted my own negative feelings could I then accept his."[5]

Before negotiating love, our healthy anger *must* be emptied out. As we express our negative feelings to our lover, they will eventually disappear. From this our passion will ultimately grow. We allow each other to relax and to be ourselves—something we all crave. The trust between us deepens. One happily married woman informed me: "If my husband and I disagree about something—even a stupid, nonsense issue—we say what needs to be said and then shut up. Sure we may yell and swear, but we never hit or torment each other. We always make sure we're finished, so we don't have to go around mad at each other."

Healthy anger is about your own emotions. It has nothing to do with who your lover is or even what s/he did. It's the human venom—hitting below the belt and deliberately hurting each other—that makes anger toxic. How do we express our anger in a healthy way? According to Dr. Irene Gad, a Jungian psychiatrist who specializes in couples therapy, there's a simple rule: "Only one person can get angry at a time. *Take turns acting crazy.* When I am angry you take care of me; when you are angry I take care of you."[6] Thus each of us has a chance to feel heard, seen, nurtured, and loved. To many of us, talking about our feelings, shouting, yelling, and using profanity are also acceptable. Hitting an old pillow with a plastic baseball bat is another option. Redirecting our energy into useful activities such as going out for a run, working in the garden, washing the car, vacuuming or scrubbing the floors is a safe, sane outlet. With regular sublimation you will both protect each other *and* get your house cleaned.

We all can learn to express our anger physically in a way that's safe and sane, according to John Lee, author of *The Flying Boy.* Before a man gets angry in the presence of his female lover he should first practice directing his impulses toward something he cannot hurt—in the company of other men. He can punch a mattress, twist a towel, or hit the ground with a rock. Then he will realize, "I'm not alone. Lots of other guys act silly like this too."[7] From my own experience at the Woman Within weekend, I believe that women can also learn to express healthy anger physically this way.

Emotional violence[8] is often the most difficult form of toxic rage to avoid. We'd like to eliminate it, but most of us will secretly admit that we inflict it occasionally on our lover. Yet words can be as deadly as actual blows. Calling names is one kind of emotional violence. "You're a wimp. Why can't you be a real man like your brother?" "You cheated on your first husband; once a cheat, always a cheat." Some other forms we may be familiar with include: throwing tantrums, making character attacks, ridiculing, hurling put-downs, making false accusations, using information against your lover that s/he gave you in confidence, keeping your lover up half the night or hounding her/him all day, shaming, using guilt to inflict pain, bribing with sex or money, and making threats.

One specific form of emotional violence is worth a paragraph of its own: prolonged withdrawal. Some people express anger by ignoring its target. When they are furious with their lover, they refuse to pay her/him any attention. They won't make eye contact, talk, eat meals together, sleep in the same bed, or make love. For many of us this is the most terrible punishment of all. We'll do anything to get our lover talking again. Otherwise, it's like we're experiencing solitary confinement in our own house. The lover who is shut out may end up ignoring her/his own legitimate feelings and pleading for mercy just because s/he cannot stand the silence. And cajoling a lover can be demeaning.

Least acceptable is physical violence, from hitting each other to throwing things. One man told me, "My wife once stood up in a restaurant and threw her entire plate of food in my lap. It was incredible. We wouldn't be together now if we hadn't each gotten help from our men's and women's support groups. We would've killed each other—and I wasn't prepared to die." He went on to say that their relationship was still difficult for him, because he never knew what either of them would do next. He wished they had a few ground rules.

Lovers need to decide exactly what expressions of toxic rage they consider off limits. Here's a typical agreement—and it should be either written down or jointly understood: "Certain ways of showing anger are off limits to us. Together we agree not to do the following . . . We are comfortable with other ways of getting angry. When we get mad, it is okay to . . . Lastly, we will both do our best not to get angry at the same time." But bear in mind, *no two lovers' standards are alike*. As we all know from reading the newspapers, there are men and women for whom physical violence is routine. Others find even name-calling abhorrent. Most of us are somewhere between these two extremes. What all lovers need to do is develop an agreement about anger that both do their best to respect. If one lover refuses to abide by the rules, then a confrontation, a discussion, and immediate action are necessary. Physical abuse by a partner is a danger signal and should not be tolerated.

One couple I interviewed, whom I'll call Anne and Bernard, demonstrated the consequences of not having such an agreement. They loved each other very much but had great difficulty accepting each other's expressions of anger. For example, after they had been living together with Anne's young son for several months, Anne became annoyed that one of their neighbors was constantly calling to see if her children were at their house. One day, after the neighbor had called repeatedly, Anne told Bernard how upset she was. "Listen to what I'm saying," she begged. Instead, he kept mocking her and making fun of her. She got angrier and angrier, lost control, and finally punched him. Had she known how to remove herself from the inflammatory situation, this unfortunate incident might not have occurred.

Bernard immediately withdrew from the relationship, started ignoring her, and insisted that she and her son leave his house. To her, his demand represented the ultimate rejection and abandonment she had always feared. "I'm still very angry; I mistrust him now," she told me. "I'm afraid that if I move back in with him, he'll ask me to leave again."

Both lovers said they were sorry about how they had hurt each other. But they were still very angry and unable to negotiate love. Bernard didn't realize that he had to expel her because by punching him, she had triggered his fear of his own capacity for physical violence. Anne didn't understand that he needed time alone to deal with strong emotions that were threatening to overpower him. I suggested that they learn healthy ways to share their anger and to set limits when it came to toxic rage. She could *tell* him about her own angry feelings without throwing tantrums and repeatedly accusing him, "You kicked me out of your house." When he needed some private time he could say to her, "I can't be with you right now. It doesn't mean I don't love you; it just means that I'm hurting and I need to be by myself for a while." Eventually they might agree that physical violence, tantrums, prolonged withdrawal, and ordering each other to leave were unacceptable expressions of anger.

The Two Stages of Powerful Communication

Powerful communication between lovers has two stages:

Stage One: Empty out your healthy anger.

Stage Two: Negotiate love.

You can't make a decision, find a solution, or come to an agreement until you've experienced your anger first. When you are full of "attack energy," you block out all your loving emotions and problem-solving abilities. Rather than cooperating with the other person in a spirit of trust and goodwill, you push her/him away. So how can you possibly negotiate love?

In the words of Dr. Brad Blanton, gestalt psychologist and couples therapist, "Put it out there. Get all the hollering, all the crying, done; say your awful things. Experience your anger. Don't try to fix things while you're still mad; it won't work. There's no point in talking about a solution too early."[9]

If your lover is expressing healthy anger, let her/him alone. One happily married man I interviewed told me, "When my wife gets upset, I just let it happen. I wait to negotiate until she calms down." His wife added, "When I yell, scream, and holler you can hear me in the next county. I slam doors; I throw things. It's so bad that you shouldn't ever come near me until I'm totally silent. We wait until it's over to talk." Phil now does the same thing with me, although it's taken him a long time to get to this point. He tells me that he has learned to say to himself while I'm venting, "It's not about me. . . . It's not about me. . . ." In fact, recently we had a conversation that ran something like this:

HE: I appreciate your telling me your complaints last night.
ME: Well, I know that I carried on a bit. I'm sorry I said some of the things I said, but I really had to get them off my chest.
HE: That's okay. I understand.

Now we were ready to negotiate love.

Can you ever get past your anger? That's a question we all wonder about. From my own personal experience I can tell you, "Yes." If you start negotiating love and one of you starts shouting again, then end the conversation *immediately.* It's a warning: You're both not on "empty" yet; you haven't gotten rid of all your anger. When you think you're ready to resume your loving negotiation, try again. You may have to do this three, four, or even ten times, but eventually, it works. Dr. Blanton agrees: "I've seen hundreds of couples who really wanted to get past their anger but believed they couldn't. I tell each of them, 'Nobody's anger is as bottomless as they think it is. Your anger will end." They all ended up saying, 'I didn't think this advice would work, but it did!' "[10]

What exactly happens when we share our healthy anger with our lover? We experience that special relief that comes from being with someone who looks into our eyes and listens to us talk without judging or criticizing us. We feel seen; we feel heard; we feel deeply understood. Underneath our angry feelings are our unmet needs, which now we are able to express.

Dr. Warren Farrell, author of the books *Why Men Are the Way They Are* and *The Myth of Male Power*, says many men do not communicate because they are afraid they may be inadequate. "What if I can't solve her problem; what if I mess up?" they ask. Dr. Farrell advises them, "Your power is not to *fix* it. Don't give her advice; don't argue; don't walk away. Heal her. Be there for her. *Listen* to her. This is what she really wants."[11] To be listened to with compassion is something that both men and women crave.

Dr. Tom Daly, a leader in the men's movement, and his partner, Jude Blitz, explain to each other how their expression of anger aids their own personal relationship:

JUDE: When I was growing up I never actually saw people venting, so when I got mad, I would think, "It's bad to feel angry. I shouldn't feel angry." But you are so generous to me, Tom. You show your not-so-wonderful side and you let me show mine. I can "kvetch," whine, and say what I really think.

TOM: I don't have any problem with my bitchiness, my stubbornness, or my crankiness. Once I get into my narrow ways of thinking and express them, then things get clearer. It's only when I resist that I really get myself into trouble.[12]

At some point the anger *has* to stop. As author and psychologist Dr. Susan Jeffers puts it, "Anger always will come up. But you get beyond it by asking yourself, 'Why am I reacting this way?' or 'What action must I take to change a situation that is not working for me?' "[13] Then you get ready for the second stage, negotiating love.

A very articulate couple I interviewed described exactly how this shift occurs for them. The woman told me, "After we've had a fight we wait awhile. Sometimes we don't talk, except when it's absolutely necessary. I go into the bedroom, close the door, and lick my wounds. I kind of let him gather himself, go to his corner, and lick his. Then I feel as if I can talk to him, whereas before I had no desire. We haven't necessarily made up, but time has passed. We're ready to talk about what's really bothering us. It takes us less time to get that second conversation going than it used to."

Sometimes the two stages, expressing healthy anger and negotiating love, rotate continually for a prolonged period of time. A happily married woman described this kind of experience: "When my husband's twelve-year-old daughter by his first marriage came to live with us, we started to fight. He and I literally fought and discussed and fought and discussed for two years. After we'd fight we'd always make up. I never thought we'd leave each other but at the time I wondered, 'Are we going to *live* through this?' Well, we did. We just kept putting it out there."

RESENTMENT: THE BIGGEST BARRIER TO NEGOTIATING LOVE

Those who go directly from expressing healthy anger to negotiating love are fortunate. They do not get stuck in the mud of resentment. There are two ways resentment starts to build up. First, anger may erupt but not run its course. The lovers slink away full of unresolved angry feelings. Pouting or sulking, each one pretends it's business as usual.

Or one lover will disagree with the other but be afraid to talk about it. If the issue keeps coming up, s/he will eventually get angry. If the anger about the issue is hidden, it becomes resentment. And each time the issue comes up, the resentment grows.

From my own experience, I have learned this: *Unexpressed anger doesn't go away*. Holding it in just makes it build up. I start off thinking, "This thing isn't very important; I'm not going to get mad over it." But I do. Two days later I'm still in a stew because I've been sitting on it all this time. By now it's so massive and unpleasant, I don't want to do anything about it. Not only am I embarrassed to be angry, but also I feel totally stupid to be upset about such a small thing. I think, "This is ridiculous. I shouldn't be so mad." So I sit on it again for a while, until eventually I decide to open up.

Resentment—stored-up, withheld anger—is like poison. If you don't let it out quickly, it can kill you. When you push your anger deep inside you, it doesn't disappear. It grows and festers like an infection. When your resentment eventually gets discharged, it shows up not as healthy anger, but as toxic rage. You suddenly unload all of the angry feelings you've been pushing down. Since they've been stored for so long, the pressure's been building up, and you explode.

One couple described how the wife's resentment had exploded as toxic rage:

HE: You were a totally different woman. You had such vengeance in your voice. That look on your face was enough to scare me to death.

SHE: There had been so many years of holding it in. It finally got to me. Before I gave it to you I said to myself, "I've had enough; I'm going to stand up for myself; I'm not going to put up with this anymore."

HE: It was absolutely awful.

Another man shared with me the tragic consequence of his own resentment when he finally decided to stand up to his wife after years of giving in to her wishes: "She told me to clean the cellar. I was slow in getting started. Then I began to think, 'Why should *I* have to be the one to clean it? She's home all day. I work eight hours a day plus I commute for two more. Why should I have to come home and do this? She's always taking advantage of me. I'm being screwed–and I've known this for years.' Then I heard her shout tauntingly, 'What's the matter? Can't you stand being in the cellar alone?' I shouted back, 'I don't want to clean the cellar; it's your job.' She came down the stairs to argue with me, and then I hit her."

This man deeply regretted the consequence of his toxic rage: his wife subsequently divorced him. He admitted to me that he had been unwilling to deal with his anger since their very first disagreement. After a decade of pushing his angry feelings down and letting them accumulate, the pressure inside him was enormous. He didn't intend to hurt his wife, but he lost control.

Before lovers can negotiate, both of them must let their healthy anger out. If you want to confront the conflict and your lover wants to avoid it, you won't ever get to the negotiating couch. It takes only one of you to short-circuit the system by burying your angry feelings. On ABC's *20/20* Barbara Walters and Hugh Downs were interviewing marriage researcher Dr. John Gottman of the University of Washington. All three of them agreed that husbands avoid conflict more frequently than wives do, and Dr. Gottman declared that regular withdrawal by husbands is the biggest predictor of divorce.[14] But men don't have a monopoly on hiding their anger. One couple I interviewed described their relationship like this:

SHE: When I get annoyed I don't want to talk about it. I show my displeasure with silence, whereas he likes to put it out on the table, deal with it, and get past it.

HE: You think that if you don't discuss it, then there won't be a problem. But even if we don't say a word to each other, I just know the problem is there.

To Break Down the Resentment Barrier: Ask Questions

If your lover's favorite saying is "I don't want to talk about it," how do you get her/him to express her/his healthy anger? *By asking questions.* "Are you upset? Did what just happened bother you? Are you annoyed at me?" This is powerful communication. People are secretly complimented when someone, especially the one they love, is interested in them. At first you may not get an answer. Or you may hear something like "I don't know. Just leave me alone." It may be necessary to ask several times—and wait a while between each time—before there is a response. One moment when you least expect it your lover will reply. Spontaneously. When this happens, put down whatever you are doing and *listen*. Do your best not to interrupt or to talk too much about your own feelings. If you allow your lover to experience her/his anger completely, eventually the hidden fear, envy, guilt, loneliness, sadness or pain will surface. (Remember the layer cake of feelings?) Then you can share these emotions together. Once you both have processed them, you are ready to discuss your unmet needs and negotiate love.

Do you have to forgive your lover completely before you start to negotiate? Not necessarily. Some couples don't make up; they simply allow enough time to pass so that they can cool down. Others apologize and forgive each other before they sit down to talk. Saying "I forgive you" does not mean "I agree with you." Nor does it mean "Let's forget about our disagreement." What it means is "I forgive you for getting angry at me; now we're ready to discuss the issue."

Negotiating love expands your forgiveness. As you explain your point of view to me, I get to understand you better. You tell me why you behaved as you did and why you believe as you do. I share the same information with you. Now we are ready to forgive each other not only for our explosions of anger but also for not meeting each other's needs.

For example, after Phil had returned from an out-of-town trip, he told me that he had spent some time there with another woman. As he put it, he had the "warms" (although not the "hots") for her. I was jealous and I got angry. He thought I was being overly possessive, so he got angry. During the next few weeks we had several heated arguments. Then we exchanged apologies. We forgave each other for the shouting but we still were unhappy about his attraction to this woman and my jealousy. Then we sat down and negotiated love. Phil learned that underneath my anger, jealousy, and possessiveness was pain. My pain arose from old wounds—memories of other women he'd been attracted to in the past. He needed to feel that I trusted him now; I needed to know that he still loved me the best. By the time we finished negotiating love, we had forgiven each other completely.

By now you may be asking yourself, "What if I have disagreements and unresolved conflicts with my lover that I've been hiding for a long time? If I've been storing away anger and building up resentment, is it too late?" *No.* Make the decision right now that you will "come clean" with your lover. First, work on your own feelings. Can you transform them from toxic rage to healthy anger? If not, ask a friend or find a therapist to help you. Then ask your lover to set aside a time when s/he will support you in letting off steam safely. Prepare your lover in advance that you are going to share some angry feelings. Warn her/him that they may come out with a "pop" instead of a "fizz," but that eventually they will dissipate.

If you believe your lover has been harboring resentment for a while, start asking her/him questions about it. Proceed slowly and carefully. "Has . . . been bothering you for a while? Are you becoming more and more frustrated about . . . ? Are you fed up with . . . ?" If s/he inquires, "Why are you asking me?" explain, "I love you; that's why. I want to make sure you're okay with this." The chances of a toxic rage outburst diminish if your lover feels that you really care. So from time to time, let her/him know, "I'm available if you want to talk."

Then wait. Be prepared to receive your lover's feelings when they erupt. If s/he is reluctant to share them, be patient. Years of resentment do not disappear overnight.

As long as you are angry, you can't resolve conflicts. So first you need to express your angry feelings in a healthy way. By doing this, you get ready for the second stage of powerful communication: negotiating love.

CHAPTER 3

Creating the Right Mindset: Ten Ways to Get to the Negotiating Couch

You and your lover have finally emptied out all your anger. Are you now ready to sit down and talk? Not necessarily. Before you can effectively negotiate love, it is essential that both of you feel like allies, not enemies. If you follow these ten suggestions and create the right mindset, you will move quickly to the "negotiating couch":

1. Don't take it for granted that you and your lover are ready to negotiate love. First confirm that you care for each other, are committed to resolving your conflicts, and are willing to compromise.

Take a moment to ask yourself these three fundamental questions: Do I really care about my lover? Am I committed to continuing our loving negotiations even when they temporarily break down? Am I willing to compromise? Then ask your lover the same three questions. Do you really care about me? Will you make the same commitment to stick with our relationship? Are you willing to meet me halfway?

Being deeply in love inspires you to negotiate. Many of my interviewees told me that otherwise they would have walked away. One woman said, "I'm willing to do a lot of things that I said I would never do because my lover is the most important person in my life. I'm even willing to postpone having a baby because he's not ready. The intensity of my passion for him simplifies everything." A man stated, "My love for my fiancée is something I feel from the soles of my feet to the hair on my head. For it not to be honored would be the end of the line." A single man who had not found a woman he truly loved commented, "If I go out with a woman and I care for her a lot, I cater more to her needs and desires. If I don't have very strong feelings for her, I tend to insist on getting my own way. That's because I don't really care if we break up." A single woman added, "If I like a man enough to spend time with him, I'll say, 'Okay, I'll do that,' when he suggests something. I won't try to have it all my way; I want him to be comfortable as well."

Second, for loving negotiations to succeed, you have to make a commitment to see them through. As you confront your conflicts, there will be difficult moments. Is your relationship worth the effort? Many of my interviewees told me that because they answered no to this question, they never negotiated with their partner. Love is the force that makes them want to try. As one man put it, "My love for my wife is worth fighting for. In my two prior marriages, I got to a point where I felt it wasn't worth the struggle. The love just wasn't there. So I stopped. I won't fight a battle I don't have my heart in. Since this time I do, I work at it." Couples seminar cofacilitator Dr. Jim Sniechowski described to me how his commitment to Dr. Judith Sherven, his wife and cofacilitator, evolved: "I never really entered into my first marriage; the back door was always open. I thought, 'There's always divorce.' In my second marriage I was ready to make a commitment. The back door was locked; I could not sneak out. Yet the back door was still there. With my third wife, Judith, there isn't even a door; the whole *wall* has been plastered over. We both have a commitment; we call it 'Nobody leaves the room.' I know she's not leaving and she knows I'm not going anywhere. As a result, there's freedom here to really open up and let whatever happens happen. It gets pretty stormy sometimes. But it's also the deepest relationship I've ever had with another human being."[1]

Both of you have to be committed to negotiating love. *If only one of you is motivated, it is not enough.* I am reminded of an incident that took place many years ago in a previous marriage. After my former husband and I had left the dance floor, an acquaintance of mine pulled me aside and commented, "I couldn't help but notice when I saw the two of you out there that you were doing all the dancing. He was just standing there, swaying his arms and legs a bit." We couldn't shine as a couple on the dance floor unless both of us were giving our best. The same holds true for negotiating love.

Another prerequisite for loving negotiations is that you and your lover both be willing to meet each other halfway. In legal and business negotiations this is called "split the difference." This strategy is often used when there's a disagreement about a sum of money. The difference between your price and the other party's offer is cut in half. By subtracting it from your price and adding it onto the other party's offer, you reach agreement. While split the difference is common practice in businesslike negotiations, it is fiercely resisted by lovers. Compromise has a bad name among both women and men. Some women see it as being a doormat. As one woman put it on one of the call-in radio talk shows I appeared on, "No man is going to tell me what I have to do. I don't care to be told when and how high I have to jump." Many men are even more resistant. I have heard them remark, "When you start compromising, you might as well get castrated," or "The ring isn't on your finger anymore; it's through your nose."

To many people compromising means being controlled. This has been an especially difficult issue for Phil and me. During the early years of our marriage, he'd buy items for the household without talking to me beforehand. When I'd ask him afterward why he didn't talk with me first, he'd reply, "That would be asking your permission. I don't need to do that." What he meant was that if we had a discussion, he might never get to buy what he wanted. It took a while before he was ready to listen to my point of view. What I shared with him is that there is a difference between total surrender and compromise. Powerless people surrender. Totally. They say, "Okay, do it your way. Never mind what I need." Powerful people compromise and also set limits. We say, "I prefer this way instead of that way." Or we say, "This way is totally unacceptable to me." If Phil had checked with me first before he went shopping, I wouldn't have told him he couldn't buy what he wanted. But I might've suggested some prices or colors I preferred. And he'd counter with his own. As two powerful people, we would each have an equal say in the negotiations.

Do you shudder at the thought of compromising? If so, you're probably concerned that your viewpoint is not going to be respected. If you're the reluctant one, spend some time alone exploring your own limits. Then you will be able to say to your lover, "This is what I am willing to do," or "This is what I am unwilling to do." If your lover is the one who is unwilling to compromise, your task is more difficult. Start by acknowledging her/his fears (which usually arise from feeling powerless). Then explain that in loving negotiations both lovers' limits are respected; you go back and forth until you reach a solution that honors both hers/his and yours.

Like affection and commitment, your willingness to meet your lover halfway develops slowly. It takes time to explore your own self, establish your own limits, and become flexible. Be patient with yourself. And with your lover.

2. Don't let your resistances to negotiating love hold you back. Think, "I can; it's worth it; and it will work."

Even caring, committed lovers who are willing to meet each other halfway still resist negotiating love. Why? Because it's a new experience. And if you've never done it before, you don't know how rewarding it's going to be. So, human nature being what it is, we tend to procrastinate and avoid taking a risk that might mean a change for the better.

Sometimes we deny that our differences as a couple even exist. You would be amazed at the number of couples I talked to who said, "Us disagree? Never. We agree on just about everything." Somehow every time I heard these words I became suspicious. It sounded too perfect. More than one of these "perfect couples" later split up.

Other times we make excuses. Some of the most common are: "I can't," "I don't know how," "It takes too much time," "It's too much hassle," and "It won't work." None of these statements is true. *Almost anyone can learn to negotiate love.* That's why I've written this book. Yes, it does take some time and it can be difficult, but it is far less painful than a breakup or a divorce. And the rewards of getting along with each other are priceless—for you, for your children, and for the world.

Women are more likely to be initially receptive to negotiating love than men are because we are used to being peacemakers in our family relationships. But because women are less likely than men to take risks, we are sometimes afraid to try.

When women do take the initiative, men often resist strongly. As one man put it, " 'Let's talk about our relationship' isn't as simple as 'Let's open a bottle of wine!' " Yet once they start, men become fascinated as they apply the negotiating skills that they already know in a brand-new way.

Is negotiating love effective? I can tell you personally that it is. Other women and men whom I have interviewed for this book and who have come to my seminars agree. You and your lover are invited to try it and find out for yourselves.

The best way to deal with your resistances is to confront them. Whenever you hear yourself or your lover making an excuse, remind yourself that that's just what it is—an excuse. Put it out of your mind and think instead, "I can; it's worth it; and it will work." Suggest to your lover that s/he do the same.

The most difficult resistance of all is "I can't." People who say these words feel powerless. What is power? It is energy. When you are full of energy you are power"full." You have your own opinions; you know what you will and won't do; and you bring all this energy to the "negotiating couch." When you are empty of energy, you are power"less." You are looking for your lover to fill up your energy tank instead of doing it yourself. But your lover can't make you powerful; *only you yourself can*. If this is where you're stuck, skip to Chapter 9 (if you're a woman) or Chapter 10 (if you're a man). Then read Chapter 12.

You can't negotiate love until both you and your partner

begin to experience your own power. When you are power-"full" you come from a place of fullness. You know who you are, how you feel, and what you need. You are able to direct your attention toward discovering your lover's preferences, feelings, and needs. Then powerful communication begins. When you start asking questions, you will soon find out that your lover's answers are not the same as yours.

3. Acknowledge and respect your differences. You and your partner are not identical twins.

Until you have a clear sense of who you are, you can't recognize how your lover is different. When you start discovering your own self you will realize that the two of you are separate people. On some issues you agree; on others you disagree.

Most of us have been taught to be ashamed of conflict. Our goal is peace and harmony. If we have an argument with our lover, we think, "Oh, no, we're at it again. Maybe there's something wrong with our relationship. I'd better fix it right away." So we give in, insist on having our way, or else deny that there's a disagreement at all. Some lovers refuse to listen to any point of view except their own. They'd prefer to have a clone of themselves, and when they don't find one, they're disappointed. That's a tragedy.

Recognizing that your lover is not your identical twin is an essential first step. The second step is to give her/him the room to be her/himself. One happily married man confided, "I sometimes wish my wife were more like me but I accept that she is not." A married woman I interviewed gave me a vivid example of how she and her husband are unique: "My husband and I express our love differently. He plants beautiful flowers in our yard and decorates our home. I'm highly verbal; I talk a lot about my feelings and write him love letters. One day I asked him, 'Please write me a love letter.' He replied, 'No, I don't write love letters. Writing beautiful words is your thing. I show you my love in my own way.' At first I was disappointed. Now I just let my husband be who he is and appreciate his unique qualities."

Lovers have not only different styles of expression but also divergent tastes. One woman recalled a moving incident: "I like long plays; my lover doesn't. One day he bought me two tickets to *Nicholas Nickleby* and said, 'Please take someone with you who will enjoy it.' I misinterpreted him and thought he was rejecting me. Later on I realized that he was doing just the opposite. He had genuinely appreciated our difference and was paying me the compliment of honoring it."

The truth is that conflict is an essential part of all relationships. If you and your lover *don't* have differences, there's something wrong. Conflicts are inevitable; *it's how you handle them that counts.* If you and your lover are continually arguing, you're stuck in the prenegotiation stage. What happens next is up to you. Will you continue fighting? Will you store up resentment? Or will you decide to empty out your anger and acknowledge your differences—which will actually make your relationship much more exciting. Jude Blitz says of her own relationship, "In many ways Tom and I are very much alike. But any differences add energy and vitality to our relationship. *We think of ourselves as training partners.* We are willing to stay at odds with each other until we reconcile our positions."[2] Experts Drs. Judith Sherven and Jim Sniechowski sum it up: The purpose of negotiating is "to go from 'my way' and 'your way' to 'our way.' So you need to have a sense of the other person being just as important as you are—in soul, in mind, and in body. Her/his perspective is as valuable as yours."[3]

You can learn more about your lover's viewpoint by asking open-ended questions, questions that require more than a simple yes or no answer. The next time you share an experience, ask your lover, "How do you feel about this?" or "What is it like for you?" When the two of you disagree, ask, "Where are you coming from?" or "How do you see it?" *Listen carefully to your lover's answers. This is powerful communication. Your lover's special gift to you is a perspective that is different from yours.*

4. Quit competing with your lover. Be willing to share your own unique gender gifts instead.

Here's a quick quiz: Are women's ways better than men's? Or are men's ways better?

If you don't believe that either of the ways is better, you are correct. If you supported either women's or men's ways, however, you are not alone. Many people still mistakenly believe that the way of life of one sex—usually their own—is more valuable than the other.

Before you can negotiate love you must value the perspective of both sexes. *This mindset is very important.* Lovers compete only with themselves, not with each other. There is a big difference between "I want to do better today than I did yesterday" and "I am better than you." When you try to overshadow your lover, you are competing in a race that neither of you will win—and both of you may lose.

Women and men are natural allies. We need each other, we nourish each other, we are good for one another. But we have different traditions and cultures.[4] Each of us has a special and unique kind of power. First we learn about our own strengths and then we discover each other's. When you value yourself, you say to your lover, "As a woman [or man], I'm worthwhile, but you don't have to be like me to be okay. As a matter of fact, I can learn from you. I can understand your point of view; I can get interested in your way of life; and I can adopt some of your behaviors."[5] As we teach each other, we both become wiser.[6]

Women and men each have their own contributions to make to loving negotiations. Writers and seminar facilitators Jean Houston and Marion Woodman have both assessed women's strengths. Accustomed to caring for children and running a household, which don't often provide tangible results, women focus on process (living in the moment) rather than on seeking goals (making something happen in the future).[7] The female perspective on negotiation is that the conversation itself is valuable, irrespective of where it eventually leads. Just sharing our feelings and needs with each other brings us closer.

According to Jean Houston, women communicate by networking. Because they talk to each other as peers rather than as superiors or inferiors, they exchange large amounts of information quickly.[8] For this reason, women foster cooperation and connection while they negotiate. This is an important female contribution.

Men bring with them a lighter, more relaxed approach. Skilled in negotiating, they view it as a game. Instead of taking the conversation seriously, they can teach us to play. Because men are so goal-oriented, they'll help keep the conversation on track when it starts to wander. When your male lover says "Let's get to the point," he's helping both of you focus on the issue you're negotiating. Problem-solving is another male strength.[9] A female negotiating style focuses on going deeper; the male style concentrates on achieving tangible results. When women are ready to seek a solution, men will have dozens of solutions in hand. Men are also more willing to take risks and to experiment with new ways to meet our needs.

Men's familiarity with teamwork is also a valuable asset in negotiating love. They are accustomed to viewing their own personal interest as less important than that of the general team, whether it be in sports or business. They are accustomed to being team players and cooperating with their team members.[10] If your male lover sees the two of you as a team, he'll be willing to put your needs as a couple first and work together with you as partners.

Because men generally have clearer, firmer personal boundaries, they tend to pull away from their lovers, while women tend to push closer. When we negotiate we alternate between moving toward each other and distancing ourselves. There is a strong tug from man to woman and from woman to man. This tension actually helps us negotiate better. Being too closely merged would keep us from recognizing our separate feelings and needs at the beginning; being too distant would keep us from reaching a common solution at the end.

Neither women nor men have a monopoly on the most important personal qualities necessary to negotiate love: empathy, sensitivity, and compassion. As we communicate with each other we nourish these traits within ourselves, and we move away from our preoccupation with our own needs and feelings to focus on our lover's as well.

5. Forget about winning, getting your way, and being right. Think, "Maybe I'm being stubborn. . . . I might even be wrong. . . ."

Probably more couples never get to the negotiating couch for this reason than for any other. One woman graphically described the problem we all face sometimes: "My ex-husband was committed to one thing: being right and making me wrong—even though I'd remind him, 'Even a broken clock is right twice a day.' In a discussion, he would always say, 'No, this way is better; I'm right.' It ended up that we would never agree on anything; when I would hear him trying to win, I would get sucked into his game. He'd trigger me and I'd play right along."

Why is it so important for us to be right? Why do we need to win so badly? With this mindset we'll *never* get to the negotiating couch. (And if we *do* sit down together, we won't stay there for long!) There are at least four reasons. First, ours is a competitive world. In the world of business, people who reach their goals the fastest are rewarded. In the world of sports, the rewards go to the winner. And we all know how much energy we spend to be victorious in war. When we talk to each other, we follow the same pattern. And so often lovers think in terms of "either–or." Either I win or I lose. Either you're right or you're wrong. We don't consider the possibility that both of us can win—or that both of us can be right.

As children we grew up in homes where our parents were always right. How many of us can remember our mother or father admitting, "It was I who was wrong"? When we competed successfully for good grades or when our team won at sports, we were praised. Now that we are adults we are still rewarded for winning and respected for being right.

Second, some experts have speculated that we have a deep psychological need to be right. Roy Schenk, author of *The Other Side of the Coin*, reminds us that psychologist Alfred Adler wrote that when people feel inferior in some way, they compensate by finding other ways to see themselves as superior. Then they treat other people as inferiors. Men see themselves as superior to women in professional achievements; women see themselves as superior in personal relationships.[11]

Other experts suggest that winning and being right bolster low self-esteem, a common problem both sexes experience.[12] Men and women with low self-esteem need to control each other.[13] Their thinking runs along the lines of "I have to be in control. To keep you from controlling me, I'll control you first." To maintain control, they need to have the last word.

A third reason that being right is so much a part of us is due to other people's expectations. Many of us secretly believe that other people will respect us more if we act as if we have all the answers. Many men claim that the other sex likes them better if they act as if they are right. One of my interviewees told me, "I've experienced a loss of respect from some women when I wasn't the great decision-maker. Many females have a certain disrespect for males who cannot always make up their minds." (However, while initially the attitude "I'm right; I'm in control; I know what I'm doing" may win a woman's respect, later on, if it becomes stubborn self-righteousness, it can keep the two of them from negotiating love.)

In my own opinion, the best reason for wanting to be right is that it feels good. One day when Phil and I were talking we noticed that we were playing "I'm right; you're wrong" with each other. "Why are we doing this?" I asked him. His reply was compellingly honest: "I enjoy being right." When I thought about it, I realized that I, too, revel in that smug, self-satisfied feeling. The problem is, we pay a price for this temporary "high" of self-righteousness: In order to be right, we have to make someone else wrong. If it's our lover whom we're continually bashing, criticizing, or putting down, we'll never reach the negotiating couch.

What happens instead is that you and your lover get into a tug of war that nobody wins. In her book *The Couple's Journey*, Dr. Susan Campbell has a wonderful activity that illustrates this point. She suggests that you and your lover hold one side of a piece of paper (I suggest a dollar bill). Both of you then try to get the paper from the other—but if either of you damages or tears it, the activity ends. It soon becomes clear that if you pull hard on the paper and your lover resists the tug, you both will fail.[14] The same principle applies if you use a rope. If either of you pulls hard enough, the rope breaks or else one of you ends up dragging the other. At the very least you both wind up with rope burns on your hands. *The only way to stop the damage is for one of you to drop the rope.*

If you or your lover insist that you're right and the other is wrong, you're in the same predicament. Neither of you is going to get the other to meet your needs by insisting. If you keep on pulling harder and harder, the conflict will escalate and you will never wind up negotiating love.

A preschool teacher whom I interviewed tells her children when they fight over a toy, "Let go of the toy. Now, take turns, or go get another toy." In this situation, each child needs the toy right then, and both are certain they are entitled to it. But neither one will enjoy playing with the toy unless one of them temporarily gives it up. As the teacher put it to me, "I want to teach these children that you can't get everything you want at exactly the moment you want it. And if you relinquish what you seek temporarily, you might get more than you imagine in the long run."

How can we apply this to our intimate relationships? If you or your lover is continually insisting that you're right, you've reached a dead end. One of you may very well have the right answers. But stubbornly insisting "My way is best" is *not* how to get what you need. Forget about winning, getting your way, and being right; there is no great scorekeeper who is counting your and your lover's victories. With this new mindset you can entertain the possibility of there actually being another valid point of view besides yours—"Maybe I'm being stubborn. . . . I might even be wrong. . . ." This is negotiating love: It means keeping an open mind.

Couples workshop facilitator Dr. Ivan Burnell gave me an excellent example of this from his own personal experience: "When I met my wife, Dahny, she had five children from a previous marriage and was determined not to remarry. I was very attracted to her, so I pursued her and finally proposed. She said no. Instead of pestering her all the time to change her mind, I simply told her, 'I will never ask you to marry me again. One day you'll either tell me yes or say good-bye. It's up to you.' A few months later she suggested, 'Let's go steady.' Soon afterward she said, 'Let's get a marriage license.' "[15] If Dr. Burnell had insisted on getting his way right away, they probably wouldn't be happily married now. So, even though it turned out that he had been right—that the two of them *would* be happy getting married—he dropped the subject rather than pressure Dahny.

Radio talk-show host Bill Thompson shared with me how he and his wife, Nancy, were able to start negotiating love. In Bill's words, "When Nancy would share her ideas, I'd take a step back and try to listen to her objectively. I would say to her, 'I may not agree with you, but I'll listen to what you have to say. I can try to convince you and you can try to convince me.' Often I'd realize during our discussion that she had made a good point. We saw things differently because we had been brought up differently. Why should we judge each other when it was possible that both of us could be right—or wrong? Nancy and I ended up making a game out of it. Whenever she turned out to be right I'd buy her a present." Nancy continued. "I got a lot of 'I was wrong; you were right' presents. One time we got into an argument at a shopping mall. A few minutes later he showed up and said, 'Here's ten dollars. Go buy yourself an "I was wrong; you were right" present.' I looked at him and said, 'Can we have another argument?' He asked, 'Why?' I said, 'Because what I really want costs twenty dollars!' "[16]

In a more serious vein, another man I interviewed told me how he and his wife had reconciled once he abandoned his either/or mindset. Although she had wanted the marriage, he had divorced her because he had felt hemmed in by family responsibilities. As she put it, "For a long time all he could see was his own point of view. All he could say to me was 'I'm under a blanket; I'm stuck in a corner.' It felt as if we were sitting on opposite sides of a table. One day he knocked on my door and said, 'I need to talk to you. I'm really concerned about what I have done to the boys.' When he said that, I felt that suddenly he was looking at this divorce from the same place as I was. It was as if he had walked around the table and sat down on my side. He didn't have to agree to return to me, but at least we could talk to each other." They began negotiating love and subsequently remarried each other.

Why is letting go of the need to be right so effective in bringing two lovers to the negotiating couch? *Because it equalizes the balance of power.* A lover who keeps insisting s/he is right overpowers the other. For loving negotiations to begin, *both* lovers must perceive that their points of view will be respected in the conversation. If one of them is constantly being told "You're wrong," this lover will start to feel powerless. Eventually s/he'll say to her/himself, "Why bother?" when the other lover suggests that they talk about the issue. When you decide that it is more important to communicate than to be right, win, or get your way, you've taken a major step toward negotiating love.

6. Stop placing blame and saying, "It's all your fault"; instead, recognize that both of you are partly accountable and focus on dealing with the situation at hand.

The majority of my interviewees told me this was one of the most common reasons they did not negotiate love. Does this scene sound familiar?

Your lover, who is supposed to meet you and your friend for dinner, doesn't show. Finally s/he arrives just as the two of you are starting dessert:

YOU: Where've you been? You've kept us waiting here for over two hours.

YOUR LOVER: You shouldn't have arranged this dinner on a night when I always work.

Suppose the issue is more serious. Your lover has dented the fender of your new car:

YOU: How could you be so careless?

YOUR LOVER: You know I'm not a great driver at night. So why didn't you drive me to the dry cleaners instead of just lending me the car?

Arguments like these can go on well into the night without resolution. Anger can consume us both. And when we're angry, the best defense is an attack.[17] But until we stop blaming each other we will never negotiate love.

How can we alter our mindset? By dealing with the situation rather than continuing to accuse each other. We can stop saying "What did you do wrong?" and start saying "What is happening now?"[18] In other words, we can direct our attention to the issue rather than to each other's personalities. We'll reschedule dinner and get the car fixed. And we'll start asking, "How do you feel? What do you need? What should we do next?"

Besides, when a mishap occurs, it's *not* just one person's fault. A man I interviewed from the construction industry explained how his business decides who's at fault when there's an accident: "Every dispute has two parties involved. If something happens, both parties are one hundred percent accountable." In other words: I'm not entirely responsible; you're not totally responsible; we're both jointly responsible for whatever took place. Maybe I assume more of the responsibility; maybe you do. In any case, we both did something wrong. It's *our* fault. With this mindset we're ready to negotiate love.

7. When your lover says "I'm sorry," forgive her/him and let go of the past.

To say "I'm sorry" is not easy for many of us. It makes us feel uncomfortable, embarrassed, or ashamed. One couple, whom I'll call Linda and Ken, told me how difficult it was for Ken to get used to giving and receiving apologies:

LINDA: When Ken would get displeased he would always look for somebody to blame. Everything was *always* my fault. He would never take responsibility for anything. He couldn't say "I'm sorry" to me.

KEN: She's right.

LINDA: If I hurt him accidentally and immediately said "I'm sorry," he wouldn't believe me. He wouldn't accept my apology. I'd have to spend hours showing him that I really meant it.

KEN: Linda helped me work my problem through.

LINDA: I showed him that there's nothing wrong with making a mistake. It's okay to say "I'm sorry" to someone and to take responsibility for something rather than blaming someone else.

Like many people, Ken was reluctant to apologize because he was afraid of being made to feel guilty. When we do, we feel unworthy and our self-esteem plummets. Unfortunately, many of us are pros at inflicting guilt on our loved ones. Here is the scenario that every lover dreads:

YOU: You're right, I shouldn't have done that. I was wrong. I'm sorry.

YOUR LOVER: No, you never should have done it. You ought to be ashamed of yourself.

Shame is frightening. A man or a woman can be devastated by a lover who tells her/him not only that s/he acted badly but also that s/he is a bad person. Even veiled threats of guilt or shame are enough to keep us from whispering, "I'm sorry." If s/he says these two words, s/he's playing right into her/his hands.

A man I interviewed described a situation in which his lover made him feel guilty and ashamed instead of accepting his apology: "I said to her, 'I did something really stupid. I forgot to buy you a birthday present. I'm sorry. What do I have to do to make it up to you?' At the same time I was thinking, 'I can't defend myself on moral grounds. So if she tells me I'm an awful person, she's somewhat justified, and I'll feel bad about myself. I won't be able to summon up the words to defend myself.' Well, the worst happened. She gave me a fifteen-minute tirade that went something like this: 'Besides this, you did this and you did that and you did that other thing too. My birthday is a mess—and so are you.' Her words tumbled out with such force and conviction that I felt like a subhuman. Now, I was aware that I wasn't as guilty as I seemed. Yet I couldn't utter a single word in my defense. Why? Because all that time I was sitting there thinking, 'It's going to take at least an hour and a half to dissect every one of her accusations! It's so much work to argue back that it's easier just to walk out and say to myself, 'I don't want to deal with it.' So I left."

This man did not have a trusting relationship with his lover. Together they had not created a safe, secure emotional climate where they both could be themselves without fear of ridicule or reprisal. If they had this trust, he could have said, "I'm sorry; I made a mistake," and she would have replied, "I forgive you. I was disappointed, but it's okay; I still love you. Here's what you can do to make me feel a little better . . ."

How do we forgive each other? *A Course in Miracles* is a superb resource on this subject. Its most precious insight is that when you forgive your lover you're also forgiving yourself. *You've* probably done the same thing sometime in the past. Did you forgive yourself? Hopefully you did, so how can you make someone else feel guilty about something that you've done too?[19]

Your lover may be totally innocent. S/he may have no way of knowing that s/he's poked at an open wound or made demands on you that conflicted with your own agenda. And once s/he realizes, you may receive an immediate apology.

Sometimes we injure each other accidentally. We respond, "I'm sorry you tripped; I promise I won't forget to pick up the kids' toys next time"—and we really mean it. We won't be able to undo what happened, but we can say, "I'll do better in the future. I'll write myself a note. And I'll make you dinner tomorrow night." *When we allow our lover to make amends we are giving her/him a precious gift.* If we also go on to say, "Maybe you can help me pick up the toys at the end of the day when I'm really tired. I'll be glad to pitch in and help you with the yard work on weekends," we are now negotiating love.

If you both decide to redistribute the household chores, you have reached a new agreement. What began as a painful interchange ended up as a fruitful negotiation.

8. Stop hiding from yourself. Recognize your own major wounds from your life history.

None of us reaches adulthood without being hurt. Perhaps we were wounded by our mother's abuse, our father's absence, or our sibling's death. No matter what our wounds are, it takes courage to look at them. We must do that *before* we negotiate love.

Self-examination is challenging. It is up to you exactly how you do it. You may choose to spend time alone, go to seminars, or work with a psychotherapist. In any case, your goal is to discover which people have hurt you, what they have done to you, and, most important, *how you felt at the time, and how you feel today.* To negotiate love effectively, you need to focus on the wounds that affect your relationship with your lover, and those that influence how you deal with conflict.

If you are uncomfortable making a deliberate search for your wounds, here's a foolproof way to get some insight. In psychologist Dr. Judith Sherven's words, "If, after an incident occurs, your feelings are nuclear, ballistic, or even astronomic, they're from your childhood. They have little or nothing to do with what has happened or what your lover did."[20] In other words, when you vastly overreact, you're connecting to something that happened in the *past* rather than in the *present.*

It's difficult to negotiate love if you don't understand your wounds. You'll be continually blowing up for reasons that have nothing to do with the present conversation. Or if you manage to reach agreement, you'll still be upset afterward. One couple, whom I'll call Maria and Ned, gave me an excellent example of how they managed to get past Maria's wounds once they determined their cause:

NED: Maria thought I was wasting my time when I watched football.

MARIA: I'm more interested in reading or listening to music. When the television set is on, it puts up barriers between people in the room. You can't have a conversation, and people *need* to communicate. I think that you're not "there" with the other people in the room if you're watching television.

NED: Despite these feelings she had, Maria was not going to stop me from watching football. Besides, we determined it's more than just football. Often she feels like I am paying too much attention to something else, like the television, or someone else, such as another woman—rather than to her.

MARIA: It finally occurred to me that my first husband used to get really involved with his computer and the television. So this whole situation really pushed my buttons. When Ned watches football, I don't feel like I'm getting any attention, and that's just how I used to feel in my first marriage. Now that I understand *why* I feel this way, it's been easier. I go grocery-shopping during a game or I go into the bedroom, close the door, and read. I know Ned will give me the attention I need when the football game is over.

Maria had started searching blindly, and gradually got at the cause of her pain. She was able to understand her wound all by herself, and take measures to diminish the negative impact it was having on her relationship with Ned. But not everyone can do this in every situation. Often we need a support group or a trained professional to empower us to explore our past.

Once you know what your major wounds are, you can tell your lover something about them. Needless to say, you must trust her/him first. You have to believe that your lover will treat the information you share with deep respect. If you are experiencing that level of trust, there are many ways to reveal yourself and your injuries. You may choose to have a series of brief conversations about your wounds before you start negotiating love. I don't recommend a marathon talk, but often this can occur. If talking directly about your wounds isn't comfortable for you, you can inform your lover if and when s/he touches on your sore spots during your loving negotiations. "You didn't mean to hurt me, but you did. It's because a long time ago . . ." etc. Or, "I know you didn't realize that what you said would cause me pain, but it does because . . ." etc. Always remember: *Your lover may be totally innocent.* Since women's and men's wounds are typically different, s/he may have absolutely no idea about what causes you pain.

9. Don't treat your partner like a stranger. Find out about his/her major wounds. What may be no big deal to you may be a very big deal to your partner.

You should not only share information about your own wounds, but also learn about your lover's. Why? Because if you don't know what they are, your negotiations will be like minefields. After you make what appears to you to be a perfectly innocent remark, your lover may suddenly blow up. For example, on Father's Day you may say dreamily, "It's so wonderful to have a dad, isn't it?" You may not know that your lover was abandoned by his father at an early age. Or after your lover washes the dishes, you might remark, "I really appreciate it when you share work in the kitchen." You may not be aware that what you said reminds him that his mother never expressed appreciation to him for any of the chores that he did. You merely intended to be pleasant—or to pay your lover a compliment. But what was no big deal to you was a very big deal to your partner.

An unmarried couple I interviewed (I'll call them Ruth and Peter) shared how this issue came up in their relationship. Their conversation went like this:

RUTH: It's been very rocky for the year we've been together. Peter's giving me a lot, but he's holding back from a total commitment.

PETER: I need more time. I'm not ready. I'm still dealing with the end of a marriage; it's fairly fresh in my mind.

RUTH: Every time we address the issue of commitment, we blow up.

PETER: I'm being cautious. I'm not sure I know her well enough. In fact, I have some doubts about her history when it comes to relationships. She gets in and out of relationships too easily and quickly. I'm afraid she'd leave me that easily too.

RUTH: Ahh. *There* it is. It's not the surface issues that have been bothering us; it's what's underneath the surface. Peter's afraid of losing someone again.

PETER: You're right. I don't want to repeat what happened with my first wife.

Until Peter shared with Ruth how he had been wounded in his marriage, they had frequent and always fruitless conversations about her loyalty. Once Ruth understood Peter's wound, she gave him a lot of reassurance whenever the issue of fidelity came up. Their loving negotiations became easier.

Of course, it's impossible to watch every single word you say when you negotiate love. In normal conversation there is give-and-take, healthy banter, and affectionate teasing. No one tiptoes all the time. But learning about your lover's wounds *can* help you keep your negotiations from breaking down. Avoid a sensitive subject when you can; be gentle when you can't. Ask your lover to alert you when you accidentally touch on a sore spot.

In all likelihood your lover has only a few danger zones where you need to proceed with caution. How do you find out what they are? Without being nosy or intrusive, ask questions. (A little powerful communication can go a long way.) If your lover avoids a specific topic that may indicate a particularly sensitive area for her/him or if your lover is reluctant to answer you from the outset, be observant. Sooner or later you'll find the information you're seeking.

When you honestly share the pain of your old wounds, you take a giant leap toward the negotiating couch. But don't get stuck retelling your life story over and over again. The purpose of connecting with your past is to build a bridge to the *present.* To negotiate love is to be together in the here and now.

10. Don't give up when you blow up; heed the presence of your "little observer."

Negotiating love requires persistence. No matter how angry you get, you should always return to the negotiating couch after you empty out your feelings. No matter how much you feel like quitting, you must stick with it. If your negotiations break down, you wait a few days and start again. You *always* leave the door open for a future conversation.

But sometimes we get frustrated with how slow this makes our progress. We'd like a shortcut to end the conflict. There is a way. Get in touch with your little observer, a little voice inside you that enables you to detach yourself from what's going on and see the whole situation in perspective.

Arguments and misunderstandings *will* happen. We're all used to trying to win, trying to be right, and trying to get our way. The trick is to catch yourself while you're doing it. Your little observer knows and points out to you exactly what's happening. When you begin to observe what's going on, you can start to shift the way the argument is heading. It gives you a choice: Do you want to continue what you're doing? Or do you want to stop doing it and do something else? You can catch yourself in the midst of an argument and put on the brakes.

For example, suppose you notice yourself saying, "I'm right; you're wrong." Your little observer tells you to ask yourself, "Is it more important to be right or to be in a caring relationship with my lover? Do I want us to compete or do I want us to *cooperate*?" Then you can say to your lover, "Do you hear me trying to make me right and you wrong? Let's stop and continue this conversation at another time." When you resume your dialogue, you can start with a different framework.

Your little observer is also useful during the anger stage. One woman told me, "At the beginning of our relationship we fought a lot. We'd just yell and yell until we were exhausted or until someone had to leave. Then there would be a calming-down period where we would call each other on the phone. Our little observers helped us realize, 'This is a ridiculous, stupid argument. There is no reason to continue it anymore.' So we'd start negotiating and end up compromising." Another man told me about a big blowup he and his woman friend had on New Year's Eve. "It was the first and only time that I ever left her. When I returned eight hours later we had both listened to our little observers. We sat down and said, 'Wait a second; what are we doing to each other?' We really committed that night to working things out, and we've been talking regularly ever since." Psychologist Dr. Susan Jeffers, author of *Opening Our Hearts to Men*, makes this point excellently: "When we get angry we become numb to the feelings of the other person. We lose sight of their pain. We attack, blame, and call the other person names without realizing, 'This could really hurt.' The only way we can stop ourselves is to take control of our thoughts. We can say to ourselves, 'Wait a minute, here is a human being who has feelings just like I do.' "[21]

Where is *your* little observer? Different people find it in different places. Some of us find it within our minds; others find it within our bodies. A few people locate it in their emotions. How does it show up? If it's in your mind, it might be visual. "I'm in a balloon hovering over the living-room couch and watching us play 'I'm right; you're wrong.' Or "I'm sitting in an audience that's watching a movie of the two of us arguing." If it's in your body, it might be tension that you experience in your head, stomach, or back when the conversation moves in a direction you don't want it to go. If it's in your emotions, you may find yourself shouting, weeping, or yawning instead of responding rationally to your lover.

Why is it so difficult sometimes to find your little observer? Because to connect with it we have to reverse the flow—and conflict has a momentum of its own. Its natural tendency is to escalate and then to repeat itself. We're programmed to keep on attacking each other and protecting ourselves, not to reach out to each other in trust and forgiveness.

In order to end a disagreement, one lover has to detach her/himself and then urge the other to do the same.[22] As soon as one of you says, "This arguing isn't getting us anywhere," and the other agrees, all of a sudden your mood shifts. If one of you then asks, "Why is it so important for me to be right?" and the other says, "That's a good question," your conversation moves in a different direction.

Once the flow is reversed, you're carried right along toward reaching agreement. But to reverse the flow the pressure *has* to come from an outside source. So you and your lover need to get in touch with your "little observers" as early on as possible. Once you start using them, both of you will stay on track until you reach agreement.

CHAPTER 4

How to Reach an Agreement That Satisfies You Both

You and your lover have had an argument. You've expressed your healthy anger and now you're sitting on the negotiating couch. What happens next? How do you resolve your differences and reach agreement? There is a definite three-phase procedure to follow.

The Three Phases of Negotiating Love

Negotiating love has three phases:

1. *The preparation beforehand*
2. *The conversation about the issues*
3. *The agreement afterward*

No matter what issue you are negotiating, you go through all three of these phases. Your issue may be relatively simple, like deciding what vehicle to buy. Or it may be more complex, such as determining which one of you is going to leave work to pick up a sick child at school. In both cases, you get ready to negotiate love, you have a conversation about the issue, and you arrive at an agreement.

PHASE ONE: THE PREPARATION BEFOREHAND

There are four steps in preparing to negotiate love:

1. *Figure out how you feel and what you need*
2. *Acknowledge and define the issue*
3. *Negotiate about how you are going to proceed*
4. *Determine your nonnegotiable issues*

1. FIGURE OUT HOW YOU FEEL AND WHAT YOU NEED

Before you and your lover sit down together, you first have to figure out how you yourself feel. Unless you know what is in your heart, how can you possibly share it with someone else? Take a few moments by yourself to breathe deeply while asking yourself, "How do I feel? Am I annoyed? Am I furious? Do I want to cry? Yell? Throw something?" If you find that you feel angry, then you are not yet ready to negotiate love, because (as you learned in Chapter 2) you need to empty out your anger in order to reach the other feelings hidden underneath. Anger may conceal fear, envy, guilt, loneliness, sadness, self-doubt, or general pain.

If you are a man, this step will probably be a very difficult one for you. Traditionally you have been encouraged to act rather than to feel. Since many deeds that are expected of "men"—such as going to war and rescuing people in danger—are painful, you may have become accustomed to numbing and distancing yourself.[1] Negotiating love requires the *opposite* approach. Learning how you feel is not unmanly, and is an essential preparation for negotiating love. Try asking yourself, "How do I feel?" over and over again when you're alone. If you find that nothing comes up for you or you're experiencing only anger and can't get past it, you may want to consider joining a men's support group. In these groups men meet together regularly to give each other a safe place to share honest feelings. They also support each other in learning how to put their feelings into words.

One man who took the New Warrior Training Adventure[2] (a weekend designed for men who want to explore their feelings and connect with other men on a deeper level) described his experience like this: "In college if you asked me how I felt, I'd say, 'I don't *know* how I feel.' What I meant was, 'I don't know how to get inside the feeling, describe it to myself, and then explain how it is for me.' As a man I've always had a hard time with feelings. So you can't imagine how much strength it took to go to the New Warrior weekend. But it was worth it; it taught me to clarify and deal honestly with my own feelings as well as with other people's. Now I'm sharing what I learned with my wife."

Lovers' negotiations are not only about feelings but also about *needs*. While feelings constantly change, needs tend to remain the same. After you've explored your feelings, ask yourself, "What do I *need*?" You may have to return to this question many times before you can sort out your answer. To help you identify what you need right now, recall what you've often needed in the past. And don't let your *need* become confused with what you *want*. For example, you've asked your husband to help clear out the attic so you can set up an office in your home. What you *want* is an office of your own, but what you really *need* is peace, quiet, and privacy for getting your work done.

If you are a woman, you may find it extremely challenging to get in touch with your needs.[3] For centuries, we women have been taught to think of *other* people's needs, not our own. We may even think it's selfish to give ourselves this much attention. Well, it's not. A martyr can't be a happy lover—or a good negotiator. Why? Because a martyr is busy thinking of everyone else except her/himself. You may find it a challenge to get in touch with your needs—and when you do, you may be overwhelmed. Some people come to recognize that their "I need" inventory is as long as a Christmas wish list! Some common needs you may recognize are: love, attention, companionship, sharing, understanding, emotional support, respect, valuing, nurturing, sex, money (or the things money can buy), fun, career advancement, closeness with family and friends, order, flexibility, freedom, time alone, and privacy.

Do you have an especially long list of needs? If so, don't panic. First, realize that you should not start negotiating love by presenting all of them to your lover at the same time. S/he'll probably feel overwhelmed as well, and this will end your conversation immediately.

There is a difference between sharing a need and making a demand. Sharing a need sounds something like this: "I just lost my job. I need extra nurturing from you right now. I need to have some plain old fun, to cheer me up." Underneath your words is the message "If you can't meet my need right now, I'll be disappointed but I'll go on." You are telling your lover what s/he can do to make you happy but at the same time letting her/him know that you can handle a no as well as a yes answer.

Making a demand sounds like this: "I know I just lost my job but I'm not going to bother looking for a new one. You make enough money to support both of us." A person who says this takes her/his inner child and places her/him squarely on the lap of her/his lover.[4] A one-way relationship like this is unfair.

An essential rule of negotiating love is this: Decide which of your needs are the *most* important. In other words, pare down your wish list. Ask yourself about each need, "How strongly do I feel about it? On a scale of one to ten, how important is it to me?" (You may want to get out a pencil and paper and rank each one.) Negotiate with your lover *only* about the ones that are at least a two. Select no more than the top two or three needs for starters, and negotiate *one at a time*. Ask your lover to do the same. You even may want to make an agreement that you won't obsess over lesser issues if you resolve the most important one. For example, I may feel that I need two things: For you to pay more attention to the children so we can become closer as a family, and for the house to be neater. However, the latter may be a lesser priority for me. So I won't worry so much about the mess in the house if you agree that all of us will spend Sundays together. One couple married over fifty years told me that this was how they managed to get along with each other so well: "If it's really important, you accommodate each other. If something really makes your partner happy, you do it." But before you can ask your lover for something, you have to know what you desire deep within. What do you really need? What is very important to you? What will make you truly happy?

It doesn't matter which you do first: recognize your feelings or figure out what you need most. What *is* important is that you spend time alone before you negotiate love.

All resolution of conflict begins within. You can sit together with your lover until the sun comes up, but you are not going to get anywhere unless you first sit down by yourself. You can't resolve a difference with anyone else until you have worked out the conflicts inside you. Take the time to establish a strong sense of personal identity. You have to know who you are, what you believe, and what you want from life.[5]

Where do you go to examine your thoughts and explore your soul? It's up to you. Walk in the woods, sit by a lake, or seclude yourself in a hotel room for as long as you need and look at your own self. Or use the hours you spend alone driving in your car, exercising, or taking a shower. Don't sit down on the negotiating couch until you have done your deep thinking and soul-searching. Why? Because when you and your lover are resolving your differences, your identity will be continually challenged: "How come you need this? Couldn't you do just as well with that?" You *have* to be sure of your own needs beforehand, or you won't get them met.

You may not know how much you need something until it's too late to ask for it. I have made this mistake myself. One Easter week, a dear friend of mine was singing at a Holy Thursday service at the Washington Cathedral. I mentioned to Phil, "It would be nice if you would go with me." He waffled for a few days and then at the last minute decided he had work to do. "I'll skip the service, if you don't mind," he said. "Okay," I replied casually. It was only when I arrived there that I realized how much I really needed Phil to be with me. My friend had been close to my late son, and being near her, I found myself experiencing losing him once again. How I would have loved to have been able to share my feelings, and also enjoy the beauty of the singing, with my husband. Had I taken the time to ask myself beforehand, "What do I need? How important is this to me?" I could have told Phil, "I know you have work to do. But I really need you to be with me tonight. It'll take only a couple of hours and it would mean a lot." He told me later that had I approached him like this, he would have accompanied me gladly. His work really hadn't been so urgent after all.

2. ACKNOWLEDGE AND DEFINE THE ISSUE

Before you can resolve a difference of opinion you have to admit that it exists. Many of us regularly practice denial. It takes different forms: "Whatever you want, dear. . . . It doesn't make any difference to me [when it really does]. There's nothing wrong here. . . . Everything's fine." First, you yourself have to recognize that there's a conflict: "S/he needs more time alone, but I require more love and attention from her/him." "S/he needs to make love less often than I do." "Both of us need to spend less time doing the housework."

Once you acknowledge there's a conflict, you can then go on to define it. What is going on between the two of you? What do you disagree about? What, if anything, do you agree about? You should be able to describe the issue in about three sentences. But there are no rules. One of you may sum it up in four words, "I need more sex," while the other may go on for five minutes about women's monthly cycles, sexual rhythms, and varying levels of desire.

Angry lovers are unable to define an issue; often they cannot even acknowledge its existence. All they know is that they're mad at and blaming each other. When they shout, "It's all your fault," or "Shut up," they cloud their vision even more. That's why we need to express our healthy anger first, before we negotiate love. Once our "anger tank" is on empty (or nearly so), we can start to figure out exactly what our conflict is about.

3. *NEGOTIATE HOW YOU'RE GOING TO PROCEED*

Let's call this "the negotiation about the negotiation." This may sound a little confusing, but it is a critical step in negotiating love. Before you negotiate about the "what," you must agree on the "how." You and your lover have to agree how you will discuss issues before you actually take on a specific one.[6]

What you and your lover are going to do is to develop a set of procedures for negotiating love: "This is how we are going to talk about things. This is the time when we will negotiate love; this is the setting where we will do it." Both of you create these rules *together*. They won't be your rules; they won't be your lover's rules; they'll honor the feelings and needs of both of you as a couple. To achieve this, each of you must see the other as an equal and feel entitled to have a say in the decisionmaking. If either one of you feels, "S/he's much more powerful than I am" (for whatever reason) or "S/he's going to get her way on everything," it will be very difficult for the two of you to create any rules. And, if you do, they'll reflect the style of the person who is considered more powerful—and will break down in the long run.

But before you start discussing procedures, you must consider the question of timing. No lover can negotiate until s/he is ready. If your lover is ready and you are not, it is a waste of time and energy to even start. If you are open and your lover is not, it won't work either. The best you can do is to offer her/him an invitation and then wait. You *have* to honor each other's rhythm. It might be that one of you is still angry; it might be that one of you is just not in the mood. If one of you is tired, hungry, thirsty, or otherwise physically uncomfortable, s/he'll most likely be irritable during the conversation—and especially if it's about a tense issue. So if one of you has had a bad day, it's best to postpone your talk.

What rules should you set in this "negotiation about the negotiation"? First, you must agree in advance how long each loving negotiation will be. We all dread those seemingly endless conversations that keep us up until two A.M. and don't resolve anything. It's better if you start off with a time limit—even if you mutually decide later on not to stick to it. Fifteen minutes to a half hour at a time is a good beginning limit. As you progress, you can work your way up to an hour or more if you both choose to.

The setting also must be agreed upon. It's friendlier if you sit side by side instead of across from each other. If you sit at a table, a round one is preferable to a square or rectangular one, for the same reason. Whatever the setting, it is important that it be relaxing for both lovers and free of distractions. One couple remarked, "We often sit down next to each other and talk together at the dinner table after we have finished our meal. We don't get into a discussion unless we have put on the telephone answering machine, shut off the television, and put away the newspaper (or at least agreed not to look at it). Our physical needs have been met already; we've worked out, taken a bath, had dinner, and taken a nap if we needed one." Another couple commented, "Our hot tub is where we have our discussions. We call it our 'communications center.' We talk every night about our problems and our differences."

You also need to agree on the particular issue to be discussed. If one partner feels that something is an issue, then it is—by definition.[7] There should be no argument about whether to talk about it. Will you discuss more than one issue at a time? The two of you will decide.

You also need to work out *how* you are going to talk to each other. What happens if one of you doesn't stick to the issue being negotiated and goes off on a tangent? Or if one of you monopolizes the conversation or interrupts continually? What is your recourse if your lover tells a lie? Or gets emotionally or physically abusive? To negotiate love effectively, many lovers prefer to have an agenda, either verbal or written. You might create an agreement that goes something like this: "We agree to negotiate one issue at a time. If by chance we find ourselves negotiating two or more, we'll stop right then and decide which one to handle first. If one of us gets off the subject, the other will call her/his attention to it and together we will bring the discussion back on track. We agree to allow each other approximately equal amounts of time—to talk, to pause, and to be silent. We agree to do our best not to interrupt each other (or we agree that it's okay to interrupt each other). We agree not to lie. We agree to use neither emotional nor physical violence. If either one of us starts insisting on not abiding by these rules, we will immediately end the conversation. We will limit our discussion to fifteen minutes [or whatever length of time you prefer] and extend it only if we both agree. Plus, before we end, we will arrange for another time to continue our loving negotiation if we find it necessary."

Just as loving sex requires fore*play*, loving negotiations require fore*thought*. So, do consider the time, the setting, and your frames of mind before you proceed to the negotiating couch. However, if you prefer to work out these agreements informally, that's okay too. Phil and I often do. For example, sometimes we sit down to negotiate and one of us will say, "I just don't want to talk. This is not a good time for me." So we try again later and see what happens then. You may prefer our casual style or find it more appropriate to set up guidelines in advance. See for yourself.

4. DETERMINE YOUR NONNEGOTIABLE ISSUES

Every person has nonnegotiable issues.[8] These are the issues that make you queasy, give you the chills, and make you want to scream—or cry—when you think about them. These "nonnegotiables" are intertwined with your strongest, deepest feelings. When they come up, your buttons get pushed; your old wounds start hurting, and you get extremely emotional. You are encountering a nonnegotiable issue when you hear yourself saying, "This is something I feel very strongly about. . . . I really need this. . . . This goes against my values. . . . This is extremely serious. . . . I simply have to have it my way, because if I don't, I will either go out of my mind or walk away from this relationship."

Nonnegotiable issues can be sweeping moral principles or just different ways of life. Common nonnegotiables are: sexual exclusivity, having children, substance abuse (smoking, drinking alcohol, or using drugs), religion, political views, and lifestyle. One couple's nonnegotiable issue was neatness. At the time we spoke, they had been seriously involved with each other for three years. Dave informed me, "We love each other dearly. But I tend to be a neat person and she's just the opposite. In her house I can't find a table to put things on that isn't cluttered. That's the reason we're not married." Carol commented, "I can live with chaos; in fact, I thrive on it. I love to do several things at once." When I went on to question him, Dave admitted that he secretly admired Carol's creativity, flexibility, and spontaneity. He actually enjoyed having her around and hoped that someday he'd be more like her, but he couldn't imagine living with disorder every day. As he put it, "I have no more right to my lifestyle than she has to hers. I'm no more correct than she is. But I have to ask myself, 'Can I live with all her mess?' And I don't think so. It would drive me *insane*." They're still together but living separately.

Other couples find themselves absolutely adamant about other nonnegotiables: "I would never convert to another religious faith. . . . I refuse to live with someone who smokes. . . . I would never marry a Republican" (or a Democrat). If your lover feels exactly the opposite, then both of you are at an impasse. And the more nonnegotiables each of you insists on, the more stormy your relationship will be. Imagine what life would be like if your lover insisted, "No, I won't eat at Mexican restaurants; I once got food poisoning in one. And I refuse to drive a Jeep; my ex-husband drove one and it reminds me of him. Plus I'll never live in the country; it's too boring." With so many dead ends, it's going to be difficult for the two of you to find a road on which you can both travel.

The only way to deal with a nonnegotiable issue is to agree *not* to negotiate it for the time being. Every six months or so, review the nonnegotiable issue and check if your feelings have changed. If they have, start negotiating love.

You and your lover need to ask each other, "What is deeply important to you that I must do my best to respect? Would it be best if we agree not to talk about it?" This does not mean "If I do this for you, then you'll do this for me." No one is bargaining here, so it's okay if your lover has three nonnegotiables while you have only one. The essence of your shared understanding is "We agree that we will both honor each other's limits."

Before you can declare an issue nonnegotiable, you need to define exactly what it is. Are you talking about a single issue like sexual exclusivity, or multiple issues such as sexual exclusivity, frequency of lovemaking, and sexual style? It's a lot easier to negotiate love if you're talking about one specific issue. Precisely what is important to you? That your partner never have sexual relations with someone else, or that s/he never *date* someone else? *Make it clear.*

If it's an entire issue area that pushes your buttons, like sex, profession, or religion, then say so. Within this hotspot, you need to lead, and your lover needs to follow. Someone has to decide the steps and the direction in which you both will move. And while your lover should lead in those issue areas crucial to her/his happiness, you should lead in yours. One woman informed me: "In my relationship with my partner, I insist that I run my business exactly the way *I* want to. I need the time and space to forge ahead with my career. Sexually, he gets *his* way. There's never any discussion about prowess; he's delighted to have a strong career woman who's giving him what he needs in the bedroom. And I'm satisfied; my career is skyrocketing. Yes, we actually made our agreement explicit. We told each other, 'You need this to exist, and I need that,' and when we put the two together, it worked."

Sometimes this kind of understanding may be implicit. For years I didn't realize that my nonnegotiables were neatness (I'm a fanatic) and time (I don't *do* mornings). Phil's were religion (I converted to his) and sex (he doesn't like me to take the initiative). Eventually our relationship evolved to the point that each of us got our way in each of our sensitive areas (what I term "hotspots" in Chapter 8) 90 percent of the time. Whether or not you choose to sit down and formally negotiate about nonnegotiables is up to you; all that matters is that you do deal with them.

When you're deciding what *not* to negotiate, include both your most important and your least important issues. Identify what you simply must have and what doesn't matter very much at all. Put those issues that don't matter aside. Your lover will do the same. What you're both left with is your agenda for negotiating love. Now you're ready to tackle the remaining issues one at a time. Start with the easiest, smallest ones and leave the toughest, biggest ones for last. You need to negotiate love *slowly*. Handle a simpler issue first, resolve it successfully, and then select a slightly more difficult one. If you can't get anywhere with a particular issue, put it on the back burner and move on to the next. That's how it is in business and law.[9]

PHASE TWO: THE CONVERSATION ABOUT THE ISSUE YOU'VE CHOSEN

Before you jump into your first loving negotiation, consider how you will present the issue. Your intention is to make your lover receptive to your needs and feelings, so think carefully about your choice of words, your tone of voice, and your body language. If you use inflammatory words ("You always . . ." or "You never . . ."), if you have anger or sarcasm in your voice, if you stiffen your shoulders and fold your arms across your chest, you will distance your lover. Similarly, if your words are supportive ("Let's try to work this out together . . ." "How can I support you?"), if your tone of voice is friendly, and if you sit close by your lover with your hands lightly resting on her/his shoulder or thigh, you will engage her/him.

Women and men also have different communication styles. Dr. Aaron Kipnis and his wife, Liz Herron, who are both experts on gender issues, tell us: If you're a woman, you're used to sitting face-to-face with your partner, using a lot of words, and talking about your feelings. If you're a man, you're accustomed to sitting side by side (face-to-face usually means a direct confrontation for men), having lots of pauses and long silences, and talking about more factual matters.[10] If you learn your lover's communication style, take it into account, and even adopt some of it, you can bridge your conversational gap. If your lover does the same, your loving negotiation will proceed much more smoothly.

How do you stay on track? Whenever you experience

confusion, remember what you're trying to do: communicate your feelings, state your needs, and figure out how your feelings and needs can be honored. Instead of letting the conversation wander, guide it.

1. COMMUNICATE YOUR FEELINGS

You have already spent time alone understanding your feelings; now is the time to express them: "This is how I feel (I'm disappointed, discouraged, disgusted). This is why I feel this way . . ." and so forth. You must get your emotions out in the open before you can negotiate about any differences. Hopefully, you have already emptied out most of your anger before you start. All too frequently lovers start getting furious at each other when they begin this step. If this happens, *immediately* end the conversation. Start negotiating love again only when you have finished dealing with your intense anger in a healthy way.

What if you feel an initial barrier of mistrust? Any expression of your feelings at all will overcome it. Even if you and your lover speak about your inability to trust each other, that's a step in the right direction. As Dr. John Guarnaschelli, a leader in the men's movement, explains, "If I stand there and say to you, 'I really can't trust you right now,' that's actually trusting you."[11] When such trust and self-revelation occur, you and your lover are negotiating love. However, you may need to make many attempts before you each are able to tell the other what you really feel.

Ideally, your lover will listen and respond with sensitivity as you tell her/him about your feelings. What if s/he scoffs at what you're saying instead? Call it to her/his attention. "I wish you wouldn't do that. Please take me seriously." If your lover persists, postpone the conversation.

When you feel you are finished expressing your feelings,

ask your lover to share hers/his. "How do *you* feel? (Are you unhappy, upset, confused?) How does what I say make you feel?" If your lover gets very angry or upset and an argument is about to erupt, put your little observer into action. "Look at how upset we're both getting about this. Is this issue really worth it?" Or else take a breather. Renegotiate love later, when both of you can share your feelings openly and kindly. It may take several discussions before you're ready to acknowledge and define the issue.

2. STATE YOUR NEEDS

This is the time to be *completely honest*. Hopefully, you took the time earlier to make up your mind about what you really need from your lover. Now is the time to tell her/him just what that is: "I need love (attention, companionship) from you." Never resort to manipulation as a way to communicate your needs. Only after you have shared where you are can you and your lover have a firm base for negotiation. If you do not tell your lover what you need, that is *your* choice. It is not your lover's job to figure out what your need is. It is *your* responsibility to communicate it.

At this point in the loving negotiation, you don't want to just let your lover know what you need; you also want to tell her/him *why*. Here is when you really get to know each other.[12]

Why do you need what you need? Everyone's answer is different. At this point you may suddenly become immersed in a sea of introspection. Or you may find yourself turning back the clock and talking about events that happened long ago. You and your lover may learn things about yourself that neither of you ever realized before. If your lover is a skilled communicator, s/he will keep on asking you such questions as "When did this need first come up for you? . . . How did this happen? . . . What is it like for you right now? . . ." These questions will draw you out, and by the end of the conversation you will feel heard.

3. FIGURE OUT HOW YOUR FEELINGS AND NEEDS CAN BE HONORED

Here's where both of you will start being creative. If you and your lover have read Chapter 3 carefully, you will have learned not to unload your own responsibility onto each other. You will avoid saying, "It's all your fault that I feel this way. It's because of you that I don't have what I need." And your lover will do her/his best not to respond in kind, "You have no right to feel as you do. There's nothing I can do about your need." Instead, you will start thinking about how you can both remedy the situation. One of you will make a suggestion: "What if your mom comes to live in the intermediate care facility near our home?" Or, "Maybe we can adopt a child instead." You will take a good, hard look at what you can do for yourself and each other. You will start asking, "What am I willing to do?" Your lover will in turn examine her/his role in what is happening. S/he will start asking, "What can I do for you? How can I support you in getting what you need?" Both of you should be committed to creating new options and remaining open to all possible solutions. Professional mediators call this process brainstorming.

Of course, not all your suggestions will work. Most probably won't. Some will not meet your needs; some will make your lover uncomfortable; and others won't satisfy either of you. You need to consider your own and your lover's personal boundaries. Some solutions may seem controlling or intrusive to one of you. You need to respect your own—and your lover's—limits. If one of you is unable or unwilling to embrace certain solutions, s/he should make a countersuggestion: When s/he says, "I won't do that," s/he will continue, "But I'm willing to do this . . ." Or, "This is all I can manage right now. . . . Is it enough?" Think carefully before you respond critically. Each of you can handle *only so much.* And the more one of you feels that an issue is nonnegotiable, the less that one of you will be able to be flexible.

The most effective loving negotiations take place when both of you take turns sharing your feelings and needs as you explore the issue. Together you find a solution that will respect the feelings and needs of both of you. "I'm willing to do this. Now what are you willing to do? Will this meet your needs? It'll work for me." If you can figure out how your needs overlap, you have a foundation for agreement. For example, you feel frustrated because you need more quiet to write poetry. Your lover is feeling suffocated in the relationship and requires more time by her/himself. Perhaps together you can work to create more "alone" spaces and times for the two of you.

It is during the conversation phase that negotiating love is most different from what occurs during businesslike negotiations. There are no offers and counteroffers; instead, there are suggestions and countersuggestions. This is because both of you are on the same team. You're not trying to make a deal; you're working together to see how you can *support* each other. If you can figure out how to meet your lover's needs, *both* of you will benefit.

Most lovers' negotiations are not well-organized, coherent, and clear. So chances are yours won't be either. It's important that you don't expect them to be. I've used the phrases, "I feel . . ." "I need . . ." "What about . . . ?" "I am willing to do this . . ." "But I am unwilling to do that . . ." throughout this chapter. In your actual discussion, your negotiations may not be stated in this order and in these exact words, but they may still be a part of your conversation. What I've given you is only a model. Words and feelings should be phrased in the way you and your lover are most comfortable with. Use the model only as a roadmap for when you run into a detour or get lost.

For example, Phil and I had the following loving negotiation after he told me he had some feelings for another woman. It sounded something like this.

ME: I'm really upset. It sounds like you're really interested in her.
HE: I don't like it when you're being controlling.
ME: Well, I don't mean to control your whole life. But it *is* important to me that you don't have sex with other women.
HE: What about flirting with other women at parties?
ME: That's okay.
HE: What about being friends with them?
ME: That's fine. But that's where I draw the line.
HE: What happens if you get attracted to some other guy?
ME: The same thing goes for me too. Whoever feels the desire will talk about it. Then we'll support each other in dealing with it so that we can remain faithful to each other.

Translated into the terms of our model, the conversation would have sounded like this:

ME: *I feel* afraid that you're getting sexually interested in someone else.
HE: *I feel* angry that you're controlling my life.
ME: I don't mean to. But *I need* to know that I can trust you sexually.
HE: *I need* to know that you're not always on my case.
ME: I'm not. I only *need* this one thing.

HE: *What about* flirting? *What about* having friendships? *What's off limits?* What's nonnegotiable?

ME: No sex. *I am willing* to support you in having friendships with other women. *I am unwilling* for you to have sex with them.

HE: Okay. *I am willing* to forgo having sex with other women and *I am willing* to continue to be faithful to you.

ME: *Do you agree* that if either of us experiences sexual desire for another person, we will share it with one another and assist each other in dealing with it?

HE: *Yes, I agree* with you.

In our actual conversation, we communicated our feelings, shared our needs, and figured out how our feelings and needs could be honored. There was no neat script.

PHASE THREE: THE AGREEMENT AFTERWARD

The goal of negotiating love is to reach agreement. You and your lover seek a solution that honors the feelings and needs of both of you. You decide what you will do for each other. Unlike businesspersons and lawyers, you never use sentences like "These are my terms and conditions. If you don't agree to them, the negotiation is over." Lovers communicate in their own language: "This solution would make me very happy. How do you feel about it? Would it meet your needs?" And, "This solution doesn't meet my needs, but I would be willing to go along with you on that other one." Or one of you may simply say, "I want to be with you so much that I'll put my need on hold for now so we can honor yours." You don't mean, "I'll sacrifice my needs in favor of yours," but, rather, "It's your turn now; we'll take care of my preference later."

Lovers' agreements are give-and-take. Temporarily you may give something up, but you also get something back: the joy of knowing that your lover is satisfied and that you've supported her/him.

One phrase both lawyers and lovers use is "Let's make sure we both have the same understanding of what we have agreed on."[13] If both parties leave with different expectations, inevitably one or both will end up disappointed. So figure out what you will do for each other; start by discussing your agreement in general terms, and then move on to specifics. For example, the summer when I was writing this book, Phil and I agreed that we needed to spend more time together. After that, I made a list of fifty-one activities that we both enjoyed and posted it on the refrigerator. When I finished writing this chapter, we already had done about a dozen of them.

It helped us to put our agreement in writing. If it helps you, *do* it. Start off with a few words about how much you love and care for each other. Then write down exactly what you have agreed upon. At the end, note whatever disagreements remain. The whole agreement doesn't have to be more than three or four sentences.

Jane and Ira firmly believe in detailed written agreements. They had learned this technique at a church seminar and started to use it when they first began dating. They would start off by developing a verbal understanding and then later put it in writing. Their first agreement was simply that they would take care of each other. They also wrote down that there was no expectation of sexual exclusivity, getting married, or his helping to put her two children through college. Since Ira's relationships normally lasted no more than three months, he had insisted that this information be included so that Jane would know where she stood. Afterward they said they both felt more comfortable with each other. They continued to update the agreement every three months with the understanding that it could be terminated by either person. Ira terminated it when he left Jane; he said that he needed time by himself. One year later he returned to her and proposed. They updated their agreement again, knowing that marriage would change the expectations in their relationship. They wisely agreed that if they grew apart, they would seek counseling. Ira said to me, "The agreement really helped me feel safe about contemplating a second marriage—especially because I'd gone through a difficult divorce." Jane agreed with him.

Despite Jane and Ira's reaction, written agreements aren't for everyone. Some lovers feel that they make the negotiation more complicated. Others feel that they imply mistrust: "I don't believe that you will do what you promised, so we have to write it down." Personally I believe that written agreements *simplify* loving negotiations. In my view, the biggest barrier to lovers' keeping their agreements is not dishonesty but forgetfulness. Often Phil and I write down our agreements, particularly when money is involved, because both of us tend to forget the exact amount and who owes what to whom. Our agreements are usually only a couple of sentences long—and they are effective.

When Couples Fail to Reach Agreement

Don't expect your first loving negotiation to end in agreement. Included in your "negotiation about the negotiation" should be an agreement about what you will do next if you do not agree. This may simply mean that before you end your loving negotiation you will arrange another time to continue. During my interviewing I found only one couple who insisted they needed only one session. The woman told me, "When we have a disagreement, we talk about it right then and there. He and I snap and then we apologize. I tell him how I feel and we keep at it until we reach an understanding. A lot of people walk away, but we feel that if we do this, it's harder to come back." Their viewpoint is unusual. You *don't* have to resolve everything in one marathon negotiation. Typically it takes several fifteen- or thirty-minute sessions over a week or more before you can find a solution that works for both of you.

A couple married for over thirty-five years described their experience to me:

SHE: When we negotiate a major issue, we talk about it in bits. I know it's there; you know it's there; and we let it simmer.

HE: I throw up "trial balloons": "I'd like to do this . . ." or "How about we try that. . . ." Then I hear how they sound and find out what your reaction is.

SHE: Sometimes I don't respond right away because my reaction can change over time. I usually need some time to think things through before I finally make up my mind.

A "trial balloon" gives a couple an opportunity not only to share their gut reaction but also to come back with a countersuggestion. If you don't like your lover's "trial balloon," then send up one of your own. Replying with "No, but . . ." or "How about another way . . ." keeps the conversation alive.

If one of you decides you've had enough, then that's the end of the loving negotiation for now. *Let your lover go.* Each of you must feel you have the freedom to walk away from the negotiating couch without guilt or fear of retribution.

Negotiating a little at a time actually gives you an *advantage.* You have the chance to think through what has been said. If you have been extremely stubborn, you have the opportunity to reconsider and back down without embarrassment. If you have been refusing to accept your lover's feelings and needs, you have a chance to make a fresh start. There is nothing like a good night's sleep to enable you to develop an open mind.

A loving negotiation that ends without reaching agreement is a temporary setback. Let it be. Put it on hold. Remember, for lovers there is *no* deadline, and that's an advantage you have over businesspersons. Sometimes it takes a while; you have the opportunity to try again. I spoke to a couple who, despite an incredible array of complicated family issues, succeeded simply because they refused to give up. For example, one conflict arose because his ex-wife would come over to their house regularly unannounced.

ELLEN: Whenever I found his ex-wife somewhere in our house—sitting in the living room, talking on the phone, or downstairs doing her laundry—I'd tell Frank how I felt. I would refuse to keep it inside of me. At least three or four times a week I would stop him and say, "I have to tell you this." "I don't want to hear it," he'd answer, "so are you sure you want to say this to me?" "Yes," I'd insist, "because I cannot live this way. She's always in my space."

FRANK: Ellen *wouldn't* walk away. She'd always persist. She had a sense of herself and her values, and she was going to stick up for what she believed in. She'd bring it up and I'd listen, even though I didn't want to hear what she needed.

ELLEN: Eventually, he did speak up. He stood up for me and told her not to come over anymore without calling first. I finally got the privacy I needed. With my first husband, there was no resolution to our conflicts. We couldn't even talk about them. But Frank and I can. That's why we're still together.

Another woman told me, "One of the things that bothered me about my lover was that he had a strong sex drive. I work pretty late hours, and I'd come home and want to go to sleep. I wouldn't be ready for a romp in the middle of the night. When he'd wake me up, I'd tell him exactly how I felt. I figured I had nothing to lose. He thought what I had to say was valid; he actually listened to me. We finally figured out some times and ways we could make love that suited both of our needs."

A third couple, whom I'll call Grace and Harry, had a more complex sexual problem but also managed to work it out with persistence.

HARRY: Grace and I have different ideas about sexuality. I've never been a sexual person; I have a hard time expressing myself this way. I'm very spiritually developed; my whole life revolves around this. But for Grace, sex is one of her most creative ways of self-expression. Spirituality is not all that important to her.

GRACE: You can see how we would often conflict. At the beginning it was complete havoc. We were very frustrated with one another. Because we're very different people we couldn't understand each other's viewpoints. I'd be talking about one thing and he'd be talking about something else. What made sense to me didn't make sense to Harry.

HARRY: But we never stopped trying to get each other to understand what we were talking about. We never let it drop completely or said "I've had it" and walked away. Instead, we just kept experimenting. We said to each other, "There'll be one way or another that will work."

GRACE: And one week there'd be no problem at all; everything would be going great. Then one day it would snap. We'd get frustrated, have a fight, and then cool it for a while, saying, "I gotta think about this for a while and figure out another way to explain it to you."

HARRY: We found that there's nothing wrong with putting everything on hold for a while. What good is it to struggle to express yourself if the other person is not in the mood to listen?

But sometimes loving negotiations can come smack up against what seems to be an insurmountable barrier. Perhaps you have made a false assumption or your lover is projecting her/his own past experience onto you. When you and your lover find yourselves getting stuck, check your mindset. If necessary, go back and reread Chapter 3. Identify the barrier that you've encountered, and start dealing with it.

If you or your lover starts getting angry, stop your conversation immediately. You're back in the prenegotiation stage now. Deal with your anger in a healthy way before you go back to negotiating love. One couple I interviewed recommended "refighting the fight." This is when you go back, taking a bad fight, and redo it. One of you asks, "What went on last night? Let's do this one over." You make an appointment for a "rematch" after you've cooled off. This time, instead of exploding, you tell each other what you were feeling while you exploded. Handling a conflict in this way short-circuits your anger until you're ready to resume a conversation that will mutually benefit the two of you: "How can we find a solution that meets both of our needs?"

Negotiating love requires patience. You and your lover must both be committed to explaining your viewpoints and to listening to each other until you reach an understanding. This truly is an act of love. As couples workshop facilitator Julio Olalla puts it, "What you are saying is, I care enough to stay with you through all your questioning, to explain to you my ways of thinking and to listen to yours."[14] You also are saying, "I will be patient. I will support you no matter how difficult this loving negotiation gets."

Every so often you and your partner will make a breakthrough. First you will learn how to negotiate love. Then you will resolve a major issue that has been dividing you. Next you will work out several major issues in a troublesome hotspot area. Finally you will manage to cool off several hotspots. What satisfaction you'll feel! Seeing the happiness that brightens your lover's face will make you feel that all your efforts were worthwhile.

Is It Ever the Right Time to Give an Ultimatum?

Ultimatums are a common tactic in businesslike negotiations. Lawyers walk out of meetings; businesspersons withdraw their offers. Both are making it absolutely clear that unless they get their way, the negotiation is over. If their fall-back position is strong, they'd rather end a negotiation than compromise. Committed lovers operate differently because neither gains anything by walking away permanently.

Should you ever deliver an ultimatum to your lover? And if so, when? An ultimatum is appropriate mainly in an emergency, when your lover's angry behavior exceeds the limits you've agreed upon. If you are in serious physical or emotional danger, this is the time to say, "Stop it, or we're through." But this is not something you should demand in ordinary loving negotiations. If your attempts at negotiating love repeatedly fail, it's better to get a neutral third party to mediate your dispute. Threatening to leave is *not* the solution of choice.

However, if your lover's behavior has been destructive for some time, you may be ready to end the relationship anyway. In this case, you may want to warn her/him first. Take some time alone to define the issue as you see it. What behavior can you no longer tolerate? How does it make you feel? What do you need to survive? Promise yourself that you will ask for it. Then pick a time to talk when your lover is receptive; express yourself clearly, and listen carefully to her/his responses. Give your lover time to think about what you said and allow her/him to make her/his own choice. In the event that your lover refuses to honor your feelings and needs, be prepared to follow through. If you have threatened to change the locks if s/he doesn't stop drinking, then call a locksmith the next time s/he goes on a binge.

How do you reach agreement? There is no magic formula. In the last analysis, do whatever works for you. What you seek is a balance between your needs and your lover's; it doesn't matter exactly how you achieve it. All the suggestions in this chapter are guidelines, nothing more. My intention is for you and your lover to reach agreement *your* way, not my way!

CHAPTER 5

The Eleven Secrets of Negotiating Love

When you and your lover negotiate love, your goal is to build a bond of trust. Otherwise you won't keep on returning to the negotiating couch. Knowing these eleven secrets will enable you to trust each other—and also to have fruitful conversations and reach agreement quickly.

Secret 1: When you negotiate love, tap into your inner power—which is infinite.

Power is energy. Your inner power is the energy within you. The emotional, intellectual, physical, and spiritual energy that comes from within you has no limits—and depends upon no one else. You are power"full" when you are full of this inner power and have extra energy to give to other people. The more power you share, the more you get back.

If you are not aware of your inner power, you feel power"less." Believing you lack energy, you try to get it from other people. You control, manipulate, make demands, or hang on to your lover to get power from her/him. You think, "The more power my lover gets, the less *I'll* have." That's not true.

To understand the enormity of your inner power, think of you, as a child, watching a big pot of hot apple cider simmer on the stove. As you see your parent ladle it out among you and your playmates, you probably think to yourself, "I have to get as much cider as I can. If the other kids get too much, there'll be none left for me." The way you see it, there is a limited amount of cider; you won't get enough unless you take it away from someone else. But as an adult, you can choose to think differently. You can say to yourself, "I can share the cider. If I want more, I can just buy more apples and spices. The amount of hot apple cider I can make, drink, and share is virtually limitless."

We're adults now, but still we often think like children. Women are afraid that they'll have less power if men have more. Men worry that women are getting too powerful, which will make *them* less powerful. When we negotiate love in this mood, we think, "If my lover gets what s/he needs, then I won't get my needs met." We *compete* rather than *cooperate*.

Increasing your lover's power doesn't necessarily mean decreasing yours. Quite the contrary. As you negotiate love, some of the agreements you make will benefit you more; others will benefit your lover more. As your lover gets her/his needs met, s/he will be more eager to support yours. Each of you will have more energy and feel more power"full." The more power your lover gets, the more power you get. And vice versa. *Inner power is infinite.*

Secret 2: Do not transfer your past experiences onto your present negotiation. Be present in the here and now.

All of us come to the negotiating couch with a history of past experiences. Often we transfer our images of our other-sex parent or our ex-lover(s) onto our new lover.

Our history affects how we see the one we love. Sometimes we have unrealistically high expectations. If our mother catered to our every whim or our father spoiled us, we may expect our lover to do the same. More often we carry deep disappointments from our past. If our mother abandoned us, we may expect our lover to walk out at any time. If we had an overbearing father, we assume our lover will be the same way.[1] If our previous spouse was unfaithful, we may be suspicious of our current lover's fidelity. Our past experiences also lead us to make inaccurate generalizations. We may transfer onto our lover a stereotyped view of the way we believe women or men behave. Instead of responding to each other as unique human beings, we think, "He's a typical man," or "She's acting just like a woman."

Our history also affects how we see ourselves. Often we unconsciously repeat the roles we saw our parents play or that we played in our previous relationships. We may assume the role of "daddy's little girl" or "mama's boy" and push our lover into a position of control. Or we may model ourselves after our dominant mother or authoritarian father and encourage our lover to become subservient or engage in a power struggle. In mimicking a distant parent, we may maintain an emotional detachment.

How do you know if you're transferring old images onto your lover when you're negotiating? The trick is to use your little observer. When you get stuck, be a detective. Ask yourself, "Why am I acting this way? Could my thoughts and feelings be about someone else, instead of my lover? Whose role is my lover playing out? Whose role am I assuming?" If a conflict keeps going on and on and on and you can't stop it, you aren't simply disagreeing with your lover. Instead, you are making a transference—and arguing with someone from your past.

To assist you in analyzing the situation correctly, psychologist Dr. Judith Sherven offers these four clues that can help you pinpoint whether you're transferring:

1. As you talk with your lover, you are reminded of feelings and experiences you had with another important person in your life. You find yourself sounding like one of your parents or behaving the way you used to in a previous relationship.

2. Your emotional response is much greater than a situation warrants. Instead of simply saying to your lover, "Don't do that," you blow up.

3. What you're feeling and thinking has no basis in fact. It's irrational. Your lover always seems to be stupid, inattentive, or unkind, when s/he is not. You think your lover has done something when in fact s/he has not.

4. It seems that you're totally innocent and it's all your lover's fault. You feel self-righteous in your anger. The madder you get, the more justified you feel.[2]

Helen and Jim gave me an excellent example of an unconscious transference. Jim had felt abandoned by his former wife during their relationship and transferred this feeling onto Helen while they were dating. As he described it, "When Helen went away on a business trip, I had this idea that she was out partying and picking up other men. Late one night I telephoned her and she wasn't there. When she finally called me back, I exploded at her. 'You're out with someone else having fun. You're not thinking about me at all.' It turned out that Helen had been attending sales meetings all evening and had called me twice, without connecting to me, from a pay phone. So we got into a big argument. Finally she said, 'Maybe you're attributing to me something you have felt before. Let's drop the subject, and we'll talk about it tomorrow.' When I thought about it later I realized she was right. I did overreact. I was thinking of Helen as my ex-wife."

Once you become aware of a transference, you can decide to withdraw it. You can start asking questions like "Who is my lover really? What is s/he really like? How is s/he different from my other sex parent or my former lover? How is s/he similar?" You'll begin to see who your lover is and how s/he differs from the person whose identity you have transferred to her/him. At this point you have a choice. You can discard your false images and see who your lover really is. You can focus on being yourself instead of continuing to play an old role. You can put your past aside and be present in the here and now. Then you will be in the right mood for negotiating love.

Secret 3: Stop making assumptions when you don't know the facts. Ask questions instead.

To negotiate effectively, it is important to get *accurate* information. The more you know about the issue you are negotiating about—and the person with whom you are negotiating—the more likely you are to reach agreement. You can figure out how your needs overlap and which solutions are likely to meet them.

When businesspersons negotiate, they don't make many assumptions about the other party. Lovers do. If we believe or feel something, we assume that our partner believes or feels it too.

When you assume that you know what your lover is up to and don't bother to check out if you are right,[3] you set a chain of events in motion. Your lover says something. You make an assumption. Because of your assumption, you feel a certain way, make certain statements, and do certain things. Then your lover responds to what you say and do. If your initial assumption is wrong, the entire negotiation goes off track.

Susan and Tom explained to me that after they had been dating about six months, Susan told Tom, "I need to devote more time to my personal life. I've been neglecting myself and my children." (Until then, she and Tom had been spending every weekend and most weekday nights together.) When Tom heard Susan say that she needed more time to be alone and with her children, he assumed that she meant, "Now that we've established a relationship, I don't need to pay much attention to you anymore. I'm going to start spending my time doing what's really important to me." Tom felt disappointed, hurt, and rejected. He angrily retorted, "How could you tell me that you enjoy being together and then say you have more important things to take care of?" and withdrew emotionally from the relationship. Several months later, when they were both able to negotiate love, Susan was surprised to learn about Tom's assumption. As she put it, "I thought I was being extremely up front about my needs. I really did enjoy being with Tom, but I also was getting behind in the things I had to do. And the children were getting upset because I was away from them so much. It never crossed my mind that Tom would assume anything else."

How do we stop making assumptions about our lover and her/his feelings? *By asking questions.* In any conversation, the person who asks for information has power. When you inquire, "Where are you at?" "How do you feel?" and "What do you need?" you guide the direction of the conversation. You put the focus on understanding your lover's needs as well as your own. If Tom had been able to ask Susan, "Could you explain to me why you feel you need to spend some time apart?" they could have spent six months enjoying each other's company when they were together instead of being at odds.

Whenever you ask a question, you take a risk: Your lover might not appreciate your inquiry, or you might not like what you discover. However, risk-taking is essential to building a strong relationship. As we move into unknown territory, we get to know our lover.

Secret 4: Don't avoid the issue or play games. Share your feelings and needs honestly.

So many of us hide from each other when we negotiate love. We put on invisible masks and pretend to be someone we are not. We clothe ourselves in imaginary bulletproof vests to protect ourselves from being hurt. We play games, make superficial remarks, or get involved in logical discussions to avoid discussing emotional issues. Sometimes it seems as if we'll do anything to avoid telling the truth. In this mood we'll never reach agreement.

Why are we so wary of being honest? *Because we don't trust each other.* We aren't sure that our lover will give us the safe space we need to open up. We're afraid that s/he might shame us, reject us, or, worst of all, use what we say against us in the future. One woman I interviewed described a typical relationship she had with her ex-husband: "Vernon and I didn't know how to negotiate. I used to say to him, 'If you can't put what you want on the table and if I can't do the same, how can we come up with a creative solution?' Both of us were so wary of one another. He was starting to use what he knew about me against me. Eventually I refused to be open with him emotionally so he couldn't hurt me anymore."

If this mistrustful mood persists, you and your lover will continue to exchange words. But your discussion will have nothing to do with the issue you are negotiating about. As one woman told me, "My lover and I once got involved in a factual disagreement. We went on for hours before I realized that our conversation wasn't the one I wanted to have: an honest dialogue about our feelings and needs." I myself have noticed that I occasionally have what I call "a conversation that is not the real conversation." In a heated debate about whether or not a spouse has the right to walk away from a marriage, I've realized that what I'm really worried about is whether my *own* spouse will leave me.

A delightful married couple I interviewed gave me an excellent example of a conversation that was not the real conversation. Early in their relationship they frequently debated the question, "When a woman gives birth, should her husband be present?" As they got to know each other better, he told her that he was a liberated man active in the men's movement. She asked him, "Well, of course you would be there for your wife during labor, wouldn't you?" When he responded, "No, I can't stand the sight of blood," she countered with, "How can you profess to be a modern, twenty-first-century man and refuse to be with your wife in the delivery room? Can't you see you're being logically inconsistent?" He was turned off. In his words, "I couldn't relate to what she was saying at all. I just didn't *want* to go into a delivery room. That was a personal decision."

After many fruitless conversations, she started sharing her real feelings and needs late one evening: "All my life I've done everything alone. Now you're telling me that if we were to get married, I'd have to give birth alone. It's one of the biggest events of my life and once again nobody's going to be with me." Tears filled her eyes. "If we were to have a child, I would need you to be there." "Ah," he sighed, "that I can relate to. If you tell me you really need me, that's different from telling me why logically I ought to show up. Of course I would be there with you. I'd just block off what was hard for me to see. Would that be okay?" Now they were negotiating love instead of having a debate.

To negotiate love, you must trust each other. What if you don't? Maintaining such façades will drain your energy. One of you needs to risk being honest.

Trust grows slowly. Be the one to sow the first seed. The first step is to admit to your lover your fear of being seen, heard, and truly known. Sooner or later your lover will also confess that s/he is also afraid to open up. Then bring up an issue—one that is not deeply important to you—and during the discussion remove your mask. Only when we speak this way do we truly connect. Say to your lover, "I value our relationship and I am willing to risk being real with you. I want you to know me as I am, imperfect and human." Then share a few of your real feelings and needs. See what happens. If your lover accepts your truth and shares a few of her/his own, try to reach agreement. Then move on to another issue that is slightly more important to you. As the months and years pass, you and your lover will become accustomed to negotiating love honestly instead of playing hide-and-seek.

Is it worth the effort? One man I interviewed gave this answer: "If somebody's got bad feelings hanging around, we don't feel in tune with each other. Lately lovemaking has been really rewarding for both of us because we don't let it happen unless the air is clear. There's nothing between us that keeps us from connecting sexually." Another man put it more bluntly: "When we talk through an issue we stamp out whatever has been keeping us apart. The honesty in our relationship is our best aphrodisiac."

Find out what you really need and ask for it. You do not negotiate love just to please your lover. Your purpose is to look within, discover what you need from your lover, and then make a suggestion. To get what you need, you need to phrase your suggestion properly. Your wording should be *specific*, not general. "I need to spend more romantic time together with you; to get this time, I would like to eat out at a restaurant one night a week" is better than "I think we should eat out more often." And you should phrase your suggestion in *positive* terms. "All my friends go out with their husbands regularly; I'm the only one who never does," or "Men are so unromantic. How can I expect you to understand that I need to go out to dinner sometimes?" will put your partner on the defensive and keep you from negotiating love.

It also helps to speak about your own experience instead of making generalizations about other people. "We haven't spent a romantic evening together since that weekend last summer when we went to the beach. I think I'd feel more cheerful and a lot closer to you if we could go out to eat once a week" is another good way to make your suggestion. But if you phrase your suggestion as a *demand*, you will not create the right mood for negotiating love. "I expect that you'll take me out weekly from now on" will invite your lover to end the conversation, not to ask you to dinner.

Once you reveal your desire, you must be prepared to repeat it several times before it becomes a reality. You may be ready to make reservations for two tonight, but you may have a faster pace than your lover. Perhaps this is just not the right moment; s/he may be overburdened with work or family responsibilities right now. Wait at least a week before you bring up the issue again. No, this is not nagging; it takes most of us a while to process information before we act on it. Two weeks or two months later your lover may finally realize, "Oh, that's what s/he needs. *Now* I understand what s/he's been trying to say."

Negotiating love is a two-way street. You shouldn't be making your suggestion in a vacuum; your lover should react to your suggestion. Ask her/him, "How do you feel about it?" or "What do you need?" It's possible your suggestion may elicit a countersuggestion from your lover: "Going out once a week might get us stuck in a routine. How about every other weekend we eat two meals out in different restaurants?" Don't automatically reject your lover's countersuggestion just because it's different from yours. Instead of replying, "Absolutely not," respond, "Let me think about it." Count to thirty slowly while you consider your lover's idea. To reach agreement you will have to accept it and combine it with your own. You might end up replying, "How about a 'restaurant weekend' once a month and then a couple of spontaneous meals out during the other three weeks?"

Secret 5: Avoid hurting each other. Be kind.

Once you become aware of your lover's vulnerabilities, you have a special responsibility: to handle them with care. What you do will determine how much your lover trusts you. You now have the potential either to hurt or to heal her/him. Once you recognize a wound of your lover's, stay away from it. You wouldn't pull on a broken arm, would you? No, you'd leave it in a sling and let it mend.

Women and men injure each other in different ways. Psychologist Dr. Karen Kahn Wilson told me that the women in her workshops say that men make them angry because "He takes me for granted," or "He doesn't appreciate how difficult it is to work full-time and run a household."[4] On the other hand, many of the men I interviewed for this book commented, "My woman friend doesn't listen to what I say," and "My wife doesn't pay enough attention to me." Most women get wounded when they don't feel valued enough; most men feel sad when they don't get enough nurturing.[5]

There's always the case when you accidentally hurt your lover while you're being honest; it can happen to the most well-intentioned of us. For example, when I once felt an attraction to another man, I told Phil about it. Initially, he was devastated. I didn't deliberately intend to hurt Phil with my honesty, but I did. While I apologized to him, I maintained my integrity: "Yes, I'm attracted to someone else, but I love *you*."

Few of us deliberately cause our partner pain. After all, s/he is our true love, best friend, and the main element in our support system. Yes, honesty hurts in the short run, but in the long run, it enables us to negotiate love.

Secret 6: Don't insist that your gender's style of communicating is best. Honor your lover's style as well as your own.

Both men and women have their own distinct contributions to make to loving negotiations. Unfortunately there is an unspoken assumption held by many people that the feminine way of relating is the only good way.[6] We have come to believe that women know how to "do relationships" and men don't. As a radio talk-show host friend of mine puts it, "Traditionally there is one person in a relationship, more often than not the woman, who is the 'relationship manager.' She is more in touch with her feelings and skilled in expressing them in words. Whenever there's a problem her solution is, 'Let's talk.' "[7]

Or as Dr. Shepherd Bliss, a pioneer in the men's movement, explained it: "Often we do a 'fishbowl' in our workshops. A group of women huddle and talk in the middle of the room. The men are outside the center; they just listen. Then the men and women switch roles. We have noticed that it is much harder for the women to be invisible—to not jump in."[8]

But what is the male communication style? How is it different from the female style? For one thing, men use fewer words. The average woman says about 25,000 words a day, whereas the average man says about 12,000.[9] Women are more skilled at expressing their feelings and describing their needs in words. Men are just starting to find their voice, and although some are working hard at improving their verbal skills, women have had a head start. They have been making suggestions to men since the rise of the modern feminist movement. Men haven't been together long enough to talk about what they want to propose in return.

And while women assume that the best way to communicate is with words, men don't necessarily feel the same. Accustomed to playing sports, they find their own kind of connection through physical communication. A man's hug or a squeeze of his hand might mean more to him than a thousand words. If his female lover says, "Why are you all over me? I want to talk" in response to his gesture of physical affection, then he is sometimes put in an uncomfortable situation.

According to Dr. Shepherd Bliss, our different ways of expressing affection create a serious communication problem. Women criticize men for being too sexual when actually what men want is to communicate more deeply. An important avenue of male expression is lost if a woman interprets a man's physical advances as purely sexual. When a man reaches out to touch a woman, he may be indicating sexual interest, but he is giving her other important messages too. Yet the woman immediately perceives only the sexual interest and says, "Stop." By doing this, she never finds out what the other messages are.[10]

Additionally, men's communication style is slower, with many pauses and fewer words. They often combine conversation with a physical activity such as cleaning out the garage or hiking. Two male friends walk and talk shoulder to shoulder; their eye contact is fleeting. Sometimes there will be long silences in which they both feel comfortable. Even if they are close buddies, each will wait until the other is finished talking. Sometimes they playfully insult each other or call each other names. Women's communication style is faster, with a rush of staccato words and few pauses. If two women are good friends, they will delight in finishing each other's sentences. Women's conversations often take place while they are sitting down together facing each other and looking into each other's eyes as they talk. But what is natural for women can be a torment for men.

Men's movement leader Robert Bly shared with me a brilliant metaphor that best describes how men feel when faced with a communication style that is radically different from theirs: "Even powerful, successful men, when they're in an intimate situation with a woman, feel weak and helpless. Why? Because a woman has this communication method that's like a 100,000-year-old mountain. Her mother's on the mountain and her grandmother's on the mountain. She's sitting on the mountain and all her experience is on that mountain—all the talk that she's had since high school. The man is hanging in a little basket off the mountain and he's looking down all the time. He's thinking, 'If she cuts the rope, I'm gone. If I mess up, it's the end of me.' No one wants to start a conversation when they're hanging from a rope.

"If men could bring to consciousness what they feel when they're with nature, with animals, and with their fathers, then each man could have his own mountain. He'd be on his mountain and she'd be on hers and he wouldn't have that fear anymore."[11]

The same can be true of women's acceptance of the male style. When I once gave a seminar at a local hospital, I asked the thirty women there to be silent for two minutes so that together we could experience the male way of communicating. Afterward, I asked, "How many of you felt comfortable with the silence?" Not a single hand was raised.

How can we create a balance between male and female communication styles? Robert Bly gave me this illustration from his own experience: "When my wife asks me, 'Will you spend forty-five minutes talking with me this evening?' I reply, 'Yes, if you will spend forty-five minutes walking in the woods with me and not say a word.' In this way, I'm accepting her way and she, mine."[12]

He then went on to share how he and his wife communicate regularly: "We set aside an hour; half an hour for each of us. One of us begins first. If it's me, I start talking about what I've been feeling for the last few days. I'm not allowed to use the word 'you' and she's not allowed to finish any sentences for me. This is very difficult for her. (I once heard her say to some other women, 'It's really true. Women love to finish sentences. We're so good at it.') My wife has said on occasion, 'In places where he's pausing, I have to realize that it is sacred space. It is Robert's sacred space.'

"There's lots of sacred space in my half hour. She has to realize it's going to be very slow and there's going to be boring times. All she has to do is keep track of the time and say, 'There are ten minutes to go.' Because it's usually during the last ten minutes when the stuff comes up that she's never heard before.

"Then she goes into her half hour. I can't interrupt her either. Nor can I try to fix it for her. For example, she recently told me, 'I've been feeling very lonely for the past two weeks.' I thought, 'I must have done something wrong.' But I didn't say anything. If I had interrupted her, it would never have become clear that her loneliness was about her father, not about me at all."[13]

Eventually, women and men must have a joint discussion. As we talk, we each bring our gender's special communication gifts to share with one another.

Secret 7: Don't forget what you and your partner agree about. Focus on what you have in common.

The goal of negotiating love is to reach agreement. To attain your goal you and your lover must remember what you have in common. This may include past experiences and future hopes, spiritual values, family members and friends, hobbies and interests, philosophical and political ideas, and things you both think are funny. Whenever you and your lover start saying "I disagree" and "I see it differently," you need to remind yourselves to move away from this divisive mood.

In spite of all your common bonds, sometimes it seems as if you and your lover don't agree on anything at all. John Bradshaw tells of a couple he saw in therapy who kept arguing loudly with each other about a variety of subjects. They just wouldn't stop. Finally, one of them exclaimed, "Dr. Bradshaw, we can't seem to agree about anything." Thinking quickly, he replied, "Yes, you do. You both agree that shouting at each other is the way to handle your differences."[14] Fortunately, most couples agree on far more than this.

Tamiko, an expert on women's issues, recommends that lovers focus on the parts of their relationship that work best. Every relationship has at least one strength, even if it's mainly sex. *Build on what binds you; deemphasize what divides you.*[15] In this mood you will reach agreement quickly.

The deepest bond between lovers is often unspoken. It is a shared spirituality. In the words of men's issues expert Forrest Craver: "It is a common commitment to serve each other. There's an aspect of the sacred that takes a relationship beyond a fifty-fifty partnership and makes it a covenant to do whatever it takes to keep going."[16] We reaffirm this commitment every time we sit down together on the negotiating couch. This is a unique strength lovers have that lawyers and businesspersons lack: Couples persist in negotiating love because they value their precious relationship.

Secret 8: Avoid making snap judgments like "This won't work," or "We can't do this." Open yourself up to all possibilities.

One of my interviewees summed up this secret well when he said, "Always keep an open mind." When he met the woman he loved, she lived three thousand miles away. He said to her, "If you lived near me, I would pursue you relentlessly." "I don't believe in long-distance relationships," she told him. "Neither do I," he replied. "But let's do each other a favor. Let's both keep our minds open." In this mood they were able to continue their courtship, negotiate love, and eventually marry. She found a job in his hometown, something she originally said she would never do.

Keeping an open mind means considering many possible ways of resolving your differences. It means listening to your lover's suggestions even when they sound bizarre at first. It also means being willing to change and grow. You have to think, "Maybe my way isn't necessarily the best way." For example, one couple, whom I'll call Fran and Ed, had gotten a divorce. Yet when Ed appeared at Fran's door one day and said he wanted to talk, she was receptive. In Fran's words, "I felt that we were entering into a discussion that was very open-ended. My concern was to really explore what was best for the two of us—whatever that happened to be."

Opening yourself to all possibilities means brainstorming. Businesspersons do it all the time. They define their problem and then write down every conceivable solution that comes to mind. They then consider each one until they hit upon a solution that seems right.

Lovers can also brainstorm. You need to start with the mindset that anything is possible. It's difficult to get past your preconceptions that only certain solutions are the "right" ones. But thinking "We have to do it my way" or "It has to be done exactly like this" will close your mind to some possibilities. Thinking "Maybe there's a way that we haven't thought of yet" will open your mind up. After you find out what you need and what your lover needs, you say, "Let's see if we can come up with a creative solution that makes us both happy."[17]

Brainstorming should be done in a playful mood. Now is the time for you and your lover to act like children—to indulge your passion for creativity and experimentation. You toss out one suggestion; your lover tosses out another one. Let your fantasies run wild as you say, "What about . . . ?" "If only . . ." "Maybe we could . . ." and "Someday we might . . ." to each other. Venture into the unknown, the unfamiliar, and the unpredictable. No idea should be dismissed as impossible. Avoid phrases like "That's ridiculous," "We've already tried this," and "Who ever heard of that?" Your purpose is to collect as many ideas as possible.

You or your lover can list all your solutions on a large piece of paper or a chalkboard. Or else record or videotape the conversation so that both of you can listen to it or watch it again. After both of you have had some time to reflect, go back to your list. This time you are free to evaluate each idea, combine the best ones, and build on them. For example, a couple I interviewed told me how they solved their problem about where to spend Christmas. He began, "I wanted to be with my parents and she wanted to be with hers. Both sets of parents were asking us to come home." She continued, "Christmas is supposed to be a time of renewal, and here we were arguing with each other instead. We finally decided to sit down and figure out what to do. Now we invite our families over to *our* house. Whoever shows up shows up."

To brainstorm effectively, you and your lover need to be flexible. Neither of you will change completely, but you must be willing to bend. Ideally, at this point each of you has made a commitment to grow closer together. So when one of you makes a suggestion, you don't mean "Do this for me." You mean "Let's do this because we value our relationship and we want it to stay alive." You're willing to give an inch (or a foot) and serve each other for the sake of your relationship.

When we brainstorm we are not judgmental. Why? If I'm playing "moral policeman," I'm saying to you, "I'm more correct than you are." If I insist we solve our problem my way, I limit the number of our possible solutions. As Dr. Brad Blanton told his wife, Amy, when they were negotiating their schedule, "There is no 'right' number of times per week to play golf."[18] Or to wash the dishes, go out to dinner, or make love.

When you arrive at a solution that meets both your needs, remember that it is not necessarily permanent. Recognizing that you and your lover change and grow means "We may not feel the same tomorrow as we do today. What we just agreed on may have to be renegotiated at a future time."

Secret 9: Use your little observer continually. Encourage your partner to do the same.

To stay in the right mood while you're negotiating love, you need to *use* your little observer continually. Actually you're having two conversations: the negotiation with your lover and a background dialogue with your little observer. Your little observer is removed from your conflicts; it monitors and defuses them. In the words of psychologist Dr. Susan Jeffers, "It's our ability to take control of our thoughts."[19]

If you start feeling healthy anger, your little observer is by your side to restore your emotional balance. It asks, "What's going on?" Then it says to you, "You need to feel this anger but eventually you must get beyond it." Dr. Jeffers shared this example from her own experience: "Whenever I feel angry at my husband, I immediately picture a vulnerable, precious man who wants to be loved and tries his very best for me. I ask myself, 'What am I expecting from him? To fix everything in my world? It's not his job to fill me up and make me happy. It's not his fault if I am empty or sad. Get off it.' As I begin taking responsibility for my feelings, my anger disappears . . . and love and appreciation take its place."[20]

If you feel your conversation is getting too grim and intense, your little observer notices. You realize that you need to do something to relieve the tension. So tell a joke or a story—or at least threaten to tell one. Laughing together enables you to enjoy negotiating love. Sometimes your little observer even defuses conflict by directing attention to your surroundings. Dr. Brad Blanton and his wife, Amy Silverman, coleaders of couples workshops, told me: "We were having this argument and getting deeper and deeper into it. While we were sitting there glaring at each other, an ad came on the radio for Steve Martin's movie *The Jerk*. Since the ad was in the background, we weren't listening to it at first, but somehow Bernadette Peters's voice got our attention. At the same moment we heard her saying, 'Aren't you going to ask me for a date?' Both of us burst out laughing, and our anger was all gone. We couldn't go back to making accusations and counteraccusations anymore."[21]

While you are negotiating love, your little observer can keep you in the here and now. If you start discussing the past over and over again, a little voice in your head whispers, "Isn't this enough, please?" Or, "Isn't it time to move on?" If you listen to its message, your little observer will enable you to shift into the present. And whatever phase of negotiation you were in, you can eventually return to it if you choose.

It helps if your lover also is aware of her/his little observer. This way your two little observers can communicate with each other. You can agree in advance on a series of nonverbal signals such as raising your hand if the other person is getting off the subject. When both of your little observers are in action, the chances of your reaching agreement are greatly enhanced.

Secret 10: To keep negotiations from breaking down, show affection.

Words can get us only so far. When we find ourselves getting strangled in our own sentences, it's time to stop talking and get physical. Unlike lawyers and businesspersons, we can hold hands, hug each other, or give each other a kiss.

Demonstrate your affection for each other continually as you negotiate love. Start out sitting next to each other on a couch or at a table. During your conversation touch each other affectionately or hold hands from time to time. This way you get a real sense of connection. As one married man I interviewed told me, "When we get angry, we hold hands very closely. It reassures us that no one will get up and walk away. The hotter the argument gets, the tighter we hold on." A married woman said that when their loving negotiations get stuck, they hug each other. "There are times we come to a dead end and we don't know what it takes to make it right. He just puts his arms around me and holds me. And I put my arms around him. Sometimes I resist at first. But I know that it's this loving energy that takes our anger away."

Keep on negotiating love as long as the conversation is comfortable for both of you. Whenever you feel conflict escalating, it's time to stop. Do one of these activities immediately afterward to defuse the tension and reestablish your loving connection:

- Snuggle together
- Lie close to each other and breathe together
- Sit on the floor and meditate together
- Dance together

- Go for a long walk together
- Look at a sunset or a sunrise together
- Listen to music together
- Pray together

These activities work because they rejuvenate your balanced, cooperative mood. You experience your togetherness instead of your separateness (see Secret 7), your unity instead of your opposition. Walking or dancing together harmonizes your body movements. When you're moving at the same speed, you're not trying to compete with each other. Lying down or sitting on the floor together is a great equalizer. No one feels taller or more important than the other. Looking at a sunset, listening to music, or praying together enables you to share a beautiful experience. When you are both silent you can distance yourselves from your verbal impasse and get inside your own heads. Later on, continue your loving negotiation if you're back in the right mood.

Should you make love during or after a tension-filled discussion? It's debatable. From my own experience, having sex in the middle of a loving negotiation just doesn't feel right. Perhaps it's because the kind of tension we experience during the push-pull of conflict resolution isn't in sync with our crescendo of sexual energy. Maybe the anxiety from the disagreement keeps us from feeling sexual pleasure. If we resolve the issue at hand first, we can sigh with relief that it's under control—and then let go sexually. Personally I don't recommend having sex to relieve the tension of loving negotiations, but use your own judgment. If it works, enjoy!

Secret 11: When you get stuck, seek outside help. You may need the assistance of a neutral third party.

Sometimes we reach a point in our negotiations where we can't go any further. No matter how many times we return to the negotiating couch, we keep having the same conversation that doesn't go anywhere. Or we lock horns in an "I'm right; you're wrong" deadlock.

When you get stuck, get outside help. Don't suffer in isolation. Reaching an impasse is nothing to be ashamed of. All lovers can benefit from the assistance of a mediator, a neutral third party who moves the negotiations along. According to Dr. Angeles Arrien, an expert in crosscultural resolution, traditionally Americans have used mediation to resolve conflict. Yet at the same time Americans are also fiercely independent. We feel ashamed if we can't handle our own problems, and find it hard to call in a third person. It's as if we have failed at something—and Americans see failure as a huge taboo.[22] But calling in a mediator is not a sign of weakness; it's a sign of strength and commitment. Once we've moved beyond the initial stages of negotiating love, many of us can get only to a certain point. Stuck in our positions and suffocated by our strong emotions, we cannot move forward all by ourselves. The choice is either to break up or get outside support.

Your third party can be a trusted friend, a support group (either same-sex or couples), a psychotherapist, a family counselor, or a professional mediator. If you choose a friend you know well, make sure s/he is really neutral and not just willing to agree with whatever you say. This is also true when you ask members of your support group for advice. A friend of mine who was deadlocked in her loving negotiations sought the assistance of the women she met with twice a month. Their unanimous verdict was "He's a snake. Drop him." Fortunately she decided to try a friend who was outside the group—me. I did my best to be objective.

Psychotherapists and family counselors are like healing catalysts. By working with one of you, they can sometimes spark both of you to start negotiating fruitfully again. Those who work with more than one person at a time practice a form of mediation. Rather than just listening to one of you, s/he can direct your conversation in some other direction besides a dead end when s/he hears your two perspectives.

While deciding to go to a psychotherapist is difficult, asking your lover to accompany you requires even greater finesse. One woman whom I interviewed succeeded in this way: "I asked him to go into couples therapy in order to help *me*. I looked at myself and asked myself honestly, 'Do I have problems?' Since I answered yes, I felt I was acting in integrity. Everybody has problems. By swallowing my own pride, I allowed him to preserve his dignity." Because she was willing to do whatever was necessary to save her relationship, this couple was able to start working out their differences.

Professional mediators are trained to help couples to stay away from the courtroom. You need not wait to use one until you have already started divorce proceedings. More and more mediation is taking place during the early stages of a relationship, when it still can be healed with minimal effort. Instead of letting your dispute fester, you sit down together with a neutral person who hears both of your sides.

There is no fixed mediation procedure, but this scenario is typical: First the mediator meets with both of you together to explain the mediation process and find out your expectations. During this session each of you gets a chance to share your feelings and needs. Then the mediator meets with each of you separately to hear what each of you prefers not to say in front of the other. These conversations are kept confidential. Finally, there is another joint session to explore options for a solution. Each mediator is trained to find the areas where your needs overlap, assist you in brainstorming for cooperative solutions, and enable you to reach agreement.[23] The mediator does not express any opinions.

Sometimes you can mediate your own dispute if you learn how. Start by assuming a neutral position. Listen to what your lover says without giving your opinion. Then initiate powerful communication by asking questions the way a mediator does. "How does each of us really feel about this issue? Are either of us overreacting or projecting? What does my lover need? What do I need?" Once you see where your needs overlap, start suggesting options. Write them down just as a mediator would.

It is difficult to be your own mediator. To have no opinion about your own dispute, you must pretend that you are neutral when you're really not. As a mediator, you have to look at the conflict through your lover's eyes as well as through your own. It takes a lot of patience, but it is possible. Avoid hurrying to reach agreement, becoming obsessed with finding a "perfect" solution, and getting so caught up in the emotional intensity of the conflict that you lose your detachment. As Dr. Angeles Arrien puts it, the very qualities that make a good mediator—visualizing possibilities, searching for excellence, and showing deep concern—can become liabilities if carried to an extreme.[24]

Lovers who ask each other questions, who share their feelings and needs honestly, and who are kind to each other build a foundation of trust for negotiating love. By keeping the eleven secrets in mind while you reach agreement, you and your lover will enjoy your conversations together—and return again and again to the negotiating couch.

CHAPTER 6

The Seesaw of Power: Who Has More Control?

In a healthy love relationship, power continually shifts from one person to the other. You and your lover strive for a power equilibrium, which is never achieved absolutely. As the two of you negotiate love, you constantly rebalance your energy. And any alliance with a third person that is stronger than your own relationship is a threat to this balance of power.

Unfortunately, for many of us, it is taboo to discuss power in love relationships. Some of us think power is evil. We'd rather talk about sex or money—anything besides power. If and when the subject of power does come up, we are ambivalent about it. Men are indicted for hoarding political and economic power but criticized for not fully developing their emotional power. Women deny that they have any power at all, when in reality they have enormous emotional and sexual power.

People who believe they don't have power fear it. People who have power are embarrassed to admit they do. Most of us pretend power doesn't even *exist* in our own love relationships.

We are uncomfortable discussing power-related issues such as competition, authority, and domination.[1]

Actually, power in itself isn't bad; it's how it's *used* that is the key.[2] Depending upon who holds it, power can be used to accomplish either evil or worthwhile purposes. So, if understood and handled properly, power can actually strengthen your love relationship.

What Exactly Is Power?

Does possessing power mean having lots of resources like money, social position, and an impressive job title? Not necessarily. This kind of power is *external*. It can be gained or lost in a moment. There's a different kind of power within you that lasts—and that's what we're talking about here. It's your energy, integrity, self-esteem, self-confidence, honesty, charm, expertise, and ability to get along with other people. If you're power"full," you are full of this inner energy. You know who you are and you value yourself. Most important, you believe that you "can do it," whatever "it" is. Self-confidence is the essence of power.[3]

In a love relationship the external trappings of power are irrelevant. Whether your ancestors came over on the *Mayflower* doesn't matter; how much money you earn is beside the point. It doesn't matter whether you are called wife, husband, fiancé, or significant other. What counts is whether you *perceive* yourself as powerful.

Your power comes from *within*. It's surprising to admit, but I've learned this from my chihuahua. Mitsy has no money of her own, no pedigree, and no job title—except "family watchdog." So how does she manage to get her needs met? Because

Mitsy acts as if she's entitled to whatever she craves. When she's hungry she sits at our feet and stares at us until we feed her. When she wants to go out she follows us around the house until one of us decides to take her for a walk. If we ignore her, she tries again a few minutes later. Although Mitsy weighs only four and a half pounds, she is a powerful dog because of the confidence she exudes and feels.

How much power do you have in your love relationship? It's difficult to know, because lovers' power isn't measured by conventional standards. Never mind who makes decisions and who gets her/his way; power starts with knowing what your needs are and believing you can get them met. Your belief in yourself enhances your ability. If you think you can do something, your chances for accomplishing it are vastly increased. When you are powerful, you are confident you can get what you need and also give your lover what s/he needs most.

Each of us has different needs.[4] For example, your lover may yearn for more time apart from you for work, privacy, and freedom. You may crave more time together for fun, companionship, and sharing. When the two of you negotiate love, you can reach an agreement in which both of your needs are sometimes honored. If you don't agree and your lover always gets lots of time alone, is s/he powerful? Not necessarily. If your needs are not met and the two of you break up, your lover isn't powerful. People who monopolize power in the short run often lose it in the long run.

To negotiate love effectively, you and your lover must both see yourselves as *equals*. Each of you must *value yourselves.* Each of you must believe, "I have a right to get what I need. I can ask for whatever means most to me: more frequent lovemaking, more help with the housework, or more time with our child. If my lover doesn't agree right away, I will not get discouraged." As you negotiate your differences and get your needs met, you will both become even more powerful.

THE POWER DYNAMIC

Do you like to play games? Most people do. In football, baseball, Monopoly, or Scrabble, you do your best to beat your opponent(s). Winning is fun. But when you win you don't intend to take away the other person's power permanently. Maybe next time your opponent will win.

In a healthy love relationship the balance of power works like a game. In the short term, you try to achieve your goal, but your overall objective is not to make your lover helpless and unable to keep playing. *Neither of you intends to conquer the other forever.* Sometimes you'll get your needs met; other times your lover will. Some of your agreements will be to your advantage; others will be to your lover's. Both of you will rebalance your power continually by negotiating love. You and your lover will strive for a power equilibrium, which is never achieved absolutely.

In a healthy love relationship, power continually shifts from one person to another. As you negotiate love, you rebalance your energy. Ultimately, there are two different power balances to achieve: the "me/you" power balance and the "us/them" power balance.

THE "ME/YOU" POWER BALANCE

In the me/you power balance, you and your lover achieve a dynamic balance of power between the two of you.

Imagine yourselves on a seesaw. One of you is on the bottom; one of you is on the top. But not for long. Inevitably the balance will change: the person riding on the top will go to the bottom. This is the way power flows when you negotiate love. You take turns being on top—and being powerful.

In an unhealthy relationship, power is static. One person holds most of the power and gets her/his needs met most of the time. With one person always on top, it's not much of a seesaw ride. For example, a male acquaintance of mine once told me that his woman friend had gotten pregnant. Against his wishes she had decided to have the child, demand substantial child support, and keep him from assuming any role in the parenting. In his words, she had "total power." He was unwilling to be a victim, and decided to distance himself from her shortly after the baby was born since she refused to negotiate love. Her continual monopoly of the power meant he couldn't stay in the relationship.

When one lover monopolizes power, s/he thinks, "I'm the only one who has the right to get my needs met." Her/his partner thinks in turn, "I'll never get what I need." The monopolizer has what s/he needs so s/he doesn't want to talk; the victim doesn't believe s/he can get what s/he needs so s/he doesn't even try to talk. One person overpowers; the other feels helpless. Neither ends up negotiating love, and eventually the person lacking power may seek another relationship where s/he can try to get some of her/his own power. One man informed me, "Ninety-nine percent of the time my ex-wife got what she needed. That was completely unsatisfactory to me. Eventually we divorced."

When power is shared, you and your lover *both* believe, "I am entitled to get my needs met. I can negotiate love." The balance of power constantly changes, and you need to negotiate love frequently to reestablish equilibrium.

Sometimes one of you is on top of the seesaw; other times it is the other's turn to be on top. But only for a *moment.* When the lover on the bottom says "What about me?" the seesaw shifts. It's time to negotiate love. It's this tension—this rebalancing of power—that keeps the ride going. Sometimes you get what you need; other times you don't. No one keeps score. Sometimes you contribute more to the relationship; other times your lover contributes more. If it were always fifty-fifty, the seesaw would stop in the middle. The secret of making the ride enjoyable is to always keep shifting the balance. Power flows back and forth continuously between the two of you. You alternate, "up-down, up-down." As couples workshop leader Jude Blitz puts it, "The truth is that, in a relationship, power is fluid. It's dynamic. In a second it can shift and turn around completely."[5]

One way to spoil the ride is to get overwhelmed when you're at the bottom of the seesaw. When the balance of energy temporarily shifts against you, you can feel powerless. And at one time or another we've all felt this way. We say to ourselves, "I can't possibly ask for what I need now. This means I'll never get what I crave." At this moment our self-confidence is low. We feel empty, worthless, and helpless. We aren't being valued and we aren't being nurtured. And we think our lover has all the power, so we get angry. We manipulate, store up resentment, or get furious at our lover. We must release this anger in order to get to the negotiating couch.

The time you need to negotiate the *most*—and feel like negotiating the *least*—is when your lover is getting her/his needs met and you're not. When this happens, you feel overwhelmed, discouraged, and hurt. It's tempting to seek an outside alliance—someone else who will buttress your self-confidence and soothe your hurt feelings. But this won't help you in the long run. Instead, you need to turn inward and restore your own energy. To start negotiating love again, you have to perceive your power as equal to your lover's.

In a healthy love relationship, you recognize that an imbalance of power will be resolved by negotiating and a new balance will be created sooner or later. You realize that the person on the bottom today will be on the top tomorrow. You know that when your lover gets what s/he needs, your power isn't endangered—because the more powerful your lover is, the more powerful you become. The more your lover thinks, "I can do it," the more s/he will inspire you in turn. By sharing your energy and your self-confidence when you have it, you get it back when you need it. When you feel empty, it's your turn to be nourished, to be seen, and to be heard. As one man put it, "In any active, ongoing relationship you're going to have to give and take. No one likes to give all the time; no one likes to take all the time. It's a delicate balance at best."

A significant change in one person's life can temporarily upset the power balance. For example, if a wife reenters the workforce after years of childrearing, or a husband decides to do a larger share of parenting, the balance of power shifts. One lover may feel that the other is getting more of her/his needs met. This means a new equilibrium must be created by negotiating love.

THE "US/THEM" POWER BALANCE

Imagine that you and your lover are riding on the seesaw of power and having a good time together. What happens if a third person climbs on, sits down in front of you, and doesn't get off? The seesaw ride will end—and the fun will stop. This is exactly what happens when you give another person outside your relationship priority over your lover.

It is essential to avoid creating alliances outside your relationship that are *more* powerful than the relationship itself. Of course, this does not prevent you from having strong, lasting relationships with family and friends. However, when you form a relationship with someone else whom you allow to be *more* important to you than your lover is, you shift the balance of power. Energy begins to flow between you and your new ally. Whether or not you keep your outside relationship secret, you take some of the energy and time you used to give your lover and share it with someone else. The power that would ordinarily flow between the two of you is siphoned away. Your splendid seesaw ride with its dynamic energy flow suddenly stops.

You and your lover have an alliance with each other. You share common preferences, interests, and goals. Each of you also has alliances with other people outside the relationship. Some of these are temporary, such as casual acquaintances. Others can be lasting and strong—for example, those with parents, sisters, brothers, children, in-laws, ex-spouses, friends, and business associates. Outside alliances that are *more* powerful than your primary one will endanger this relationship.

Remember when you were a child and played with magnets? The magnet you held attracted small steel objects—until someone else came along with a more powerful one. All your steel objects gravitated toward the stronger magnet instead. So it is with relationships. A third person can pull you and your lover away from each other if the outside relationship has *more* energy than your own.

For you and your lover to negotiate effectively, there must

be a strong flow of energy. It is not enough to balance power between the two of you; power must also be balanced between the two of you and outsiders. The us/them power balance is an even greater challenge than the me/you one. As one married woman said, "If it's just the two of us, it's easy!"

When the Seesaw Gets Stuck

In businesslike negotiations you are advised to create as many outside alliances as you can. Get together everyone on your side—supervisors, clients, and coworkers—and build a coalition of supporters. Then use the power of your coalition as leverage to get what you want from your opponent.[6]

This strategy may work for lawyers and businesspersons, but it is deadly for lovers. A lover who is excluded from an alliance feels powerless, gets angry, and becomes unable to negotiate love. Whenever either you or your lover forms an alliance that endangers your relationship, you must negotiate with each other as soon as possible—if you want to maintain your relationship. If the center of power has moved away from the two of you, you need to restore it to its rightful place: yourselves.

There are five major ways to shift energy away from your love relationship:

- Putting a third person's needs ahead of your lover's
- Talking to a third person instead of negotiating with your lover
- Making a third person the issue, rather than facing your own issue
- Using a third person as an intermediary

- Siding with a third person who is in a dispute with your lover

PUTTING A THIRD PERSON'S NEEDS AHEAD OF YOUR LOVER'S

If you truly want your relationship to work, your alliance with your lover must be stronger than with anyone else. Power should always be concentrated in the hands of the two of you. Happy couples describe their outlook like this: "My lover always comes first. . . . My husband is my top priority. . . . Among all her relationships, I come first." One man described how their agreement evolved: "When we were dating each other, I started to feel 'locked out.' My fiancée was spreading her emotions so thin that I wasn't getting my fair share. I felt I was entitled to more than just the little bit that was left over after she finished with her family and friends." His wife continued: "Once we started living together, it was understood that our relationship was more important than any others I had. It was difficult because I still wanted to spend a lot of time with my mom, sisters, brother, and even my ex-boyfriend. But I realized that I couldn't do everything, and my fiancé and I started spending more and more of our time with each other."

Deciding on your priorities is difficult when you have a job and children to contend with. When you're absorbed in a project or a child becomes demanding, you instinctively feel like putting your lover's needs on the back burner. But common sense should tell you otherwise: You and your lover need a strong foundation to survive the stresses of work and family.

In fact, your ties with your lover should be even stronger than those with your family of origin.[7] At first this idea may be difficult to accept. As one of my single colleagues recently remarked to me, "Blood is thicker than water. Family always comes first." "Of course, you should give your relatives loving attention," I replied, "but you must never let a family member take *over* your life."

If your father, mother, or sibling is a more powerful magnet than your lover, your balance of power with your lover will be destroyed. One woman who was very close with her father persuaded her husband to work for her dad's business. They even went so far as to live on her father's farm. As her husband put it, "I felt powerless. Generally things went the way her dad programmed them." He left her, and they divorced. Several years later they remarried, moved away from her father's farm, and eventually built their own house.

A man who was closely tied to his mother was unwilling to marry his lover, whom he had been dating for seven years. His family was Jewish and his mother wanted him to marry a woman of the same heritage. Although his lover was willing to convert, his mother remained adamantly opposed to the marriage. It was only when he separated himself from his mother that he could ally himself closely with the woman he loved and get married.

Another man had a strong relationship with his younger brother. Although he and his wife had not been to New York together (and he knew she longed to go), he invited his brother to take a trip with him instead. "George and I are going to New York," he informed his spouse. "If you can get a baby-sitter, you can come too." His wife was furious. At first he was surprised. "I was too much of a dunderhead to realize what I had done. She let me have it after my brother left—and I realized she was right."

If a situation arises in which you are the outsider, negotiate love as soon as you perceive an imbalance developing. Start the discussion by explaining, "I feel excluded. It seems you're putting someone else ahead of me. I need you to put me first." Say it again and again and again until your lover hears you.

A man and woman in their twenties with a very strong marriage told me, "We've never talked to our families or friends about our problems. When we got married, our families disapproved of our relationship and our college friends had mostly graduated and moved away. It was a distinct advantage that we didn't have anyone to fall back on when the going got rough. We were left to confront each other. Now we are our own family. We never let our extended family get between us."

If you've been previously married, the balance of power shifts when you remarry. More energy goes to your new lover and less to your ex-spouse and children. These family members may not accept their loss of power gracefully and may try to get it back. Many of my interviewees dealt with threats to their new power balances effectively. They encouraged their other family members to be friendly to their lover. They included their lover in their relationships with their ex-spouses and stepchildren. But whenever there was a dispute, they supported their lover.

In turn, their partners initiated loving negotiations whenever they perceived an imbalance starting to develop. One woman married to a man who shared custody of his child told me, "His ex-wife would frequently call and come over to pick the baby up. I didn't understand what was going on. Was their relationship really over? I shared my concerns with my husband. He explained to me that they were working through the situation themselves. Ultimately, we agreed that it was best for the child, Yvonne, if we all got along. After all, Yvonne was *our* kid, not just her kid. He paved the road for our relationship, and now his ex and I get along quite well. He always made me feel a part of what was going on. He never ever said, 'Deal with it yourself.' "

Another woman who remarried found herself dealing with an ex-wife who had a key to their house. As the second wife told me: "His ex would come over to wash his car and launder his clothes. She'd call on holidays, especially on their anniversary. The phone would ring even while we were making love. I kept telling my husband how invaded I felt until he was willing to set boundaries. He finally told her, 'You do not enter this house until one of us says you can. And you do not call late in the evening except in an emergency.' "

A third woman told me, "I had never been married before, but my husband had an ex and two children. It could have turned out to be a love triangle, but it didn't. When she kept calling our house collect, I confronted her and asked her to stop. My husband was very supportive. He encouraged his ex and the kids to be nice to me. Eventually we all became very close."

When you remarry you also have to rebalance your energy between your new spouse and your old friends. This can be scary. Your buddies may get angry. Or you may feel threatened. "I *need* my support system," one of my single interviewees remarked. "What happens if my marriage breaks up?" While this fear is understandable, you have to take the leap. Maintain your relationships with your old friends, but remember your mate is number one. When s/he really needs you, be there for her/him.

In a healthy relationship you and your lover both share your energy with your families and friends. Outside alliances enhance your relationship, not endanger it. In an emergency, one or both of you may temporarily focus your attention on the outsider. But in the long run you always remember to put each other first.

TALKING TO A THIRD PERSON INSTEAD OF NEGOTIATING WITH YOUR LOVER

I call this "emotional infidelity."[8] It happens on the telephone, at lunches, and in support groups. A couple has a dispute. Either member discusses it with a friend or a support group *instead of* negotiating love. A third-party confidant responds, "Gosh, this is really terrible. You're so brave to put up with it." Or s/he says, "How could you allow this to happen? Get rid of the so-and-so." The moment you start agreeing with the confidant, you create an outside, hurtful relationship.[9] The two of you start colluding against your lover. As your new connection energizes, you drain power away from your love relationship.

If you go to a neutral third party for *advice*, with the intention of taking it to your lover later, that's a different situation. Often a neutral person can help you get ready to negotiate love. As you talk to her/him, your anger cools off. You realize how you really feel and what you need. You return to your lover with a different perspective. However, make sure that your neutral friend keeps your conversations confidential just as a professional mediator would.

Confiding in a third person is destructive only when you don't negotiate love afterward. Often, we are afraid to express our anger directly to our lover. Fearing we'll be abandoned, we talk about the situation behind our lover's back instead. You'll find groups of these people seated together at lunch or at a party commiserating with each other. "You poor thing. How terrible for you." When each one goes home afterward, instead of confronting her/his lover and sharing her/his feelings, s/he continues to seek her/his approval.[10] Again, in this case, emotional infidelity replaces negotiating love.

MAKING A THIRD PERSON THE ISSUE, RATHER THAN FACING YOUR OWN ISSUE

A woman I interviewed told me about a typical triangle. When she began living with her lover, his best friend Umberto would constantly come over to visit. Umberto was willing to listen to her talk about her problems with her lover, and she thought he was befriending her. One day after she had finally decided to leave her lover, the "best friend" asked her to go for a walk. Much to her surprise, he invited her to move in with him. After she told her lover, he became furious and accused her: "You used him to make me jealous. You provoked him." They continued arguing about the incident even after she moved out. Finally she realized that they had both been focusing on the best friend instead of dealing with the issues that divided them. "Because we couldn't face our own issues, Umberto became the issue." They both lost their power by giving it away to a third person. Once they realized their mistake, they started discussing their real feelings and needs—and negotiating love.

USING A THIRD PERSON AS AN INTERMEDIARY

When you use a third person as an intermediary, you temporarily give up your power. Instead of saying, "I can communicate," you say, "I can't communicate." You lose the opportunity to express your feelings, share your needs, and listen to your lover. Instead, an outsider interposes her/himself between the two of you.

Friends and relatives make poor go-betweens. They aren't qualified for the job and usually they don't want it. Most of them resent being put in the middle and eventually tire of their role. Worst of all, they can distort your messages.

Making your child your spokesperson is emotional abuse. No young person should ever be forced to say, "Daddy wants me to tell you this," or "Here is a message from Mommy." Only a professional, objective adult mediator can properly serve as an effective intermediary between you and your lover.

SIDING WITH A THIRD PERSON WHO IS IN A DISPUTE WITH YOUR LOVER

More often than not, this third person is your child. The most powerful outside alliance *is* with a child. One man, whom I'll call Oscar, told me how a serious imbalance of power in his romantic relationship began. He and his wife, Diane, had a precocious five-year-old daughter named Wendy. In Oscar's words: "Every weekday morning Wendy has to meet the school bus, which arrives promptly at ten minutes to eight. As seven thirty approaches, I start getting anxious. By the time it's seven forty-five, if she's not downstairs, I am frantic. I go upstairs and say to her, 'You must be downstairs by the count of ten.' Then I start counting. If she still isn't ready, I tell her, 'No allowance this week if you miss the school bus.' Wendy starts crying. What happens? My wife intercedes and takes our daughter's side; she can't stand to see our daughter upset. When Wendy plays one of us against the other, it's an affront to me. I get so angry I could put my fist through a wall."

The more the balance of power shifted against him, the more helpless Oscar felt. What could he do? I told him that he felt powerless because he was stuck at the bottom of the seesaw. I advised him to sit down alone with Diane and share his feelings and needs with her. A few weeks later Oscar told me: "Once Diane and I began talking honestly with each other, the negotiation went smoothly. We agreed that whenever Wendy would appeal to the other parent, she would be sent back to the parent she had already discussed the issue with. So there was no way Wendy could get between us. You know, it was only when I started listening to Diane that I realized how difficult mornings have been for her. Now *I* get Wendy dressed, and after that I leave her alone with Diane upstairs. I sit in the living room, have coffee, and read the paper instead of griping at them. If my wife and I have an argument, we excuse ourselves and talk together in another room. Sometimes we fall back to our old habits, but not for long. We're putting our own relationship first now."

When one parent starts giving most of her/his energy to a daughter or son, the balance of power between lovers is upset. Lovers spend less time talking with each other as one of them spends more and more time communicating with the child instead. When the child exchanges confidences with one parent, then one parent is withholding important information from the other. Agreements that used to be negotiated between the couple are now being made between one of them and their offspring—and the other lover feels like an outsider in her/his own home. No wonder so many marriages break up after a baby arrives!

A common complaint of new fathers is that they feel excluded from the mother-child relationship. The balance of power shifts even before the baby is born. When a pregnant woman turns her attention inward to her fetus and her own special needs, the father often feels that his needs are being neglected. One woman told me how her husband insisted that she cook dinner for him every single night while she was pregnant even though she worked full-time. His implicit demand was "Pay attention to me instead of giving it to our unborn child." As she put it, "He was angry that the energy I had been giving him was now focused on someone else." Other fathers feel nervous and insecure when faced with the prospect of having a child.[11] Instead of saying "I can parent" and owning their own fathering power, they fall back into old modes of thinking and say, "I can't deal with kids. This is more women's work anyway. Let her do it." When a father backs off and chooses to relinquish his own power, the flow of energy between mother and child increases.

Other mothers have a baby to gain an identity separate from their husband's. Being pregnant makes them feel that they have their own special area of expertise,[12] and instead of including their husband, they exclude him. Their message is "As a woman, I know how to raise a child and you don't. Your job is to provide for us financially so that I can take care of the children." From the father's viewpoint, then, the baby immediately becomes an intruder who has upset their balance of power. Often he is overwhelmed by feelings of helplessness and inadequacy. He's stuck at the bottom of the seesaw and doesn't have the energy to start it moving again.

Imbalances of power can develop with older children as well. One man told me, "My wife and I had excellent communication until our daughters became teenagers. That's when she entered the workforce and we got a dog. Our relationship became less and less important to her. I came after the girls, the job, and the dog." Eventually the marriage ended.

A couple whom I'll call Barb and Arthur had the same problem. As Barb told me, "When our girls entered junior high school it was the most difficult time of our marriage. Our younger daughter Carla was in an emotional crisis; I had to turn my attention to her. Carla confided mainly in me. If she told me something she didn't want her daddy to know, I wouldn't tell him." How did Arthur feel? "I felt left out to some extent," he admitted. Nevertheless Barb and Arthur managed to restore their balance of power, and he stayed in the marriage. "Now I tell him everything—and the girls know it," Barb admitted. Arthur shared some of the advantages of their new arrangement: "It helps me feel closer to Barb. I can understand more clearly the problems she is dealing with—and I appreciate her efforts on the girls' behalf. Now I also can identify the areas where I can support her *and* my daughters."

One couple who both had children from previous marriages had a double imbalance of power. She felt jealous of his eldest daughter; he, of her youngest son. He would sometimes say to her, "Why don't you just go down the hall and sleep with your partner—your son?" She in turn started asking him, "How can I compete with your daughter? Who's the real team here anyway?" Finally they both agreed that they, the couple, must come first. Only then could they start negotiating love and figure out what to do about their children.

An imbalance of power also can occur if one lover frequently sides with her/his interfering parent. In my first marriage, my husband consistently put his mother first. Whenever she criticized me, he defended her. When she moved to Florida, he announced we were moving there too, whether I liked it or not. Eventually I began to feel that my husband was more allied with his mother than with me. Had I been able to articulate my feelings, we might have been able to negotiate love. "When I'm with you and your mother, I feel like an outsider. I need you to be on my side, not hers."

So be careful about allowing an outside alliance to upset the balance of power between you and your lover. Whenever you or your lover feel the center of energy shifting away from your relationship, it is time to negotiate love and rebalance your power. Your lover's needs come first.

Riding the Seesaw of Power When Three's a Crowd

You and your lover have been enjoying a seesaw ride together; first one has more power, then the other. So what do you do when another person climbs on your side of the seesaw? You have three choices. One is to remove the outsider from the seesaw completely. Break off your extramarital affair, tell your parent that you're an independent person now, or ask your ex-wife to return her key to your house. (Even change the locks if you have to.) Or, you make the outside alliance an occasional one. Visit your brother once a month instead of once a week. Call your mother twice a week rather than once a day. Instead of staying home with the baby every night, get a baby-sitter and go out with your lover on the weekend. Or you can move the outsider from one *side* of the seesaw to the *center*, where the outsider won't upset the balance you and your partner share. Invite your new friend to have dinner with you and your spouse—so long as your spouse agrees. If you're an insecure father, roll up your sleeves, change some diapers, and get involved in parenting your newborn child. If you've gone through a divorce, ask your lover to join you when you visit with your children from your previous marriage. In this way, you negate any adverse influence another person might have on the power dynamic in your own relationship.

All balances of power are temporary. The seesaw always has the potential to shift whenever you negotiate love. When you are on the bottom, appreciate your own power. Know what you need, and believe you have the right to ask your lover for whatever you desire. Say to yourself, "I can do it." The moment you begin negotiating love, you will start moving toward the top of the seesaw again. When you reach the top, always remember to be empathetic. Draw your lover out; ask her/him what her/his needs and feelings are.

As power shifts back and forth, you can feel like you're riding on a roller coaster instead of a seesaw. The experience can be exhilarating—or frightening. Keep in mind that the balance of power constantly shifts. Whoever has the most power today may have the least power tomorrow.

CHAPTER 7

What to Do When Romance Fades

Never underestimate the importance of the romantic tie. It is the magic of romance that instantly connects two lovers and encourages them to start communicating with each other. But no matter how they try, the glow of infatuation eventually disappears. A man described his experience: "In all my previous relationships with women, I'd get these early feelings of passion and think, 'If only I keep trying, this exhilaration will last.' But it never did. I couldn't make the transition from the "teenager-in-love" feeling to what seems like the "ordinariness" of commitment. I couldn't ask, 'What's really going on with us?' and begin to create something more long-term."

Particularly when we are young, we are reluctant to face our differences. One couple told me, "We met, fell in love, and got married while we were in our early twenties. My parents were against the marriage. The family pressure of 'no, no, no' drove us to always respond to each other—and outside influences—with 'yes, yes, yes.' We didn't allow ourselves to face our differences—ever. They were kept under the surface and remained hidden until we started divorce proceedings ten years later." But mature couples often can hide from the truth. A woman in her late thirties told me that after she moved in with her lover, she found out that he had been an intravenous drug user four years earlier. In her words, "Until then we had both been looking at just the good stuff, instead of at the real person."

Everyone yearns to fall in love, escape to a fantasy world, and find an ideal lover. Like the media heroes and heroines we worship, we pretend that we are perfect and seek a perfect mate. Romance temporarily makes us forget our pain, grief, fear, and anger. We may say we don't trust women or men, but we choose to make this particular person the exception to our rule. Intoxicated by the euphoria of romance, we want to make, not negotiate, love.

WHAT ARE OUR RESISTANCES?

Why don't most lovers confront and negotiate their differences early on? The most common reasons my interviewees gave were:

- It's threatening: "It might break us up."
- It's frightening: "It'll get us too close."
- It's too difficult: "I don't know how."
- It's unromantic: "It takes the mystery out of the relationship."
- It's unnecessary: "My lover should know what I need."
- It's demeaning: "It embarrasses me and hurts my pride."
- It's destructive: "We might hurt each other's feelings."

Let's consider these resistances together one at a time.

IT'S THREATENING: "IT MIGHT BREAK US UP."

This is probably the number-one reason many couples don't negotiate love early on. When people are dating, they often don't negotiate with each other, because if they do, they may find out that their relationship isn't going to work out. They'd rather repress their needs and feelings than experience the loneliness of being without a partner. It's scary to think about being alone: "Who knows when—and *if*—I'll meet someone else." But you have to take the leap. Without loving negotiations, the relationship will founder and eventually fizzle.

For example, a woman confided in me that she was reluctant to discuss controversial issues with her lover; she was afraid if she rocked the boat, he'd leave. According to psychotherapist Laurie Ingraham, this outlook is common among women who aren't in touch with their own power. "For example, a woman who needs a man for economic reasons will start noticing his faults only once they get married. Either unconsciously or purposefully, she closes her eyes so she can close the deal."[1] Actually, women with this viewpoint are often mistaken in their assumption. A man revealed to me that he proposed to his wife in the *middle* of an argument! "What we were arguing about didn't matter; what counted was that she was standing up for herself. I wanted a whole person for a wife. I wanted negative as well as positive information."

Think about it: The negotiation you fear may break you up could actually bring the two of you closer together. For example, suppose you're afraid to tell your lover how you feel about country music.

YOU: I really don't want to go to Lonesome Larry's Country Dance Hall again this week. My feet hurt, and besides, that place is so smoky. I think we're getting into a rut.

YOUR LOVER: I'm glad you spoke up! I'm getting tired of it too. I suggested it only because I thought *you* liked it. How about a jazz or classical concert, where we can sit down and hold hands for a change?

You can't hide from the truth forever. If you don't face the issues you have now, you may spend years with the wrong person—only to have your resentment and frustration build, build, and build until, finally, you head to the divorce court in the later half of your life. *Wouldn't you rather have spent those years creating a relationship that would last?* Being with a person who is wrong for you will keep you from finding a person who may be right.

IT'S FRIGHTENING: "IT'LL GET US TOO CLOSE."

At first glance, this argument is the opposite of the one we've just discussed. Lovers are not only worried they'll break up; they're also afraid they'll get too close to each other. Actually, both of these concerns are part of the "push-pull" dynamic typical of dating relationships. "Don't leave me, but don't come too near" is the message lovers frequently communicate to their prospective partners. What we actually fear is getting closer to our *own* selves, not to each other. One woman candidly admitted, "I'd love to be able to sit down and talk honestly to my husband. I want this piece of heaven but I'm afraid of it. I might discover something about *myself* that I'm scared to confront, admit, and support."

It's also true that many lovers are afraid to admit their weaknesses or character flaws to each other, especially early in the relationship. We're embarrassed about our insecurities, uncertainties, and "selfish" desires. Maybe we're hard to get along with at certain times, we're not into housework, or we're uncomfortable around children. We wonder, "Will my lover still like me if s/he finds out I'm heavily in debt? Will s/he reject me if s/he knows I never finished college? What will s/he think of me if I reveal how much I spend on my computer equipment?" When we share our feelings and our needs, when we ask for understanding and support, we make ourselves vulnerable. Since we may have not yet fully established trust in our lover, we fear we may be hurt. Women who would freely ask for help from a female friend are often reluctant to request it from their lover. "If I asked for help, I wouldn't be showing him my liberated self," one woman revealed.[2] She was worried that negotiating love with her male lover would make her appear weak.

If you want your relationship to last, you'll find out what your lover feels, needs, and expects early on—and make a sincere effort to honor that information. You'll share your own feelings, needs, and expectations as well. As you continue negotiating love, both of you will update this information periodically. There are always unplumbed depths of each other's personalities to explore.

IT'S TOO DIFFICULT: "I DON'T KNOW HOW."

Say to yourself right now, "Negotiating love sounds like an excellent idea. I can do it!" It's true. *Everyone* can learn loving negotiation skills—and it's essential that you do so.

In any romantic relationship, conflicts emerge sooner or later. As Jungian couples therapist Dr. Irene Gad puts it, "The moment romance goes out the window, power comes through the door."[3] Instead of being a fantasy image, our lover becomes a real person. We start experiencing each other in ordinary situations instead of always going out on dates. We start sharing our feelings and needs instead of always accommodating each other. We start asking honest, pertinent questions and seeking truthful answers. At first we may be disillusioned as our lover tumbles off her/his pedestal. But if we initiate loving negotiations as soon as the first conflicts appear, eventually we will grow closer together.

IT'S UNROMANTIC: "IT TAKES THE MYSTERY OUT OF THE RELATIONSHIP."

Does negotiating love *destroy* romance? One woman I interviewed described her dilemma this way: "I'm having brunch with a man and we're discussing the issue of having children. Is this a good time to say, 'I'd really like to have a baby and it seems as if you don't want kids at all.' No. It's easier to avoid confronting the issue. I prefer to stay fascinated with my handsome stranger."

A couple who had been married for almost fifteen years had opposite positions on this issue. While the wife wondered, "How can someone possibly prefer fantasy to a real relationship?" her husband explained his point of view: "Fantasy and reality aren't mutually exclusive. We are governed not just by our intellect but by our heart and imagination as well." This couple began negotiating love as soon as they met. As she put it, "Our romantic evenings were carefully planned. Before a date we would talk about what activities we wanted to do together, what we liked about our relationship, what we weren't happy with, and what we'd like to see changed. We would shift modes: First we'd have loving negotiations and then we'd have candlelight dinners."

Another couple, two graduate students whom I'll call Karen and Len, also told me that negotiating love and maintaining a sense of romance *are* compatible.

KAREN: When we met we were both sick of playing games and not knowing what was going on. At the beginning of our relationship we both agreed that we wanted to know where we stood all the time. If we didn't know, we would ask. We would tell each other about whatever bothered us. We'd confront it directly, talk about it, and make a plan for dealing with it. There would be no sneaking around, hiding, or second-guessing each other.

LEN: Does this take the romance out of our relationship? Absolutely not. We can still be spontaneous and have fun.

KAREN: Len and I can be really silly together. The structure enables us to play and opens us up to new experiences—things we would have been nervous about doing otherwise. We enjoy being with each other.

Whether or not you start negotiating love on the first date, at least make an agreement to "lay it all out" *before* you commit. A man who had been married for twenty years told me: "Long before I proposed, we talked at great length about careers, children, and the other issues we might face as a couple. We resolved ninety percent of conflicting issues *by* our wedding day—not after. This way, we headed off a lot of arguments." A pair of newlyweds with whom I spoke agreed. According to them, "We see pretty much eye-to-eye on the big issues: time, money, and lifestyle. There has never been any game-playing between us. We talked these things out before we got married."

A couple in their fifties echoed these sentiments. Both married for the second time, they had learned from their mistakes. The man explained, "Before our marriage we made agreements with each other about issues that were important to each of us. She said to me, 'I plan on visiting my hospitalized child regularly. Will you come with me?' I replied, 'Some of the time, but not always.' I asked her, 'I want to spend part of each year in Montana. Is this okay with you?' She answered yes. The clarity of our understanding has allowed room for romance—room for it to grow, room for it to flourish."

Negotiating love before you commit to each other is *not* unromantic. When you do, you both know where you stand. Couples who take the time to discuss their important issues keep their relationship *alive*. Your shared understandings provide a foundation for romance, excitement, and play.

IT'S UNNECESSARY: "MY LOVER SHOULD KNOW WHAT I NEED."

We all yearn for the perfect soulmate. By magic or by imagination, our alter ego will always know exactly what we need and grant our every wish. But this is fantasy, not reality. As Daphne Rose Kingma writes eloquently in her book *True Love*, "Your sweetheart isn't psychic."[4] Aside from a few people gifted with extrasensory perception, we aren't mind readers. Your lover doesn't know what you need unless you *tell* her/him. If there is a difference of opinion, it won't be resolved until you negotiate love. Up to now, women have been more skilled in expressing their feelings and needs in words. Men need to catch up—and to educate women in the male mode of expression. In *The Myth of Male Power*, Dr. Warren Farrell cautions men specifically when he writes, "Women cannot hear what men do not say."[5]

Loving negotiations about one's unmet needs and unfulfilled desires must take place between a woman and a man in order for their relationship to last. Whether with actions, with silence, or with words, men must share what is in their hearts.

And women must support them in their efforts. One woman told me, "I always wanted him to call me 'sweetheart' and 'darling.' He would never say these words. So eventually I started saying these words *to* him. I also told him, 'It would mean so much if you would talk tenderly to me.' Finally, on my birthday, he gave me a card on which he had written, 'Happy Birthday to My Sweetie.' It was a great thrill for me."

IT'S DEMEANING. "IT EMBARRASSES ME AND HURTS MY PRIDE."

A single man in his twenties, still upset about the breakup of his three-year relationship, told me this story: "Our first conflict came up early on. Her ex-boyfriend was constantly interfering in our relationship. Because we had been dating only six weeks, I chose to overlook it. I told myself, 'We're having a good time. Let's not bring it up. It's no big deal.' It was only after she moved in with me that I felt I could tell her how much her ex was bothering me. He was sending her love letters, calling her three or four times a night, and hanging up the phone when I answered. She even started hanging out with him. But when I finally brought up the subject her response was, 'We're just friends. He's not in love with me.' It was embarrassing to keep talking about it, so I just stopped. Later on she realized that I was right but she didn't want to admit that she had been wrong." Neither of these lovers could overcome their embarrassment and negotiate with each other. They are no longer together.

Sometimes you must overlook your pride and open up to your lover. That's when true intimacy occurs—and true love flourishes. "I find it difficult (or embarrassing) to tell you this; please support me in opening my heart to you" is a good way to start. Honest conversations facilitate romance.

IT'S DESTRUCTIVE: "WE MIGHT HURT EACH OTHER'S FEELINGS."

Women in particular are susceptible to this argument. It's true that if you confront your disagreements you might say something that offends your lover. And if you yourself are sensitive, your lover may hurt your feelings. But while neither of you may like what you hear, once you get past the initial discomfort you'll reach an agreement that will keep both of you from hurting each other in the future.

One woman told me about a heated argument she had with her husband: "He'd never help around the house—not even pick up his clothes. Finally, I told him I was fed up doing all the cleaning, cooking, and child care. His response surprised me: 'Well, I'm sick of working two jobs to make all the money to support us. When I come home, I'm dead tired.' We finally agreed I'd start working part time and he'd pitch in around the house."

Why Negotiate Love Early On? Why Not Wait?

The romantic tie that initially bridges a couple is a superficial one. While they are fulfilling each other's fantasies, lovers are expressing only their acceptable feelings. Their negative ones are hidden or disguised. But once the infatuation starts to fade, a couple's deep, underlying differences emerge. Only if a strong relationship bond has been formed will they stay together. A couple in their late twenties told me how this transition occurred for them. The woman began: "On our first anniversary we had a big fight; it was the first and only time I ever walked out. When I came back we sat down and said to each other, 'Wait a second, what are we doing?' It was the turning point for us." Her husband continued: "We started creating our own framework for resolving our issues. They were family issues at first; our financial ones we worked out later. We laugh now about the weekly fights we used to have during those early years, but they were really good for us. We got a lot of issues out in the open that we wouldn't have confronted until well into our marriage."

Why should a woman and a man in the throes of romance begin negotiating love? Because conflicts will inevitably develop in the relationship. A lover who doesn't know how to negotiate differences will go from one romance to another without ever resolving them.

So start negotiating love as soon as you begin dating. The successful resolution of your disagreements will pave the way for a long and lasting union.

Handling Typical Dating Dilemmas

When you and your lover are just dating you're not jointly managing a household. You don't have a home, a couple of cars, kids, and an elderly parent to care for. Not distracted by these logistics, you and your lover are free to focus your attention on romantic issues.

So what emotional issues do single lovers need to negotiate? First they must determine who takes initiatives in the relationship: Who pays for dates? Who calls whom? Who initiates sex? What kind? How often? Exclusivity is another issue that must be negotiated. Do we date others? Do we have sex with them? What happens if one of us gets jealous? Last, and the most important issue of all, is commitment: Shall we live together? Get engaged? Get married? If so, when? As we negotiate all these issues, we define our own boundaries and set standards for our lover.

WHO TAKES THE INITIATIVE?

Had I negotiated "who calls whom?" while I was dating, I could have avoided much of the time I spent waiting by the phone. When I was single, it was a nonnegotiable issue; "nice" women didn't phone men. We weren't supposed to be so assertive. Fortunately, women and men now have equal telephone rights. You can phone your lover; your lover can phone you. It's up to the two of you. Perhaps both of you may agree to call each other at the office only in emergencies and to talk on the phone at length when you are home. Or you may decide to talk every other night to give each other some "alone time." Rather than being the three words women hate most, "I'll call you" is now an invitation to negotiate love.

Another issue to negotiate while dating is who pays. There are many ways to resolve this question. Either you pay for everything or your lover does. Or you split the expenses. Or one of you pays two-thirds of the bill and the other pays one-third. Or one of you pays and the other contributes home-cooked dinners and other non-cash items. It doesn't matter what your agreement is, as long as *both* of your needs are met. For example, if one of you is a wealthy businessperson and the other a struggling artist, you may agree that the businessperson will pick up the tab—until the artist strikes it rich. One couple I interviewed had a huge disparity of income but did not negotiate love. As the man told me, "My woman friend was rich and horribly spoiled. Time and time again I would ask her to pay. I'd tell her, 'Don't take it for granted that I will come up with the money.' But she never paid. Eventually we broke up.

It was only when she started earning her own living and realized the value of a dollar that we got back together again." Another man whose woman friend lived out of town always traveled to see her and always paid their expenses. Instead of hiding his feelings, he told her how he was hurting: "It's very hard for me to keep giving and not receive something back." She listened. Now when they go out to dinner, she contributes instead of assuming he's going to pay for it all.

Expressing affection is another emotional issue to negotiate. You may enjoy displaying your affection publicly, including hugging and kissing; your lover may want to draw the line at hand-holding. If you have differences, you need to work them out. "No hugging or kissing in public, but when we're alone together, I'll make up for it." Or, "We'll hold hands in front of our families and friends, but not at the office party."

When it comes to words, "I love you" means different things to different people. Some of us are comfortable using these words early on, while others prefer to wait until the relationship gets more serious. One couple I interviewed, two graduate students whom I'll call Tanya and Sam, told me how they negotiated this disagreement:

TANYA: I fell in love with Sam before he fell in love with me. I needed to tell him in words because I couldn't keep my feelings inside. But I did ask Sam, "Is it okay if I tell you I love you? I don't want you to feel pressured." I wanted to respect his feelings. He said, "You can say it, but I'm not ready to do so myself." I responded, "It really hurts not to hear you say it, but I understand."

SAM: I *did* feel pressured because she said "I love you" a lot. When someone says "I love you," you're supposed to say it back. I was running out of things to say to her: "You're special to me . . . You mean a lot to me . . ." But I didn't want to tell her "I love you" just for the sake of saying it; I wanted to really mean it.

TANYA: Finally he was able to tell me he loved me. And I knew then it came from his heart, because Sam is a very genuine person.

As Tanya and Sam learned to negotiate this emotional issue, they laid the foundation for the practical issues they would face later on.

Sooner or later the questions arise, Who initiates sex? How often will we have it? What kind will it be? No longer is the man always expected to take charge. Women and men need to reach agreement about these issues together. In this arena, often our negotiations are nonverbal and subtle. A glance may signify, "Do you want to?" A shake of the head may indicate, "Not now." A gentle touch may mean, "Yes, let's do this" or "No, let's do it another way."

You also need to respect each other's sexual needs. One of you may have had a tough day and not be in the mood. You can agree to say, "I'm stressed out. I can't handle sex tonight. How about waking up a little early in the morning when we're both feeling refreshed?" Or if you're uncomfortable using words, you can hold up your hand like you do if you're stopping traffic. When you're consumed with desire, you can simply say, "I want you"—or you can open your arms to your lover as if you want to give her/him a big hug. While you're making love, you can gently guide your lover's hand to where you want it. If your lover inadvertently does something that is uncomfortable or painful for you, you can move her/his hand away or you can say, "Please don't do that." If your signals don't work, have a loving negotiation to clear the air. A couple who is comfortable negotiating about sex is usually able to negotiate about other issues as well.

IS OUR RELATIONSHIP EXCLUSIVE?

Sooner or later the issue of exclusivity comes up. If one lover is dating or having sex with other people, the other may become jealous. If lovers can sit down on the negotiating couch and reach an agreement, there is an excellent chance that their relationship will last. But this is an incredibly sensitive issue, and there are many possible ways the issue of exclusivity can be resolved. One woman told me how she and her lover negotiated it:

HE: I want to date other women.
SHE: Well, if you do, I won't be seeing you anymore. That's it; I won't change my mind.

Regretfully, neither was receptive to the other's feelings and needs, and their negotiation quickly ended. Eventually they broke up.

Another couple negotiated the exclusivity issue differently:

HE: I want to date other women.
SHE: I'm not happy with this, but I'm not going to beg you not to. If you want to go out with other women, it's okay. Just don't tell me the details. And this means that I may start dating other men. Can you handle that?
HE: Well—yes. I guess I have to. It's only fair.

A third couple had a different resolution of the same issue. When the woman expressed her desire to date, her partner countered that he expected to do the same. Their loving negotiation revealed that what she really wanted was an opportunity to go dancing, an activity he did not enjoy. They agreed she would attend dance lessons—but not date anyone in the class.

While the future of the latter two couples—like all others—is uncertain, at least they shared with each other their real feelings and needs. Dating, expressing affection, and making love with other people are all subjects for loving negotiations. Whether a relationship is exclusive or somewhat open, chances are good that it will last as long as some kind of agreement is reached.

SHALL WE COMMIT?

The most important issue of all is commitment. Eventually every couple in romance needs to make a decision whether or not to live together, get engaged, or get married. There are four possible alternatives: Both want to commit; both don't want to commit; the woman wants to commit and the man doesn't; the man wants to commit and the woman doesn't. Couples in all four of these situations need to work things out.

How the commitment issue is resolved will often set the tone of a couple's future relationship. When there is a conflict, it is *vital* that they negotiate love and reach a mutually satisfying agreement. If one lover wants to wait, s/he must feel that her/his needs are being respected. If her/his partner "pressures" and the other "gives in," the stage will be set for an unequal balance of power (as discussed in the previous chapter).

Several couples told me about the different ways they reached agreement about the commitment issue. One couple dealt with the commitment issue only as a response to external pressure. As the man described their situation: "All her friends and business associates knew that she was seeing me regularly. She was getting pressure from them, so she put heavy pressure on me to commit. She told me, 'I want to be able to show my friends that you care for me.' I resisted. A month later she called me and said that if she didn't get a commitment from me right away, she wouldn't talk to me again. I let her hang up on me."

Not to stereotype, but it is often the woman who puts pressure on a man to commit. A couple whom I'll call Ursula and William were experiencing this dilemma when I interviewed them.

URSULA: I am deeply concerned about this, William: The way things stand now, you can walk out the door at any time. I've already been through a divorce, and then my fiancé died; I don't think I can go through another loss like that.

WILLIAM: I feel that you're pressuring me. What you said makes me feel responsible—that I need to "fix it" for you so you don't feel this way. And I don't want to be pushed into making a commitment right now.

URSULA: I don't intend to lay a guilt trip on you—but I really do feel this way.

A couple in their mid-twenties with whom I spoke had a similar negotiation, in which they were uncomfortable with each other's desires. In her words, "I've told him, 'I'm the happiest I've been in a long time. I think we'll be married one day.' But when I say this, I make him uneasy." He continued: "She always says, 'I won't bring marriage up,' but she keeps on talking about it. And that's not right." A single woman who was dating a married military officer told me, "We soon started arguing all the time about his getting the blasted divorce [from his wife]. Often I got anxious about the situation and couldn't refrain from pressuring him." All three of these women were giving notice that they were uncomfortable with the current situation, and they wanted to take control of the relationship. Although their own feelings and needs were being ignored, they did not show respect for their lovers' feelings and needs either.

It is important for couples to balance their power as they negotiate the commitment issue. A man I interviewed described how he and the woman he married reached an agreement together. "She asked me to marry her first. I think her words were, 'Isn't it time for us to get married?' She took me by surprise. I told her, 'I'm really not ready.' Then we took it a lot slower. When I finally did ask her to marry me, *she* was the one who hesitated."

For many couples, time eventually works in their favor. One woman explained, "Our main area of conflict was getting married. I set my cap for him, but he was terribly indecisive. So I waited; I didn't pressure. I wasn't going to drag him down the aisle if he didn't want to go. We remained friends. After two more years he decided he was ready to marry me."

If you're the one looking to get married, you need to examine whether it is worth sacrificing the relationship with an ultimatum. The answer, for you, may very well be yes. If the answer is no, see if you can respect your lover's feelings and needs and simply wait. Perhaps you can check with her/him every few months to see if her/his feelings have changed. Or, if both of you agree, discuss the situation with a third party—a trusted friend, relative, or counselor.

Every emotional issue that comes up is an opportunity to learn to negotiate love. While reaching agreement early in the dating phase of the relationship won't *guarantee* that you'll "live happily ever after," it *will* increase your chances of forming a lasting relationship.

Moving Beyond Dating Dilemmas to the "Relationship Spirit"

For a relationship to last, lovers must transform the initial glow of infatuation into the reality of a relationship. As lovers learn to successfully negotiate typical dating dilemmas, they eventually form a bond that constitutes a relationship.

How do you make the transition? Both of you must develop the relationship spirit. To understand it, start with what you know. Men have experienced team spirit; women are familiar with the spirit of friendship; and vice versa. The relationship spirit is closely related to both.

During the initial stages of a romance, each person's orientation is "me, me, me." Both lovers think, "How can you make *me* happy? How can you be *my* ideal person? How can you fulfill *my* dreams? I won't compromise if it means giving up what *I* need in favor of what *you* need." Since the element of trust hasn't fully developed, lovers in romance are self-protective when they disagree: "You promised to bring me flowers and you forgot. How could you?" Or, "You're working late again. Don't you ever have any time for *me*?"

After a couple forms a relationship bond, their orientation changes to *"you and me."* They say to each other, "What interests you interests me. I care about what you care about." Both people think, "How can we meet each other's needs? How can we facilitate each other's dreams? What is our agenda as a couple? How can we work together to make our relationship better?" The same disagreements are handled differently. "You didn't bring any wine with you. Well, there must have been a good reason. We'll just find something else to drink." Or, "You're working late this week. It must be difficult for you to put in all that extra time. How can I help you out?"

When there's a relationship bond, there's mutual understanding. Your goal is to create a common core of ideas—with room for individual differences. Whenever you negotiate love, you say to each other, "I want to know your point of view. I want to know how *you* see it." This doesn't necessarily mean you have to agree all the time. As one of my college alumnae told me, "Until I met Michael (the man I'm living with now), I never knew communication could be synergistic. Instead of shutting down or saying something flip, Michael tells me what is important to him. When he listens he lets me know that what I have to say is valuable. Michael and I understand each other. We sometimes say to each other, 'I don't agree with you, but I can feel how you must feel.' "

Guided by the relationship spirit, you and your lover take turns listening attentively to each other when you negotiate love. You both use phrases like "Okay, I've said my piece. Now it's your turn to be heard." How comforting this can be. My hairdresser, Henry Noufal, once commented, "The only thing worse than not being allowed to speak at all is to speak and not be listened to." When you learn something from your lover, you acknowledge it. Jungian couples therapist Dr. Irene Gad points out that a precious gift lovers can give each other is validation. The words "You're absolutely right. That's the way it was" can heal if they are sincerely meant. When you receive your lover's messages with empathy, you are giving her/him a special kind of nurturing.[6] As author Dr. Warren Farrell has observed, "I've never heard anyone say 'I want a divorce; my spouse understands me.' "[7] Feeling deeply understood is an essential ingredient of the relationship spirit.

Most important, the guiding principle of the relationship

spirit is *mutual support.* You and your lover both give of yourselves. No one keeps score. Neither of you says, "I took care of you Monday through Wednesday when you were sick; now you owe me three days." Or "I shopped last Thursday; even if you're busy, you have to do the shopping this Thursday." Couples with the relationship spirit don't think in terms of "my needs" and "your needs." They realize that they have common as well as individual needs.

One man I interviewed explained: "Our relationship is like a corporation. We both work for us. When she gets a raise in salary, we have more money to spend. If I pitch in with the housework, our house is cleaner. The more each of us gives, the more we both receive." Liz Mitchell, book reviewer for *Today's Chicago Woman*, summed it up perfectly: "It's not my mother, my kids, my money, or my house, it's *our* mother, *our* kids, *our* money, and *our* house."[8] You and your lover together are a special unit: a family.

When the relationship spirit is present, it becomes easy to negotiate love. Both lovers have equal power over the long run—and neither is powerful *all* the time. One man declared, "Although I'm earning more money than ever before, Nancy's income is still considerably higher than mine. And she owns the house we live in. Yet Nancy has never made me feel I'm not pulling my weight."

Another couple living together, whom I'll call Paula and Richard, went into greater detail:

PAULA: Richard has more income than I do. But we don't keep track of who earns what. When we have money, *we* spend it. If one of us really wants something, then we buy it whenever we can. If it costs a lot, like a car, we talk about it first. Then we enjoy it together.

RICHARD: When Paula knows more about something than I do, I listen to what she says. When she's right, I give her credit.

PAULA: We're totally equal—even when it involves tasks like making the bed, cooking, washing the dinner dishes, or taking out the trash.

RICHARD: We never say, "It's your turn" or "It's my turn." We say, "If you're coming over, please pick something up." It just flows.

PAULA: We each know what is really important to the other. We have a great awareness of each other's needs, and we both operate from this awareness.

Lovers with a true relationship spirit don't compete with each other. One woman I interviewed told me she lived with a man for three years who insisted on paying for everything. She complained bitterly, "When you don't pay you don't get equal say. There are certain rights you don't have. I couldn't ask him, 'Was it really necessary to spend five hundred dollars on a new living-room couch?' I always felt he overshadowed me." The relationship spirit is different. As one man told me, "My wife and I see it like this: My success does not diminish her. My success enhances her, as hers enhances me. We want only the best for each other." Ann McGill, a performance coach I spoke with, has a similar philosophy. "The better you do, the better I look."[9] When one of you succeeds, you both benefit. You support each other as you work toward your common objectives. If you have a special project, your lover backs you. When your partner has an important need, you encourage her/him to fulfill it.

When you negotiate love with this mindset, you get further a lot faster. Both you and your lover speak to each other about "our goals" as well as "your goals" and "my goals." You ask each other, "What do you need? What do I need? What do we need?" The three may coincide. But if they don't, you and your lover start working to find a solution.

Lovers who embody the relationship spirit often take turns pursuing their goals. One married couple formally agreed to do this before they got married. He explained to her, "In my business we're going to have to move a lot during the early years to advance my career. But there will come a time when I will have reached a plateau. Then it'll be your turn to go back to school." After living in six states in seven years, they finally settled down. His wife then got her degree and a job she wanted in her chosen field. Another couple, married forty-five years, also alternated in giving each other's needs priority. During the early years she stayed home with their children while his engineering career flowered; after their children were grown, he encouraged her to pursue her interests in charitable work. When she needed his financial support, he was there for her. When he subsequently lost his eyesight and needed her help, she was there for him.

The relationship spirit means supporting each other daily—and over the long term. How can you best give of yourself? When you negotiate, ask your lover, "What do *you* need the most? What is *your* heart's desire? What is *your* most cherished dream?" Each person's answer is different. "To open my own private law practice." "To pay off all my debts and retire." "To travel." "To parent a child." Find out your lover's deepest need—whatever it is—and enable her/him to fulfill it. Your support can take different forms. It may be material; earning money or providing services may be the contribution your lover needs. Or it may be emotional; you may enable your lover to achieve her/his goal by showing your faith and offering encouragement. Sometimes your support may encompass both kinds. I would never have been able to write this book without my husband's material and emotional support.

Giving support is a generous act. You make your offer without demanding something back, "tit for tat." And although we all want support, few of us are willing to give it unconditionally. Just look at the personals ads; no matter the wording, each one cries out, "These are my fantasies. Please grant them."

It takes courage to give support, especially during romance. If you and your lover don't yet trust each other, you take a risk when you make your offer. Each lover thinks, "If I'm the first to offer my support, I might get hurt. I might be the one to get rejected." But if neither of you takes the initiative, a relationship bond will *never* be formed.

Receiving support also takes courage. To get your needs met you have to know what they are—and be willing to risk revealing them when you negotiate love.

Sometimes your lover's desire may be something that is hard for you to fulfill. Perhaps you want to get married while your lover wants to distance her/himself temporarily to make a decision. Honor your lover's need while you continue to ask her/him for what you need most. The more support you offer, the more you will receive.

Offering your support is *not* codependency. It is a healthy, loving gesture as long as you maintain your sense of self and set clear limits as to how far you will go. As long as you know who you are, you don't lose your identity when you support someone else. Being generous does not mean allowing yourself to be taken advantage of. Codependent people don't know *when* to stop giving; they always put their lovers' needs ahead of their own. When there's a healthy relationship bond, you and your lover don't become martyrs. On the contrary, you both strengthen each other as you negotiate love—fulfilling each other's desires and honoring your needs as a couple as well.

CHAPTER 8

Handling Relationship Hotspots

How do our conflicts arise? Typically a specific incident triggers a whole issue area we disagree about. I call these issue areas hotspots. In order to form a strong relationship bond, you and your lover must negotiate twelve hotspots: money, careers, housework, neatness, time, religion and spirituality, family backgrounds, substance abuse, sex, sexual jealousy, children, and outsiders (relatives, friends, and business associates). The last three of these hotspots are the most difficult to negotiate because they involve people outside your relationship.

Which particular hotspots are you and your lover likely to be negotiating now? Generally speaking, it depends on which decade you're in. In your twenties, you focus on separating from your families and launching your careers. Different family backgrounds and religions may cause disagreements. In your thirties, your main issues are money, sex, housework, neatness, and, if you have them, young children. In your forties and fifties your attention often turns to issues of changing careers, time, and sexual jealousy. In your sixties, seventies, and eighties you may be preoccupied with your own or your lover's retirement, loss of beloved family members and friends, and the problems of grown children and grandchildren.

Within each decade each couple has its own unique pattern of hotspots. One couple may argue endlessly about sex and jealousy; another couple, about money. And two different couples may have financial disputes for different reasons. One of the couples may be negotiating their conflicting dependence and independence needs, while the other may be balancing their respective needs for security and growth. And as soon as a couple reaches an agreement on one issue, another disagreement may arise. The moment one hotspot cools off, a different one may heat up. Sometimes, two or even more may heat up at the same time.

Instead of panicking, withdrawing, or endlessly arguing when you're faced with a hotspot issue, ask yourself these questions: Is it a *nonnegotiable* issue (see Chapter 4) for either of us? Are we having nonconversation, a conversation that is not about the real issue? What am I feeling? What is my lover feeling? What do I need? What does my lover need? What do we need as a couple? What possible solutions can we find that honor our feelings and meet our most important needs?

No matter what hotspot area is being negotiated, your unmet needs are *always* the real issue. Let's examine the twelve hotspot issue areas to find out what these needs usually are.

Money

Money is at the root of many lovers' conflicts. We all need money; most of us would like more of it. Why, then, does it divide us? The divisiveness comes not from the money itself—the green pieces of paper and the shiny coins—but from what money symbolizes to us. Money is a means for attaining many of our deepest needs. We don't need just money, we need what money can buy: necessities and luxuries, fun and relaxation, adventure and retirement. With money we can fulfill our healthy needs for security or self-expression, connectedness or independence, being generous or feeling valued. It's also true that we can fulfill our *un*healthy needs to overcontrol or put down our lover.

One couple I interviewed admitted that they often argue about money. "We look at money differently," the man explained. "For my wife money is a means to financial security; she wants a comfortable cushion for our retirement and savings to fall back on in an emergency. For me money is most valuable when I can give it away. I like to take risks and embark on projects that benefit my community. Do we think money is worth arguing about? No. For the most part, we agree that we can disagree about it. Sometimes we save it and sometimes we spend it."

When I appeared on the *Sally Jessy Raphael* show during a program entitled "My Husband's Middle Name Is Cheap," the three couples on my panel all had the same disagreement about money. The husbands wanted to save it in order to gain financial security; the wives wanted to spend it on luxuries that would make them feel valued and pampered. Rather than negotiating the disputes, the men tried to overcontrol their spouses. One man proudly boasted about how he had forced his views on his reluctant wife. And rather than privately complaining to their husbands about this tyranny, the women expressed their criticisms publicly. Two of the women seemed to take particular pleasure in insulting and ridiculing their lovers. *All three of the couples lacked the relationship spirit:* They spoke about "your money" and "my money" but not "*our* money." I explained to them that they needed to stop conflicting in this unhealthy way and start negotiating love.[1]

A young woman I interviewed for this book needed to feel independent from her live-in lover. She was a full-time student while her lover was working forty hours a week to pay their bills, and she was determined to keep an exact financial record of their expenditures so she could pay him back in the event they broke up. He, on the other hand, had the relationship spirit: "I don't see her as a financial burden," he told me. "Although I haven't bought anything for myself in a while, I'd rather have her than material things." The money he earned enabled him to connect with the woman he loved. He enjoyed being generous to her. She didn't have to contribute the same material amount; eventually, over time, it would even out.

For a couple who share the relationship spirit, money is an opportunity to meet individual and joint needs. It isn't used to meet the needs of only one lover—and it is not a tool for one lover to use to overcontrol the other.

To resolve the money hotspot, couples first need to recognize that there are several legitimate ways to earn money. Having a paying job outside the home, being self-employed, performing household services, and parenting are—and should be perceived as—equally valuable. Dr. Ivan Burnell and his wife, Dahny, who teach a course for couples entitled "Love and Live," suggest that every houseperson have a weekly paycheck (not an allowance). In this way, the services one partner performs within the home that enable the other to work at a job outside the home would be formally recognized and valued. Dr. Burnell goes on to say that after the household expenses have been paid, whatever is left over should be divided in half. Both lovers should have the same amount of money to use at their discretion to meet their individual needs for luxury, adventure, or security. They should also have the option of contributing to a collective fund to be used for the benefit of the couple.[2]

On major expenditures it is critical that, ultimately, you both agree.[3] If one of you is strongly against a particular item, *this* is the time to negotiate love. You need to discuss your respective spending priorities and balance your conflicting needs. One successful negotiator admitted, "How we spend our money is the source of a lot of our conflicts, but we've managed to resolve the issue." His wife agreed. "I enjoy his traveling to Latin America with me. But if he sometimes doesn't want to go, I am not going to spend my energy convincing him to do something he doesn't want to do. I was very surprised when last summer he *asked* to go. He told me later that he did it because it was important to me."

This couple, whom I'll call Beth and Aaron, went on to tell me how they resolved their different financial expectations and style. "When we got married, Aaron didn't trust me at all with the checkbook," Beth began. "He balanced it every month for the first year of our marriage. He insisted that it be kept in the top desk drawer. Slowly I earned his trust. After a year, he had gained confidence in my spending; he knew that I wasn't going to go wild writing checks." Aaron continued: "When we got married, Beth didn't know a thing about managing money. About a year and a half later we bought a computer program and she learned how to use it. Now Beth pays all the bills. Every month she knows exactly how much money is left over to spend. Yesterday she bought a couch for our living-room. But she didn't just show up and say she bought it; we discussed it first." Aaron and Beth demonstrate how sharing decisions about spending money is a hallmark of negotiating love.

CAREERS

What healthy career needs do we have? Careers mean different things to different people. Some see their work mainly as a means to earn money. They prefer to limit their hours at the office and have as much leisure time, and time to spend with their family, as possible. Others are willing to work overtime in order to achieve promotions and pay raises. Still others see a career as a mission; they are dedicated to their life's work and put it ahead of everything else.

Most often, one lover needs the other's support to pursue or to change her/his chosen career. The required support may be emotional, practical, or financial. Sometimes simply saying, "You can do it. I believe in you," or listening sympathetically to your lover's small victories and frustrations is all your lover needs. Running errands, doing household chores, and assuming responsibility for child care can be an incredibly valuable contribution. One of you may be asked to support the family financially for a while so that the other can lay the groundwork for a new career. Either the man or the woman can be the provider. After a while, you may switch roles. Phil supported me financially for seven years while I wrote until I was ready to start supporting him.

But in a two-career relationship, conflict can arise over whose career gets priority. Supposing your lover has an opportunity to relocate; what happens if the job s/he wants is three thousand miles away from where you presently live? Do you give up your job or does your lover forgo the opportunity? One happy couple in their twenties, whom I'll call Charlotte and Dan, effectively negotiated this issue.

Although Dan had always wanted to go to medical school, he worked as a laboratory technician instead. Charlotte had an excellent fund-raising job. After they got married, Dan was accepted by a top medical school in another city. Since this was an opportunity Dan had always dreamed about, Charlotte agreed they would move. Then they started negotiating about money; Dan was getting nervous about the future and their savings. About six months before they were due to relocate, he suggested to Charlotte, "I think you should update your résumé and start sending out copies now."

Charlotte responded, "I'm concerned about the future too. But I don't think I should carpet the city with my résumé six months in advance. I've been thinking about how to find a job and I've worked out a timetable." But Dan still wasn't satisfied. Charlotte realized that the real reason he was eager for her to find a job was that he needed to feel financially secure. So she said to Dan, "We should consider the possibility that I might not find a job in six or seven months. What then? What if we start getting desperate and we have only one box of cornflakes left? *Let's develop a plan now.* What about borrowing some money? Or moving to a less expensive home? Or what about my doing some temporary work? We could start spending less money now and start building our savings faster; I'm willing to give up spending on weekend fun if you are." Once this couple started brainstorming, they realized that there were many possible solutions to their problem that could satisfy them both.

It may be necessary for you or your lover to give up your own career for a while for other reasons. For example, when you have children, one or both of you may prefer to stay home and care for them. If this is your career need, *plan ahead.* Negotiate an agreement before you get married and certainly before the baby arrives. "I need to be with our child while s/he is young. How do you feel? What do you need? What about taking turns pursuing our careers?" These questions should get the discussion flowing.

Another less recognized career need is one lover's need for the other to work. If both lovers are employed, the size of the family budget stretches proportionately. So to insist that your lover support you by *not* working instead of striking out on her/his own can be financially as well as emotionally unhealthy. Your lover's career, especially if it is one s/he enjoys, may make her/him a happier and more stimulating person; through it s/he gains new interests and meets new friends.

One couple in their fifties was having a serious conflict about career issues. After being employed for fifteen years as a supervisor in a hardware store, the husband lost his job. After he had been turned down for a couple of jobs, his wife suggested, "Why don't we take our profit-sharing money and buy a business?" He told me later, "When she said that, I felt like a thousand-pound weight had been taken off my back. Unfortunately, I took it a step too far; I just assumed that any kind of business would be okay with her. I thought she was behind me all the way."

Rather than complete the negotiation with his wife, he started to call prospective sellers immediately, and shortly afterward bought a hardware store. Until the business took off, he would need his wife to work as his cashier. Unfortunately, he had neglected to find out two vital pieces of information: First, she wasn't interested in a hardware business. Second, she didn't want to work for him; she preferred to continue her own career. She was focusing on her own needs, not his. He was thinking only of his needs, not hers. Until they negotiated love, they would continue to argue bitterly.

HOUSEWORK

When it comes to housework, it seems our main preference is that our lover should do more of it! That's when our conflicts begin. Before you negotiate with your lover about this hotspot, discover your true needs and motives. When we say, "I need more help with the housework," usually we mean physical help. Each of us finds certain household jobs time-consuming, unpleasant, or just plain boring. But sometimes we also need *emotional* support. Few of us receive appreciation from our lover for cleaning the bathroom or taking out the trash. I once told my husband how delighted I would be if he would occasionally say, "Thank you for washing the sheets and towels." Now he does—and that makes me feel incredibly better about performing any task around the house.

Sometimes we need to recognize that our needs in this area are unhealthy. We ask for help and then require our lover to do a task according to *our* specifications. "Vacuum the floors; don't just sweep them." "Presoak the clothes before you wash them." "Use organic, not commercial, fertilizer on the lawn." Women in particular frequently suggest that the only "right" way to do a household job is their way. Some women overcontrol their lovers by taking over all the housework, which they label "women's work." They give the message, "I can do domestic chores; you can't." When men insist, "I can do yard work; you can't," they also exclude their partners without being aware of it.

Every woman who asks her lover to "help with" the dishes immediately puts herself at a disadvantage. Implicit in her request is the assumption that doing the dishes is *her* job and she is supposed to be grateful to him for helping her. The thought that doing the dishes might not necessarily be her responsibility doesn't cross either of their minds. The notion that, as one of my interviewees put it, there are "boy jobs" and "girl jobs" has to be discarded before we can even begin to negotiate effectively about who does the housework.

We also have to recognize whatever wounds we carry from the past about doing household tasks. For example, one man confessed, "My mother always used to nag me to do the dishes. So whenever my wife asks me to wash them, I hear my mother's voice."[4] If you understand your lover's wounds you will respond to her/his pain, instead of complaining that s/he isn't fulfilling household responsibilities. You will openly discuss the issue and arrive at a mutually agreeable solution. Maybe you can figure out a way to phrase your request gently so it sounds like an invitation to help instead of a demand. Or because it's a sensitive issue, you can assume responsibility for the dishwashing and ask your lover to do other chores instead.

To negotiate about housework, start by assuming that running a house is like running a business. *No one job is more important or more valuable than another.* Make a list of all the household jobs that have to be done, and identify those you don't mind doing. All tasks should be assigned to the best qualified person—unless this weights the tasks unfairly. If you like it or you're good at it, then do it—your way. Do other less fun jobs together; companionship makes them more enjoyable. If neither of you wants to do a particular job, laugh about it until finally one of you decides to do it; hire someone to perform the task; or just forget about it. As one happily married couple commented when they were discussing housework, "It doesn't matter who does what; eventually it all gets done. Don't sweat the small stuff."

If you can occasionally trade off jobs, you and your lover

will grow closer. By sharing household tasks, you develop common understandings. When you clean up the kitchen or mow the lawn once in a while when these tasks are normally not your responsibility, you know what the experience is like for your partner. If the garbage disposal malfunctions or the gutter becomes clogged, you and your lover can say to each other, "Let's *both* see how we can fix it." Neither of you should insist, "Let me fix it. I'm the only one who knows how." Encourage your children to follow your example. One woman revealed, "I taught my boys to cook and to knit. I taught my daughters to understand what's underneath the hood of a car and how to take apart a washing machine and repair it." How fortunate her children's spouses will be!

You and your lover also need to negotiate how to ask for help with the household chores. Learn to make your request in a healthy way and at an appropriate time. During my interview with pastoral counselor Dr. Daniel Henderson, we did a role-play together: He played a man who needs to relax by watching a Sunday afternoon baseball game on television, and I played his wife, who needs him to help clean the house:

ME: Because of my work schedule, the only time I can clean the house is this afternoon between one and five. I'm sorry, because I know that's when you watch the baseball game.

HE: That's right.

ME: Just give me half an hour of your time; that's all I'm asking for.

HE: No, I can't help you out now. I'm absolutely exhausted.

ME: But my parents are coming for dinner tomorrow night and the house is a mess!

HE: Look: I can either stay here and listen to you complain or

I can go to a bar and watch the game. If I stay home, relax, and build my strength up a little bit, I can be available to you later on. But if you don't want to wait, I'm going to go to a bar and watch the whole game there.

ME: I'm in a bind *right now.* I need to get this house cleaned because I'm going to feel very embarrassed tomorrow if it's dirty. What can we do about it?

HE: *Let me relax for a couple of hours and then I'll help you.*[5]

Once you understand each other's feelings and needs, you can work together to get an outcome you want. A woman told me how she negotiated another housework issue. "When I got totally exhausted because I was doing most of the housework, I wrote down all the tasks I did every day and showed the piece of paper to my husband. I told him, 'Afterward you expect me to be in the mood to make love. Well, I'm too tired by then. If you want romantic evenings, this is what you can do. It's up to you.' Then I gave him a list of jobs he could do." Another man shared with me how he and his wife frequently negotiated love. She would ask him, "How about helping me fold the laundry while we talk about our next vacation?" They would use a normal sit-down discussion time as a chance to also complete some household chores.

Neatness

Do you crave order in your life? Or do you prefer disorder, even chaos? Many couples disagree about this issue. Underneath a neatnik's desire to arrange objects is a deeper need. Many of us (including me) have a yearning for security and predictability which is met by knowing exactly where our possessions are. We also need efficiency. It takes less time to straighten up the house and file away your papers than it does to search for something you must have. When you can say, "I know where it is" instead of "I think it's here someplace," you save time in the long run. Other people are comfortable in what some people would characterize as disorder. Because they crave spontaneity, they feel constricted by constant demands to put things away.

One couple I interviewed, whom I'll call Elizabeth and Fred, openly shared how they negotiate the neatness issue.

FRED: Elizabeth is superorganized. She likes the house "just so." And she has the energy, drive, and determination to keep it that way day in and day out. I, on the other hand, just don't feel like putting my energy into straightening up. So I tell her, "If you take the lead, I'll hang in with you and keep it going." But there are times that it's just not important for me to pick my jacket up off the chair if there's something else going on. Maybe we have football tickets and we need to leave right now. As far as I'm concerned, we're out of here. But my wife won't leave without washing the breakfast dishes first. She's like a tornado coming through.

ELIZABETH: I know my neatness drives him a little bit crazy. So I try different approaches depending on my mood. Sometimes I ask him, "Please hang up your jacket." Other times, I'll put it away; it doesn't take but a second. If he's going to be short about it, I'll do it myself. Now he hangs it up more times than not.

FRED: It's not a big deal to hang up a coat. And I do like the place to be straightened up.

ELIZABETH: What we're both trying to say to each other is "Maybe my way isn't always the best way."

By valuing your lover's different way of being, you are honoring her/him. While Phil's own casual approach has been difficult to get used to, it's part of what I love about him: His life just flows. It's not perfectly segmented. Phil doesn't concern himself about small details like where he puts his jacket down; he's focused on the big picture. While I have urged him to be more orderly, I don't want to suppress his individuality either.

When it comes to neatness, it's a challenge to find a solution that meets both your and your lover's conflicting needs. One woman with whom I spoke told me about how she resolved their disagreement. "I'm a neat freak; I'm very organized; I'm a detail person. I don't like to come home and find things in disarray; it gets my head all mixed up. My husband is a big-picture person. His philosophy is 'Until the house gets extremely messy, it doesn't bother me.' While he realizes the benefits of being neat and organized, it's just not that important to him.

"When we first got married I had to live with more disorder than I'd ever been accustomed to. Although I had explained to my husband that it was important to me that he help me straighten up, all the work was falling on me. So I had to figure out a way to get us organized that would fit within his framework.

"I asked him, 'If I make drawers, shelves, and cabinet spaces available for certain items, will you put them there?' He agreed. So I bought shoe cartons for his shoes, hangers for his clothes, and boxes for his papers. Now he always puts his things back where they belong. While I'm out of town for a week or two he lets everything slide. But when I come home everything is back in its place."

These couples negotiated love to work out agreements that would respect their individual differences. Whether you're neat or casual, it's unhealthy to try to make your lover be "just like you." And it's unrealistic.

TIME

Do you need to spend more time together with your lover? Would you like your lover to give you more companionship and attention? Or do you need more time apart? Do you wish your lover would understand that you need the freedom to work, be creative, and enjoy some privacy? Do you and your partner conflict about "when's": when to wake up in the morning, when to go to sleep, when to eat dinner, when to have fun, and even when to negotiate love? Or do you disagree about time management—how to budget the precious twenty-four hours each of us gets in a day?

If you're a night person and s/he's a day person, you need to confront and resolve this issue. You may decide that both of you will keep an early schedule on weekdays and run late on weekends. Or you may prefer to each honor your own rhythm but have shared meals and other fun times together.

Phil and I are still negotiating our differences about "when's." The time I want to start an important conversation is often the time he's ready to go to sleep. The time he wants to go out on a date may be the time I have a project deadline. Once when he asked to use my computer printer at eleven P.M., I blew up. Then we negotiated love. We agreed that neither of us would do "business" with each other after ten-thirty at night except in an emergency. We wrote down our agreement and posted it on the refrigerator. Now we violate it only by mutual consent.

If one of you has a heavy commitment to work or school, the other may feel that s/he isn't getting enough of your time. A first-year dental student who had recently gotten married told me, "Many of the disagreements my wife and I have are because I cannot give her the time she needs from me—or that I need to give her. She knows that I am very committed to my career, but it's still hard for her."

Balancing your needs for privacy and companionship is a challenge you will continually face. Both of you may need your own private time which the other must learn to respect. One of you may be an introverted, creative person who craves a lot of time alone, while the other may be an extroverted person who yearns for connection. One of you may be an independent "free spirit," while the other may have a clinging, dependent personality.

Your needs for independence and companionship also may shift over time. At the beginning of your relationship you may both seek each other's companionship frequently. But when children arrive, the primary caretaking partner may get absorbed in them instead. Or the primary wage-earning partner may start meeting most of his/her relationship needs with coworkers and colleagues. Agreements about how much time to spend together must be continually renegotiated. When one of you isn't getting your social needs met, this is the time to say, "Let's talk."

It's difficult to find enough time to spend together. If you and your lover have different commitments to work, school, or children, negotiate to get your schedules in sync. From time to time, spontaneously go out to dinner or jump in the car and head for the beach. Or pick a regular time to send the children to your parents' or friends' home, shut off the phone, and stay in bed all day. You will emerge closer and better able to tackle the problems you both face.

The most important time agreement you must make is when to negotiate love. No matter how many other urgent concerns you have, it is vital that you schedule time to share your lives—and work out your disagreements. If you have children, you can talk when they're asleep or when you go out for the evening. *There is no priority higher than finding time to communicate with each other.*

Religion and Spirituality

All of us need opportunities to express our spirituality, and many of us to practice our religion. This is part and parcel of what we value about ourselves. We need our lover to understand our spiritual and religious needs and to accept our way of manifesting them. We also need her/his understanding if and when we choose to change our spiritual values and religious practices.

What happens when lovers practice different religions? For many, religion is a nonnegotiable issue. Sometimes one lover may choose to convert voluntarily. S/he can say, "I realize my faith is not as important to me as it is to you. I know it will mean a lot to you if I convert, so I will." Other times, conflicts arise. It is unhealthy if one lover insists that both of them practice her/his religion and the other must "give in." If the lover who goes along does so grudgingly, eventually s/he gets angry. The anger becomes resentment and can damage the intimate relationship. When one lover practices a particular religious tradition or ritual, such as lighting candles on Friday night, the other can offer respect even if s/he does not choose to share it.

Lovers who openly discuss their religious differences can create ingenious solutions. One married couple I interviewed negotiated their religious conflict effectively. The wife told me, "We have different religions. Because we know they're important to each of us, we've never asked the other to convert. Sometimes our child goes with me to my church; sometimes our child goes with my husband to his church; sometimes we all go together either to my church or his." Other couples choose to resolve this conflict by picking a third church that meets both of their religious needs.

The spirit that unites two people with each other—and with God—is far more powerful than whatever doctrinal issues divide them. As long as you have a shared spiritual foundation, you can always brainstorm about how to use different religions to express your beliefs.

Family Backgrounds

Most lovers come from different family backgrounds. You may be from an upper-class family; your lover's may be working-class. You may be Italian; your lover may be Vietnamese. You may come from a large family; your lover may be an only child.

It is natural to want your lover to understand your family history and to desire to hear the details of your lover's. But sometimes you'll find that the differences in your lifestyle are enormous. One couple who talked to me came from dissimilar social classes. Hers was a working-class family; his was upper-middle class. It took patience on both their parts to accept that her idea of fun was to go to a bar, while his was to stay home and read. Another couple I interviewed was biracial. He was African American and she was European American. As he put it, their differences "took a lot of getting used to." Fortunately, both of them had an excellent sense of humor. Sometimes she would say something and he would start to laugh. "That's so 'white,' " he would comment. She'd point out to him with amusement when he'd say something that sounded very "black." When they didn't understand each other's needs, they'd negotiate love.

Lovers from the same generation can support each other as they face common family issues. But what happens if you are from *different* generations? One twenty-year-old man I interviewed shared with me how his family issues divided him from his lover. "I'm trying to come to terms with my mom and dad—how they wounded me and how my family was dysfunctional. I need to get away from them, to be on my own and to find myself. My lover is eighteen years older than I, and she doesn't understand that. She also doesn't realize that I don't know how to stop repeating the relational patterns that I've learned from my family. I build brick walls all around me to cover up my insecurity; how do I explain to her that I'm trying to stop adding more bricks?"

When one lover doesn't listen, refuses to discuss differences, and insists that the other conform to her/his standards of acceptability, it's unhealthy. It's foolish and harmful to believe your partner comes from the same mold as you do. Acknowledge your differences and negotiate love instead.

Substance Abuse

Lovers who are addicted to food, caffeine, alcohol, or narcotics have difficulty negotiating about their substance-abuse problem. If you are in a relationship with an abuser, it can be hard to understand her/his needs. All you know is what *you* need—which is for your lover to quit the habit. Meanwhile, your lover may be insisting that the only way to meet her/his needs is to tolerate the abuse. Or s/he may be denying that there is a problem at all. On the other hand, if your lover is in recovery, s/he may need you to understand and share her/his healing.

If your lover has a severe substance-abuse problem, sometimes the only way to deal with it is to give an ultimatum. One couple I interviewed, whom I'll call Gloria and Hal, negotiated this way. For several years Hal had been abusing alcohol. Gloria's negotiations with him always ended in his agreeing that he'd try to cut down, but he never did. They told me how they finally negotiated successfully:

HAL: Recently Gloria drew the line and said that my drinking was intolerable to her. If it continued, it would ruin our relationship.

GLORIA: I had thought about what was wrong with our relationship for a long time and concluded it was Hal's drinking. When I first recognized that I was actually going to have to confront him, I went into a depression. Then I said to myself, 'Whatever decision he makes, I have to be able to deal with the consequences.' And I mentally prepared myself for any eventuality.

I picked a time to negotiate when Hal was not drinking. I made sure we didn't have any plans for the weekend because I knew that once we started our conversation we might want to continue it for a long period of time. I also arranged for my daughter, Irene, to visit her dad, so she wouldn't overhear us.

For several weeks I thought first about what I was going to say. I knew I had to express myself clearly so Hal would understand me and realize I meant what I said. What I told him was this: "You need to understand that if you don't cut back on your drinking, our relationship will have to end. I don't care if I have to sell some of our furniture and move into a tiny apartment. It's that serious. I can't stand wondering every night whether you're going to come home sober or drunk. Which personality of yours will I be dealing with? My daughter needs to grow up in a peaceful atmosphere, not in turmoil. The right thing for Irene is the right thing for me."

HAL: After that I did agree to cut down. I know that Gloria's a very determined person and that she means what she says. She's also extremely protective of her daughter.

Gloria's ultimatum worked because she delivered it properly. But she also might have dealt with their conflicting needs by asking Hal to go with her to mediation.

No one can force an addict to give up a habit; the decision has to come from within. If your partner is in recovery, both of your needs may change. A married man candidly shared the experience he had had with his wife. In his words, "I was addicted to pot for many years. Finally I entered a twelve-step program. By going to meetings, I freed myself from my habit. Suddenly I began to develop a spiritual life and I started working toward my dreams. I was discovering my 'self.' My wife became concerned about my devotion to my recovery. I explained, 'There's something going on inside me that's different.' Then she told me she was afraid she wasn't growing spiritually as quickly as I was. 'I feel that you're getting away from me. I may lose you,' she confessed. So I suggested to her, 'Why don't you come with me to my twelve-step meetings?' We agreed she would. Afterward she changed careers and became an ordained minister." By expressing their needs and feelings honestly to each other, this couple was able to grow in a new direction . . . together.

Sex

Every couple disagrees about lovemaking. Which of these possible conflicts do you and your lover have?

- Do you differ about who should take the sexual initiative?
- Does one of you want sex more frequently than the other?
- Does one of you need to be "in the mood" to make love, while the other does not?
- Do you or your lover wish for more than one sexual partner?

While most of us would rather *have* sex than talk about it, sexual issues arise that must be negotiated! A fundamental issue couples have to resolve early on is "Who asks whom for sex?" One husband in his late twenties explained, "In college whenever I went out with a woman, we would always have sex. So I was somewhat surprised the first time my wife said to me, 'I don't want to make love tonight.' I didn't understand what she meant. I wondered, 'Does this mean she doesn't want me anymore? Is this a rejection?' I felt that she didn't care for me. So I overreacted; I started to pull back, and I began losing some of my sex drive. Since I no longer initiated sex very often and she was waiting for me to make the first move, our sexual relationship became pretty tenuous. Finally we sat down and discussed what was going on. We realized that sex was only one of several issues that were dividing us and we decided to go into therapy. Once we resolved our other issues, I understood that she did care for me. Initiating sex was easier after that." By consulting a therapist who acted as a mediator, this couple was able to communicate better about all their issues, including lovemaking.

Another couple I talked to, whom I'll call Kathy and Josh, had a disparity in their sexual drives. His was low; hers was high. After they shared their needs with each other, they brainstormed to find workable solutions. As Kathy put it, "We realized we both had to find creative ways to deal with our different needs. Josh wouldn't be interested in sex for a couple of weeks, but then he'd start something sexually in the middle of the night when I was sound asleep. So I learned to wake up and enjoy it." Josh continued: "We've learned to express our love physically without necessarily having sex. We sit close to each other when we're out to dinner or at the movies. We even hold hands when we ride in a car."

Several married couples told me that they had arguments when one of them wasn't "in the mood." One husband put it like this: "My wife's sexuality is different from mine. My wife would rather talk before we have sex. For me it's the opposite. Only after we have sex can I have a real conversation with my wife. How do we resolve our differences? All we can do is negotiate. 'This time we'll have sex first and next time we'll talk for an hour before we make love.' "

Another married couple with the same conflict saw a therapist to mediate their dispute. The wife told me, "When we got married, my husband felt that it was my duty to give him sex whenever he wanted it; he expected me to be able to turn myself on physically whenever he was in the mood. When I'd say no he'd feel rejected and get angry. He didn't understand that if I wasn't in the mood, I couldn't enjoy it. As soon as he demanded it from me, it was no longer a pleasure. Finally we went into therapy and worked it out together. My husband realizes that if I'm not in the mood, it's because there are other things going on in my life; it's not because I don't love him. He no longer tries to push lovemaking on me. If he wants sex, I'm willing to try . . . but if I can't get in the mood, he accepts that."

What happens when one or both lovers need variety in sexual partners? This can be the most difficult issue of all to negotiate. A couple who had been married eight years told me how they resolved their conflict. He began, "My wife and I are both turned on by other people. She once had a one-night stand, and I used to be physically attracted to another woman. Although it was very difficult for us, we told each other about our desires. Finally we decided that our sexual relationship wasn't strong enough for either of us to have an affair with anyone else. But it was difficult for us to promise we'd be monogamous forever. So we agreed to put our energy into developing our own sexual relationship for a while. During this time we'd be faithful. If either of us ever decided to have an affair, it would be when our own sexual relationship was *strong*, not weak."

Monogamy is possible—but it requires great love, effort, and compromise. Both of you have to ask each other for sexual fidelity: "I need you to have sex only with me. This is very important." Both of you may even have to demand it: "This is a nonnegotiable issue." If one of you still desires another partner, you have to get beyond your sexual needs and look at your deeper psychological ones: "What is driving me to be unfaithful? What are my fears? Am I angry? Am I bored? Is the answer to my need simply finding another body? How can I improve our relationship so that my needs are met?"

A lover with an outside sexual relationship is often seeking whatever is missing in her/his own. The focus of your loving negotiations should *not* be on the outside person (or people), but on how the *two of you* can fulfill each other's deepest sexual longings.

SEXUAL JEALOUSY

Sexual jealousy stems partly from low self-esteem. If we feel, "I'm not good enough. No one can really love me," we tend to get jealous if our lover so much as glances at someone else, whereas if we feel, "I have no doubt that my lover wants to be with me," we find that any jealousy is minimized. And if we have confidence that we ourselves can be sexually faithful, we'll be more likely to trust our lovers. *Mutual trust is the best antidote to sexual jealousy.*

Yet sometimes even the most secure and trusting lover gets jealous. If you suspect your lover has the hots for someone else, you may, in fact, be right. The only way to handle your feelings of sexual jealousy is to share them. Ask for what you need: reassurance that your lover values you, information about your lover's outside relationship so that you can feel "in control," assurance of your lover's sexual fidelity, and contact with the other person so that you are not excluded and do not feel like the outsider.

A couple with whom I spoke at length, whom I'll call Louise and Mannie, negotiated an episode of sexual jealousy effectively. They had been dating about a year when Mannie told Louise that his ex-girlfriend Nanette wanted to go fishing with him. "It will involve going away for the weekend. Will that be a problem for you, Louise?" "Do what you want," Louise casually replied. "I don't like it but I'm not going to stop you from going." From her remarks, Mannie assumed that it was okay and he called Nanette to confirm. But after that conversation, Louise became cold and hostile. Their conversation went something like this:

MANNIE: What's the problem?

LOUISE: What do you mean, "What's the problem?" You know I don't want you to go away with her.

MANNIE: I don't understand. You said you didn't like it but you weren't going to stop me.

LOUISE: *Read between the lines.* You should've known what I meant.

MANNIE: No, I didn't know.

LOUISE: Yes, you did. *Anyone else would know.*

MANNIE: I took you at face value. I assumed you meant what you said.

LOUISE: Look, I wasn't going to order you not to go. You needed to make the decision yourself. I was putting the choice in your hands.

Their conversation continued. "Well, are you going to object if we stay in the same room?" Mannie asked Louise. This time Louise expressed her feelings more openly. "You can if you want to, but I'll hate it if you do." She was already envisioning the two of them opening a bottle of wine, talking about old times, and getting amorous. Suddenly she decided to reveal her real feelings and needs. "Actually, I'll feel very threatened if you share a room with her. I'd appreciate your staying in separate rooms." Mannie sat quietly and thought for a while. Suddenly he said, "Would you like to join us?" Louise considered his suggestion and then nodded slowly. "Okay," Mannie continued, "I'll ask Nanette if she wants to invite her significant other." He called Nanette, but she chose not to extend the invitation to her current partner.

Louise continued. "Soon afterward I started thinking, 'If Mannie and I feel slightly uncomfortable about this situation, so must Nanette.' So I picked up the phone and called her. I suggested, 'Let's discuss the weekend. Instead of wondering what's going to happen, why don't we make plans? Who's going to shop for the food? Where will we stay?' Once we started talking, we smoothed things through."

Mannie concluded, "Our neighbors laughed when they saw all three of us climb into our car with fishing poles the following Saturday morning. The woman who had introduced me to Louise told me later that she was amazed that we had even tried this whole thing. Louise, Nanette, and I all worked hard at getting along and we had a very nice time that weekend."

Louise and Mannie negotiated their sexual jealousy issue effectively once Louise started expressing her feelings and needs honestly. Mannie also reassured Louise by letting her know that Nanette had a significant other, and enabled the two women to connect. Once they spent the weekend together, Louise realized that Nanette wasn't a threat after all.

If our lover is the one who's acting jealous, we need reassurance that s/he still trusts us. We also need to feel that we have the freedom to choose our friends. These are *healthy* needs. Penny was forced to confront her lover's sexual jealousy when she started feeling she had lost her freedom. Ralph was an exceptionally jealous person and hounded Penny from the moment they met. She told him that she felt trapped and needed him to stop, but he continued to follow her around and accuse her of infidelity. In her words, "One day I realized that I couldn't take it anymore. I had lost my peace of mind. So I sat down and wrote Ralph a letter. I told him, 'I can't continue living like this. It's tearing me apart. Either things are going to change or we're going to say good-bye.' All of a sudden he stopped being jealous. It was the most incredible turnaround I'd ever seen." Why did Ralph's sexual jealousy stop? He explained, "I *knew* Penny meant what she said. She was prepared to deliver on her promise. Since she'd already gone through one divorce, I knew she could make it alone."

But give this kind of ultimatum *only if you mean it.* Another way this couple might have benefited would have been by bringing in a neutral person to mediate their dispute. An ultimatum, if ignored, leaves you only two ways out—to return to the relationship disempowered, or else to break up.

Sexual jealousy becomes unhealthy when one of you needs to have an outside affair that excludes the other. When the excluded lover then becomes overcontrolling, you are headed on a collision course. For your relationship to survive, you must negotiate love.

CHILDREN

The first issue couples have to resolve in this area is whether to have a child. If a couple agrees, fine. If a couple disagrees, the conflict should be negotiated *before* the baby arrives—not after.

A man shared with me what happened to him when he and his wife didn't reach an agreement about having a family. "I've never wanted to participate in the creation of a baby," he began. "Maybe it's because I've seen a lot of men impregnate women and then leave them. Or because I've done so many drugs I don't want to create a child with a birth defect. But I think that it really has to do with the pain of growing up in my family. There was so much conflict there and I didn't want to repeat it. Ten years ago my wife stopped taking birth control pills without telling me. Then six months after our first baby was born, she announced that she wanted to have a second child. She told me, 'I'm not going to take birth control pills anymore.' What could I do? I had a vasectomy. It was a procreative suicide, but it was the only way I could protect myself." This couple did not trust each other enough to negotiate love, and eventually they got divorced.

As Jungian couples therapist Dr. Irene Gad points out, *both* lovers have to be ready to be parents. If one lover reluctantly gives in to the other's need to have a child, an unhealthy emotional climate is created even before the baby is born. How can a couple resolve their disagreement? One woman I interviewed told me how she and her lover negotiated. "My fiancé, who's seven years younger than I am, has told me that he'd like to wait five years before starting a family. I'm inclined to agree with him; putting off having children would be good for us as a team. But it would put me in a tough place biologically. I'm almost forty and the chances of having a child with a genetic disorder increase rapidly after that age. But I really value my relationship with my fiancé. If he doesn't want to be a father, it wouldn't be right to force him into it. I do want a baby, so we have been looking at alternatives. We've asked each other, "Does it have to be our own child? What about adopting a baby later on?"

Once children arrive, a couple has a whole new set of issues to negotiate. Each has a healthy need for her/his ideas about childrearing to be respected by the other. It is also normal for each new mother and father to need to be physically and emotionally close with their baby. But parents can have unhealthy needs as well. If one lover needs to overcontrol the other, s/he will attempt to impose her/his ideas about childrearing: "Our child is going to be raised my way. My ideas are the best ones." No matter how sure you are that you are right, it is better in the long run to convince, rather than coerce, your lover.

It is also unhealthy when a natural parent favors her/his own child(ren) over her/his stepchild(ren). One couple I interviewed who both had children by previous marriages shared their experience. In the wife's words, "We call this issue 'your kids; my kids.' And in our marriage, it's a firebomb. We still haven't resolved it. Every day one of us complains, 'Your kid is treated better; my kid is treated worse. Your kid has privileges that my kid doesn't. Your kid gets things my kid lacks. Your kid gets away with more than my kid does.' What do we do when one of us starts up? The other one says, 'Let it be.' We put our argument on hold and talk about the situation later, when the children aren't around. But we still haven't fully resolved this issue."

When one or both lovers have children by a previous marriage or lover, they must take special care to maintain the balance of power. If a stepparent disciplines a child, the natural parent should support the stepparent even if the child sulks. And vice versa. It is important for your children to see you as a united front, so that they will not erode the support you give one another. Any differences of opinion you and your partner have should be negotiated in private.

Most unhealthy of all is when one lover starts paying more attention to a child than to her/his partner. The seesaw of power stops and the ride resumes *only* when energy is redistributed so that the excluded lover gets her/his fair share.

OUTSIDERS: RELATIVES, FRIENDS, AND BUSINESS ASSOCIATES

Relatives, ex-spouses, coworkers, and same-sex and other-sex friends can shift the balance of power between you and your lover—but we all need to have relationships with people besides our lover. We hope that our lover will like—even love—some of our precious family members and friends and share our experiences with them. If your lover doesn't like one of your friends, you can always make it a twosome when s/he comes to town or when you plan an evening together. But if your lover is at odds with your parents, other relatives, or business associates, you have to negotiate. S/he needs to be able to interact with these significant others in your life.

One couple I spoke to reached an agreement that satisfied both of their needs. She described it: "My husband's boss, who is about thirty years older than we are, had invited us to his home for dinner. I really didn't want to attend; I expected the evening to be boring. But the day before my husband had asked for extra time off from his job to travel to the South of France with me. That meant a lot. The South of France is my favorite place and I had carefully planned the trip. Because I knew the boss's dinner was important to my husband, I agreed to go. If it means a lot to the other person, my husband and I will always run the extra mile."

When your lover doesn't care for certain members of your family, both of you must confront these feelings honestly. You need to reach an agreement both of you can live with. One man told me what happened when he and his wife didn't. "We were having an anniversary party for my wife's parents, and I wanted my folks to be invited. It was a nonnegotiable issue for me, but I didn't realize it at the time. First my wife said we could invite them; then she changed her mind. Finally I had to call my parents and say, 'My wife says you can't come.' When I hung up the phone I was enraged. I cornered my wife in the kitchen and shouted, 'I want them to come.' 'But I don't want them here,' she hollered back. My fists were clenched, and I started screaming at the top of my lungs for at least fifteen minutes.

"Later on, when I thought about the incident, I realized we both lacked communication skills. I didn't know how to explain to her how important it was to me that my parents be included in our social life. She couldn't get me to understand that I could love my wife and love my parents, but they didn't have to love each other." This husband and wife had to release their anger before they could negotiate their issue. They never did and subsequently divorced.

A friend of mine found herself with a real dilemma when her mother-in-law died, and her elderly father-in-law was no longer able to live alone. Her husband wanted his father to move in with them. She was reluctant because their eldest son had just moved out, and they had already agreed she would use the spare bedroom as an office. After a loving negotiation, they decided to build another bedroom above the garage, enabling her to keep her newfound (and long-awaited!) office space. His father was also pleased to have the extra privacy.

Sometimes your lover may pay too much attention to her/his own family and friends. A man told me how he moved to another city to live with his woman friend. After he arrived she went out almost every evening with her friends without inviting him along. Fortunately this man was able to communicate his feelings and needs honestly. "I feel kind of alone. I need you to come home from work and spend time with me," he told her. Once they agreed to spend half of their evenings together, their energy was rebalanced. The couple is now happily married.

How to Negotiate Hotspots Safely and Effectively

When you and your lover sit down on the negotiating couch to discuss a hotspot issue, there is an undercurrent of strong emotion. All hotspot issues are significant, and undoubtedly, both you and your lover feel strongly about your own particular ways of handling them. How, then, do you reach agreement? It is essential that both of you have the relationship spirit: "What nourishes you nourishes me. If you get what you need, we both benefit." You have to trust each other, respect each other, and be willing to invest considerable time and energy in the conversation. It takes two committed people to negotiate love; only one won't do.

As you work through each of your hotspot issues, remember the eleven secrets of negotiating love. But you should also keep in mind these three additional guidelines:

- Contain your conflict
- Maintain your balance of power
- Make up your own rules

CONTAIN YOUR CONFLICT

Limit your negotiation to the issue or issue area you are discussing. If you're working out a conflict about your spending habits, don't bring up changing your job. If your hotspot is money, don't bring up your need for privacy or time spent apart. These two issue areas are interrelated, but you'll get sidetracked if you try to cover them both. Sometimes it helps to write down the particular issue you're negotiating before you begin—for example, "We want to reach agreement on a family budget." When you do so, make sure the statement is not biased in favor of either one of you. "Let's talk about how you're going to spend less money" is not a promising way to begin a negotiation.

MAINTAIN YOUR BALANCE OF POWER

If you constantly reach agreements that meet your needs but completely ignore your lover's, don't gloat. Eventually your lover may become angry and resentful—and you would react the same way if the agreements were constantly being tailored to your lover's needs. Negotiating love is a give-and-take between two *equal* partners. You and your lover cooperate to create a *balance* between both of your needs. On issues that are very important to you, your feelings and needs are honored. On issues that really matter to your lover, hers/his get priority. The dynamic shift of energy keeps your seesaw of power moving up and down.

MAKE UP YOUR OWN RULES

The guidelines in this book are all *suggestions.* They are a launching pad for you and your lover to use to take off in your own direction. Every couple's negotiating procedures and agreements are unique. Yours will be too. As long as you maintain a balance of power, all that matters is that you reach agreement.

CHAPTER 9

How Women Can Get Ready to Negotiate Love

Before women can negotiate love, we have to heal the wounds we already have. If we are not in touch with our past pain, we cannot communicate in the here and now.

If you are a woman, you need to look deep within. You may hurt so badly that you feel powerless, angry at men, and incapable of negotiating love. If you can identify your major wounds, you can begin to heal them and get yourself ready for loving negotiations.

If you are a man, you need to understand women's pain. If your female lover has been badly hurt, she cannot negotiate love for long. Whenever you say something that touches a sensitive area, she will overreact and become furious at you. Whether or not she understands that beneath her anger is agony, your loving negotiation will end abruptly.

Healing Women's Wounds

What are women's wounds? The pain of feeling unworthy—of saying to ourselves, "You're no good"—haunts almost every one of us. Because men have traditionally overpowered women, some women infer that men are responsible for their suffering. Although many men now treat women as equals, we still have painful memories, and some of us are still being injured every day.

There are five major wounds that most of us carry. I call them the self wound, the mother wound, the father wound, the date wound, and the boss wound. Identifying which ones hurt you the most is the first step toward healing them.

THE SELF WOUND

Our self wound—when we are insecure, when we don't value ourselves—can be the deepest of all. When our self wound aches, we don't know who we are, why we are worthwhile, what we can accomplish, and how much we should give to other people. We feel helpless and defensive. In this frame of mind we cannot negotiate love.

To get ready for loving negotiations we first must develop a strong sense of self. How? *By getting to know who we are.* Then we can learn to value, love, and accept ourselves as women. Slowly we can become more self-confident and self-reliant. We can learn to set limits and insist that other people respect them.

As long as women allow themselves to be defined by men, we will never heal our self wounds. Liz Herron, coauthor of *Gender War; Gender Peace*,[1] wisely tells us, "It is time to stop waiting for someone else to tell us who we are. Instead, we should start asking ourselves, "Who are we as powerful women? What is it like to be strong and feminine?"

Our power lies in our own selves; it doesn't come from pleasing others. A woman can negotiate love only after she goes within and finds out what she really feels and needs. *Before there can be a "we" there has to be an "I."*

Many women I spoke with told me about their journeys toward self-knowledge. One interviewee got pregnant at age nineteen and then married the baby's father, who was frequently drunk and abusive. "I never thought of getting out. I saw myself as an appendage to him; I wasn't a person in my own right. I didn't know who I was at all until many years later." Another woman, Quincy, described her first marriage like this: "I was Steve's wife and Tommy's mother. Who was Quincy? I didn't know—and I didn't find out until Steve walked out and left me kicking and screaming."

How do you get to know your inner self? Jungian analyst and author Marion Woodman says, "Self-knowledge begins when you stop judging and blaming others for what has happened or is happening to you and look within. Then the real work starts. Ultimately you quietly say, 'This is what *I* believe.' It doesn't matter what others think. Inside yourself you know your own truth. It resonates in your gut. You don't have to shout or yell or argue. You *know*."[2]

Seminar leader Jude Blitz shared her own journey with me. "I used to believe that women's authority rested in being with influential men. My first husband was ten years older than I; I loved listening to his opinions. I wasn't yet in touch with my own knowledge. Slowly I started experiencing it—in a closet kind of way. One day I started taking science classes and decided to enroll in chiropractic college. I asked him to support me in my career, and he couldn't do that. It was hell at first being out there by myself, but later on it wasn't so bad. I was exercising my own authority."[3]

Once you acquire self-knowledge, you can negotiate love as an *equal*. Some women own their power naturally. As one woman declared, "I've always felt I have a right to pursue my goals and desires. I don't have to be in anybody's shadow." Other women realize their power only gradually. One, whose first husband beat her regularly, finally left him. "I waited ten years before I remarried," she told me. "First I found out who I was, what I needed, what I wouldn't put up with." She and her second husband now negotiate love frequently.

But self-knowledge is not enough. *We must also value ourselves.* And most women don't. According to a recent survey, the number-one source of depression among women is low self-esteem.[4] Why do so many women feel worthless? *Because we seek approval from other people instead of ourselves.* One attractive, intelligent woman I interviewed told me about her experience with her first husband. "Vinny never paid me a compliment. He couldn't say to me, 'You're a worthwhile person.' And I would beg for it: 'Please say it. I need to hear it from you.' Sometimes he would say the words to me, but in a falsetto, mocking tone."

According to anthropologist and author Dr. Angeles Arrien, whenever you receive praise for something, your self-esteem in that area increases. If another person says you are inferior in skills, character, or appearance, your self-esteem gets lower—but *only if you believe that person.*[5] You can say to yourself, "This person is right," *or* you can say to yourself, "I'm valuable, even though this person doesn't think I am." One woman I interviewed told me, "I felt inferior to my husband; his way of doing things was different from mine, and my way was never right. He'd always tell me, 'You're doing it wrong.' Believe it or not, I used to agree with him."

To complete a loving negotiation, your self-esteem has to

be at least as strong as—or stronger than—your self-critic.[6] If you ask for what you need but secretly believe that you don't deserve to get it, then you probably won't. As public speaker and author Dr. Ivan Burnell says, "It all starts from thinking, 'I am important.' You have to believe in yourself before you can contribute to someone else's life."[7] You can either wait for others to pay you compliments or appreciate your own accomplishments. You can either accept a put-down or reject it. You can either criticize or praise yourself.

None of us is perfect. In order to have self-esteem, we have to accept our whole selves *with all our faults and limitations.* We can say to ourselves, "I like you, but I don't like what you're doing."[8] We can forgive ourselves when we make mistakes. Only then can we forgive our lover and get ready to negotiate love with him.

Once you value yourself and own your power, you become self-confident. You believe, "I can do it." After that, anything's possible.

Your life experience teaches you either "I can" or "I can't." A father nurtures his daughter's self-confidence by encouraging her to take risks. Dr. Roy Schenk, an expert on men's and women's issues, told me this story: 'I have a male friend who has a little daughter. He would take her to the playground and she would run over to the jungle gym. When she started to climb up, he would let her climb. The mothers would pull their little girls down and say to them, 'Be careful, dear. You might hurt yourself.' But he didn't—and his daughter learned what her capabilities were. From time to time she would fall and get hurt, so she did learn her limits. But she developed a confidence in herself which the other little girls were denied."[9]

But it's never too late to learn. Even if you've had a lot of experience with "I can't," it is possible to develop self-confidence later in your life. One woman I interviewed told me, "Going through a divorce and raising a child alone gave me incredible strength. When I remarried and things got rough, I reminded myself, 'I have been on my own before. I can do it again if I have to.' "

Having been a single parent myself for ten years, I too have learned to be self-reliant. Yet from time to time I still doubt my own capabilities. Once when I was in an "I'm not sure I can" mood, I asked Phil for reassurance. "I can't give you confidence," he replied. "Only you can give that to yourself." And that is true.

Self-confident, self-reliant women are willing to share responsibilities in their relationships. If you let your lover know that you can take care of yourself, he will be likely to treat you as an equal when you negotiate love.

You can also heal your self wound by developing self-respect. You get clear exactly how far you will allow someone else to go. Before you can ask another person to respect your limits, you must define them. You need to ask yourself, "What are my nonnegotiable issues? What is absolutely essential for me? Having time alone to meditate? Spending time with my friends? Being treated with respect?" Then decide what you will not allow your lover to do. If he violates your limits, you will say, "Now, hear me. I refuse to be a victim. If you want to go on the attack, you'll have to find someone else. I'm not going to tolerate this behavior."[10] When you are able to say to your lover, "You may not . . ." without anger or bitterness, you are ready to negotiate love, no matter what you have learned in the past.

THE MOTHER WOUND

A mother exerts enormous influence on the development of her child. Mothers who don't value themselves don't value their daughters, and pass on to them their personal beliefs about women, which in these cases would be, "We're not worth much." Poet and men's movement leader Robert Bly told me about a workshop he gave together with Marion Woodman where many women were present. "The women devalued their daughters but not their sons. I even heard one woman say, 'My boy will get violin lessons and college, but my girl won't.' "[11]

Some mothers (or mother figures) are overpowering. They do not set clear boundaries between themselves and their daughter. Since mother and daughter share a common feminine energy, the daughter does not feel the same urge to break away that a son does. Then, once the daughter becomes a woman and finds a lover, she in turn doesn't set limits for him. When she negotiates love she allows him to overpower her and then gets angry at him without knowing why. Before she can be an effective negotiator, she has to establish her own boundaries and define her nonnegotiable issues. Then she will be able to hold her own.

Other mothers (or mother figures) are absent, disinterested, or abusive. One of my friends had a disinterested mother. Instead of being nurtured by her own mother, she had been raised by a nanny and sent away to boarding school at an early age. Much to her distress, my woman friend observed herself mirroring this pattern of disinterest when raising her own children. I myself had an emotionally abusive mother who invaded my personal boundaries just as hers had been invaded. To this day it is easier for me to be emotionally intimate with men than with women. While my mother wound will never completely heal, at least I am conscious of it.

Every woman who has suffered emotional neglect longs for love, appreciation, and respect. Our childhood wounds create our deepest inner needs. When we start expressing these needs to our lover, we move toward the negotiating couch.

If unresolved problems with your mother are causing you pain, attending a Woman Within weekend may help you make a breakthrough.[12] You may also find the five-step strategy in the following section (The Father Wound) helpful.

THE FATHER WOUND

If you're angry at men, chances are you have a father wound. A few of us were lucky enough to have fathers who doted on us. The rest of us had dads who were absent, distant, overcritical or abusive, or who exhibited a combination of these traits.

Your first experience with a man *is* with your father. If he was rarely at home while you were growing up, you may have felt that you (and your mother) weren't worth spending time with. If he was physically present but emotionally withdrawn, you learned not to share your feelings and needs with the other gender. If he paid more attention to your brother(s) than to you, you got the message that girls were less valuable than boys.[13] If he was hypercritical, you sensed that whatever you did, it wasn't quite good enough. If you were emotionally, physically, or sexually abused by your father, you became deeply mistrustful of men.

Whichever feelings you had, you take them with you into your relationship with your lover. Before you can negotiate love, you have to heal the original wound you experienced at the hands of your father, or perhaps an older brother or other male relative.

What can you do? This five-step strategy can be used with either a father or a mother wound. First, become aware of your wound. Once you allow the pain from the past to enter your consciousness, you can start to come to terms with it. Second, start talking about your wound to relatives or friends you trust whenever you are ready. A friend who has experienced the same kind of wounding, or a family member who was present at the time, can be particularly helpful. Third, find a healer, a person of the same sex as your wounding parent with whom you feel comfortable. As you establish a healthy relationship with your healer, you can replace your past pain with ongoing love.

Fourth—and most difficult of all—reconnect with your wounding parent in some way. If your wounding parent is alive, you may decide to personally confront her/him. If your wounding parent is deceased, or if you are uncomfortable sharing your feelings in person, you may prefer to make a mental connection with her/him. Communicate by writing a letter, making a tape, doing a painting, designing a quilt, or composing a song.[14] Although you may never talk directly to your wounding parent, at least you have allowed yourself to express what's inside.

Fifth—and most important—you need to forgive your wounding parent. Once you let go of your resentment, you will experience inner peace. Although your wound may never heal completely, at least you'll be able to negotiate love. Your anger toward your wounding parent won't haunt you. If your partner accidentally reinjures you, you will be in control of your feelings.

If your father or mother wound is very deep and painful, it may be in your best interest to join a women's support group, get professional counseling, or seek individual or group therapy.

THE DATE WOUND

I call it the date wound because we first experience it while we're dating. Early on, we learn that certain women rarely get asked out: If we're not young, thin, attractive, and virginal, most men perceive us as less desirable than our sisters who are.

Then, whenever we hear "I'll call you" and the call never comes, we start to feel as if we're not worth much. If this happens after we've made love, it makes us feel even more worthless. Why don't we make the call ourselves? For those of us with low self-esteem, it's difficult to take the initiative. So we end up feeling either used or powerless or both.

What some men think is a compliment often wounds us. No woman, no matter how attractive she is, enjoys being regarded as a piece of flesh. There is a big difference between "You look attractive" and "You have nice legs." There is an even bigger one between "That dress is lovely on you" and "That dress really shows off your breasts." A woman yearns to be valued for her whole self, not just for her body parts. When she isn't, she hurts. And a woman in pain cannot negotiate love effectively.

Men's put-downs cause us pain too. As a teenager, we may have been ridiculed for having small breasts, fat thighs, or large buttocks. We may be ashamed of any part of our body that we perceive doesn't measure up to society's exacting standards of beauty.

If you have frequently been injured by men while dating, it will be difficult for you to negotiate love. You will be extremely sensitive to any remarks you perceive as devaluing your sexuality or your body. As soon as possible, you must tell your lover about your date wounds. "I'm uncomfortable when you focus only on my body; I'd like you to get to know me as a person before we have sex." Or "I have a surgical scar that I'm embarrassed to show you." Or "As a child I was sexually abused by my uncle, and I'm still afraid to have oral sex." Ask your lover to be gentle and patient while you heal.

THE BOSS WOUND

Thirty years after *The Feminine Mystique*,[15] women's on-the-job abilities are still being questioned. In some workplaces, women are not perceived as team players, not allowed to exercise the full range of their skills, or not recognized as achievers because of their commitment to home and family. And women rarely achieve pay equity. Some women are criticized if they act too much like men; others are condemned for being too different from them. *Can women win?*

A boss who does not take us seriously, who ignores our opinions, who makes us feel wrong, or who disparages our talents wounds us. Her/his innocent teasing may shake our self-confidence, and her/his saying "It was just a joke" or "You have no sense of humor" does not ease our pain. And what about when we are fired? This can make a woman feel inadequate; we may know we're competent, but it seems as if no one else respects or recognizes our ability. Instead of saying to ourselves "I can do it," we start asking, "*Can* I do it?"

Our boss is responsible for creating a workplace environment that is comfortable for both genders. If s/he permits sexist comments and jokes that insult females, s/he is promoting disrespect for women. Sometimes s/he does not even encourage talented females to fully develop their potential, while s/he may do so with their male counterparts. A woman who is treated as an unequal in the workplace finds it difficult to negotiate as an equal at home; she often carries the resentment at her unfair treatment into her romantic relationship.

I myself am an example of a woman with a boss wound. During the fifteen years I spent in the corporate world, I was always given clerical work to do—even when I had an executive-level job. That's why, when Phil once said to me, "I need you to type a draft of a legal paper," I replied with indignation, "I don't do typing. Nor do I do windows. I'm a professional writer. Go hire yourself a typist." After my anger had cooled, I reviewed the incident: It occurred to me that what Phil really wanted was my help. It was not just typing he needed; it was support that he needed to get him started on a difficult task he had been putting off. I realized I had been unfair. After all, whenever I would ask him, "I need you to move these heavy boxes," he never replied, "I don't do moving." Needless to say, I apologized. In this instance, I recognized that my boss wound had put a strain on our relationship.

If you have a boss wound, how can you heal yourself? If you are having difficulties with a supervisor or coworker, talk to your human resources professional, your employee assistance counselor, or a trusted coworker. You may decide to risk confronting your abusive boss or coworker, or else find another way to stand up for yourself in the workplace. Eventually you may decide that the best solution is to leave your job. Join a professional organization and network with your peers. You will get the support you need—and hopefully find a better position.

All of us can appreciate our own value, notwithstanding society's, and specifically the work world's, negative messages. We can learn to accept, love, and respect ourselves as competent women. Once we realize our own inner worth, we will start thinking, "I can do it." We will begin to understand our own feelings and needs, establish boundaries, and take charge of our lives. At last we will experience our own power. Then we will be ready to negotiate love.

Sharing Our Special Powers

As women, we have special powers: emotional, sexual, and maternal. Once we realize their enormity, we will become even stronger. As women's seminar leader Liz Herron tells us, we can redefine the word *hurt* to mean *h*uge, *u*ncontrollable, *r*ough, and *t*enacious. It is possible to be wounded *and* be a powerful woman.[16]

OUR EMOTIONAL POWER

Women have tremendous emotional power in personal relationships. We give men the love and respect they crave. We nurture them. We offer them a safe place to express their feelings. We give them what they need, and we support them with our strength.

When you nurture your lover, you give him comfort. How? By listening to his deepest feelings—whatever they are. In your presence he can bare his wounds. He can open his heart to you without being put down or shamed. You show him compassion as he tells you about his painful struggles with the outside world. After you soothe him, he is empowered to return to the fray with renewed vigor.

Sometimes it requires extra effort to create a safe emotional space for your lover. You have to resist the temptation to interrupt, to give advice, or to focus on your own feelings instead. As you get in touch with your own strength, this comes naturally. As Daphne Rose Kingma writes in *The Men*

We Never Knew, when we empower ourselves, we find it easier to support men emotionally.[17]

As a powerful woman, you understand that your lover needs to be himself. You let him know that you accept him with all his faults and imperfections. You tell him, "You don't have to be strong all the time. How you perform from day to day doesn't matter. I respect and love you for all the good things you are."

To nurture a man emotionally is a sign of *strength*, not weakness. You enhance your achieving self when you complement it with your feminine gifts. When you and your lover negotiate, you give him emotional support. From time to time you let him know, "I enjoy talking with you. Your ideas are valuable. I may not agree with everything you say, but I'm willing to listen." These are the words of a powerful woman who understands men.

Women have the power to connect our lover to—or cut him off from—his emotional self. As men's issues expert Dr. Aaron Kipnis tells us, men seek from women what they feel is missing within themselves. "They come to us hungry for a connection with nurturing, beauty, erotic power, and grace."[18] Every time a man loves a woman he connects with his own lost feminine side. When this connection is made, he feels complete and satisfied. Women also have what I call the power of completion. According to Dr. Joseph Palmour, director of the Archon Institute for Leadership Development, many men can't express their feelings by themselves; they need to be in the presence of a woman.[19]

Yet some men can—and do—learn to express their own feelings alone and with other men; when this happens, women's power of completion diminishes. This is a healthy occurrence. However, upon returning to women, these men expect the emotional "toughness" they found in each other. In author Dr. Warren Farrell's words: "When a woman appears fragile, men are afraid to level with her because she might be destroyed."[20] It is difficult to have honest, powerful communication when you're afraid to hurt your lover's feelings.

But often women's emotional power scares men. What are they afraid of? *Losing our love and respect.*

Gordon Clay, head of the National Men's Resource Center, comments: "If we displease women, we feel it in our bodies. We really hurt. We 'go into our cave'; we don't want to deal with our pain. Men can insult other men freely. But if we talk against women, we don't have anyone to love."[21] *Playboy*'s men's columnist Asa Baber adds, "Men are terrified of female disapproval. If there's anything that scares men, it's not fire, or nuclear weapons; it's the anger of women. When a man hears, 'You terrible man. I've never been so disappointed in you in all my life,' he folds. All he can think of to say is, 'I'm sorry.' "[22]

OUR SEXUAL POWER

One recently divorced man candidly shared what kept him from negotiating love: "Men have to deal with their own fear of the consequences of conflict. How can we say what we really feel? When I fought with my wife, I was never really comfortable giving in to her way—but I never said no either. Why? Because I was afraid I'd be rejected and I wouldn't get sex anymore. For us to have an honest conversation, she'd have to say to me, 'It's okay; no matter what happens, I'm not going to kick you out of bed.' "

The sexual power women possess is simply amazing. Asa Baber described its scope to me this way: "Many men just want to get laid. And when you are that needy of sexual contact, the female has *all* the power. Our message is, 'Please, please approve of me, because if you do, we might have sex.' "[23]

Sometimes women abuse their abundance of sexual power. Rather than making a direct statement about what their needs are, they withhold sex to manipulate men. These women will avoid having sex until they get what they want: an expensive piece of jewelry, a romantic vacation, or simply an abject apology.

Other women pretend they are interested in sex when they really aren't. Onaje Benjamin, director of Men's Work, declares, "When a woman gives mixed signals concerning a sexual encounter, it establishes a climate which can be interpreted as abusive by either party."[24] If a woman says no when she really means maybe, she is implying that having sex is a negotiable issue. The man may get confused and angry—and act inappropriately.

Couples seminar leader and radio talk-show host Alice Forrester adds, "When it comes to sex, women are the gatekeepers. We have this incredible power. But women aren't always straightforward about their true desires. Some women think they have to act as if they want marriage and children when all they really want is to go to bed. Pretending to have long-range goals helps them rationalize their desire. If women would say exactly what they wanted from a relationship, we all would enjoy sex a lot more."[25]

OUR MATERNAL POWER

The power of becoming a mother is ours alone. Many men envy women's capacity to carry a child and to give birth. Others fear women's potential power to make the fundamental choice, "Shall there be life?" If she prefers, the decision can be hers alone.

One man told me this story: "You think women are afraid of men's power? Well, we're afraid of women's power too. Listen to what happened to me. My woman friend went off the pill without telling me. She became pregnant and went ahead and had the child, even though I had always told her, 'I'm not interested in being a father; I'm done with parenting.' Then she sued me for a fifth of my gross income. Now I feel absolutely powerless; it's as if I've been raped."[26] This woman made a decision that affected three people without taking the time to negotiate love. Instead of making an effort to reach agreement with her lover, she destroyed their relationship by acting unilaterally—and made it difficult for him to be a parent to their child.

Women have not only the power to bear children, but also the power to rear them. Whoever takes care of a child determines the child's values—and in effect is molding the next generation. Often women monopolize childrearing. Why? Some women allege that they are better at parenting.[27] Other women do so because they are afraid to share their maternal power; they secretly believe that the only reason they are valuable is that they're mothers. These women lack a sense of personal worth and identity. A woman who has both a strong sense of self and confidence in her lover's ability to be a father, can give him—and the baby—a precious gift by *sharing* parenting power.

HANDLING OUR POWER

When we feel truly powerful, we are not afraid to trust our lover and share our strengths with him. We go to the negotiating couch ready to give him emotional safety and sexual honesty. We view a decision about whether to have a child as a joint one. Realizing that an equal division of labor frees us both to pursue our careers, we invite our lover to share the joys and responsibilities of parenting.

But nobody's perfect. Sometimes we'll retreat behind our old walls of fear and mistrust. Other times our lover will ignore our feelings and disrespect our needs. While women learn to be compassionate and forgiving, men must also understand how they inadvertently cause us pain and how they can stop reinjuring us. To do this, men need to come to grips with their own wounds.

CHAPTER 10

How Men Can Get Ready to Negotiate Love

Men also need to heal themselves. If you are a man, you need to find out why you are hurting. Beneath your anger, depression, or withdrawal is usually pain. Before you can negotiate love, you have to be aware of it—and understand its origins. If you are a woman, you want to know what men's wounds are. Understanding what is in your lover's heart and mind will enable you to be more sensitive to his feelings and needs when you negotiate love.

Healing Men's Wounds

How do men really feel? It's often difficult to discover. What are the barriers that keep them from expressing their feelings to themselves, to each other, and to women?

Men have five major wounds. I call them the father wound, the mother wound, the buddy wound, the spousal wound, and the self wound.

THE FATHER WOUND

Unlike women, who often feel hurt and devalued, most of the time men feel sad.[1] Why do they feel this way? First, men are grieving for their lost fathers, grandfathers, and other male ancestors they never knew. If their father died many years ago, they may have never bonded with him at all. If their parents divorced, they may have seen their father only a few times a year, or for short, sporadic visits—visits far different from actually living with a parent. Even in a two-parent household, the absent, distant father is commonplace: Fathers get up, leave the house, and go to work. Some commute long distances. Others work at two jobs and are away from home in the evenings and/or on the weekends. So while growing up, sons lacked a warm connection with a grown man who could show them how to fix a car, take a hike with them in the woods, or talk to them one on one. Few men have had the opportunity to work and play side by side with their fathers.

When a man's father was around the house, he may have been emotionally unavailable. How many men remember their dad hiding behind his newspaper or staring at a television screen? In both instances, Dad was oblivious to whatever was around him—including his son. Other fathers may have been physically as well as verbally abusive. The boy who waited until his dad got home might have received a beating instead of a hug.

A man who didn't get enough healthy fathering feels empty inside. Since he hasn't embraced his manhood, he isn't ready to negotiate love with a woman. The five-step strategy recommended to women to heal their father wound (discussed in the previous chapter) can also heal men. Become aware of your father wound, share your pain, find a "healer," reconnect with your father, and finally forgive him. As you come to terms with your father, you get in touch with your male energy—and prepare yourself to negotiate love.

THE MOTHER WOUND

Every grown man grieves for his mother whether or not she's still alive. He yearns for her nurturing, and he misses his own feminine self, which she represents. Above all, he is grieving the loss of the unconditional acceptance he received from her as a boy.

The relationship between a young boy and his mother is enormously important. He desperately needs her affection and approval, yet by the age of four or five he may discover that he can't have her all to himself. He gets the message, "If you and mom love each other too much, dad will get annoyed. Keep away from her." Why? Both parents may be afraid of a mother-son sexual relationship. Or they may fear that their son will grow up to be overly dependent. Or they may be concerned that he will interfere with their intimacy. After the age of five, a boy frequently finds that he can't have all the hugs and kisses and pats on the head that he used to enjoy. The loss of closeness is so painful that many boys end up feeling that their mothers rejected them even though this was not the case at all.[2]

At the age of six or seven, a boy learns that he can't even act like her, because if he does, he'll be labeled a sissy. When he feels like crying, admiring a sunset, picking flowers, or asking for a kiss, he often hears, "*Girls* do that. You don't. Be a man." So he starts to disregard, to ignore his deep emotional yearnings. As soon as he rejects what is regarded as his feminine self, he starts devaluing and ridiculing girls[3]—without even knowing why. He becomes afraid of women, while at the same time he longs to connect with them.

A grown-up man still longs for that special time when he

could enjoy his mother's love unconditionally. So he searches everywhere for a deep connection with a woman like the one he used to have with his mom. Having found a female lover, he is simultaneously overjoyed and sad, for she reminds him of his early loss,[4] and he wishes that she could be just like his nurturing mother of long ago. He desperately wants to connect with his female self—and his female lover—but often he doesn't know how.

The men who are the most wounded are those whose mothers pushed them away completely. There are a variety of reasons why mothers ignore their sons—for example, "I've got a job. I'm too busy to parent."[5] These rejected boys grow up to be men who completely dissociate themselves from their feminine selves, devalue women, and refuse to even consider negotiating love.

Men who feel overwhelmed by their mothers are also wounded, but in a different way. They bring into their adult relationships with women their childhood experience of feeling powerless. While a boy is growing up, his mother seems omnipotent, especially when his father is absent. She feeds the boy, clothes him, rewards him, punishes him, and teaches him her view of life. Lacking strong inner boundaries, sometimes a little boy doesn't know where he begins and his mommy ends. He may feel suffocated by her. When he grows up this feeling will persist and he is afraid to negotiate love. Until he establishes strong inner boundaries and learns to defend them,[6] he will not be comfortable negotiating love.

If his mother is verbally or physically abusive, a boy may feel completely overpowered. If Dad is not around to defend him, he is totally at his mother's mercy. If she physically or sexually abuses him—which happens more often than is commonly known—he may be ashamed to report it or speak against her,[7] and may keep his experiences a secret. Before he can enjoy a successful relationship, he must confront the painful memories of his overpowering mother.

Men must realize that their father and mother wounds aren't going to heal overnight. It takes time and patience to surmount these barriers to healthy communication. But they *can* be overcome. Become aware of your feelings, share them with others, create relationships with "healers," reconnect in some way with your parents, and, most important, forgive them for their flaws.

If you're a man determined to have a relationship that lasts, read this chapter carefully and do its activities (at the end of the book). You may find—as other men have—that the New Warrior Training Adventure can help you deal with your father and mother wounds.[8] If you need additional support, you may want to go into therapy, get professional counseling, or join a men's group.

For women the experience can be overwhelming once your lover finally opens up to you. Don't be put off by the urgency of his needs; it's like unlocking a door after waiting decades for it to open. He needs to be reassured that expressing his innermost feelings is not "unmanly." He needs to know you will be there to support him as he grapples for ways to share his concerns.

When you negotiate with your lover, remember that the influence of his father and mother is still with him. If either of his parents was absent, he never had the opportunity to observe them negotiating love. If his mother was distant, overpowering, or abusive, he'll probably see you the same way at first. He may fear that you will render him powerless. Before he can sit down on the negotiating couch *he must feel just as strong as you.*

THE BUDDY WOUND

This wound occurs because men give it to each other. In sports, in war, and in business, men expect each other to keep a stiff upper lip. No matter how much you hurt, you're not supposed to show it; "real" men *don't* say "ouch." Men's issues expert Gordon Clay explains why: "If we play 'victim' with a bully, we're going to be destroyed. So we've been taught, 'Don't complain. Take it, go on with your life, and hope that it doesn't happen again.' We're programmed to solve problems and keep busy, not to act upset."[9]

Dr. Aaron Kipnis, author of *Knights Without Armor*, describes how the buddy wound develops. "To achieve manhood, a man must become a hero and a provider, out of touch with his emotions and his spiritual self. Consequently he feels divorced from the richness of his soul and from the depths of his feeling."[10] John Lee, author of *At My Father's Wedding* and founder of the Austin Men's Center, adds that in this culture men are rewarded for numbing out. A man who feels deeply can't play such aggressive games as football, go to war, or work sixty or seventy hours a week.[11]

When men with this wound approach the negotiating couch, it's often difficult or even impossible for them to share their feelings and needs. Dr. John Guarnaschelli, who has founded over forty support groups for urban working-class men, told me, "Men know how to conduct themselves in the office; they know how to act in a bar. They know how to argue and have opinions. They know what to do on the football field and on the baseball diamond. But if it comes to something below that level—something intimate and personal—they go into an aloneness. Why? Because they believe that what they feel is fundamentally unacceptable. Since revealing what they feel is unmanly, they must stay in isolation. Even if they can get to the point where they think they can share it, they believe that what they have to say is itself unacceptable."

Dr. Guarnaschelli continues. "A man in pain hurts other people. He can't say what he feels because that will hurt him even more, so he'll either yell or be violent. Or else he'll keep his feelings under 'white knuckle control'; eventually, though, he'll explode."[12] But, paradoxically, existing in a state of numbness hurts too. As one man said to me, "As a man I can't stand not feeling anything anymore."

Pastoral counselors Dr. Dan Henderson and David Ebaugh, who have run an ongoing group for middle-class men, told me, "It's a lot easier for men to stay numb or get angry than to feel their pain and loneliness. If they're with a woman, they fear that they might be ridiculed if they start to cry. Fortunately the men who have wept in our group haven't felt embarrassed. They know that we're not going to say to them, 'You're not being a man. . . .' "[13]

How do you break through your surface numbness? Spend time alone accessing your feelings. (Exercise 3 for this chapter at the end of the book will help you get started.) Find a male friend who will support you while you open up. If you still feel "stuck," sign up for a New Warrior Weekend, join a men's group, seek counseling, or go into therapy.

THE SPOUSAL WOUND

Men who are married or in a committed relationship may have a spousal wound. These men suffer physical, sexual, and emotional abuse. Sometimes their spouses hit them or force them to have sex when they are unwilling. More frequently, their spouses overcontrol or subtly manipulate them by shaming them, making them feel guilty, or threatening to abandon them.

Gordon Clay, who runs a hotline for men, talked to me about male-battering: "There is no support for a man who's been physically abused by his wife. Everyone says to him, 'What do you mean, you can't stand up to her? How can you let a woman beat you? You're a man; take care of yourself.'

"This kind of battering doesn't happen at nearly the same rate it happens to women, but when it does, the man is lost: There are few shelters for battered men. He has nowhere to go. Since he's not supposed to hit a woman back after she hits him, the only acceptable response is 'block yourself or leave.' Sometimes this abuse occurs when the man intervenes in his wife's violence toward their children. While women in this situation are told, 'Grab the kids, get out, and be safe,' men can't do the same. In some states, if they take the kids, they may be charged with kidnapping. Men who love their children often have to stay there and take it."[14]

Wives also abuse their spouses emotionally. To wear her husband down, a wife may "talk him to death"; eventually he'll give in just to get her to stop. If outtalking him doesn't work, she can shame him. Char Tosi, founder of the Woman Within, has commented: "Women use their tongues to put men down, to shame men's sexuality, and to shame men's success."[15] When this happens, some men are reminded of early experiences with an emotionally abusive mother. And they subsequently feel like this: "She's talking so much and she's accusing me of all these things. I feel guilty and so ashamed. But if I fight back, she might leave me. . . . I guess I can't do anything about it." No wonder these men refuse to negotiate love: They feel completely powerless.

Why do wives treat their husbands like this? Sadly, some women abuse men intentionally. Others are unaware of what they do. They learned a pattern of abusive behavior while they were growing up and they repeat it. These women do not realize how their behavior injures men. Becoming conscious of the terrible consequences of emotional abuse is a big first step in ending it.

A man who is being emotionally or physically abused by a woman needs support in getting her to stop. Members of a men's group, a counselor, or a therapist can help.

THE SELF WOUND

Men as well as women have a self wound. But a man's is different. While a woman has a clear mission as a mother (even if she decides not to pursue becoming one), a man is often confused about what his purpose is. Before he can express his needs and negotiate love, he must discover himself. Otherwise he is beset by feelings of insecurity, ambivalence, and disempowerment. One woman told me, "My husband and I both would have benefited from being on our own before we got married. Maybe that's why we pulled apart to find ourselves during the first four years. If you don't do your homework in your own personal growing up, there comes a time when it catches up with you."

To heal their self wound, men must learn to access their own feelings and meet their own needs instead of depending on women. How can they do this? *By bonding with other men.* Men's issues expert Dr. Aaron Kipnis explained: "Men used to find themselves by separating from each other. This helps if you're trying to accomplish a very focused task, like fighting a battle or taking over another company. But what we're seeking is much broader—the recovery of the masculine soul. The men's movement helps men return to their bodies, to their deep feelings, to nature, and to each other through brotherhood. When men gather together to tend their own wounds, they become more firmly grounded in their masculinity. They return home with a sense of fulfillment that comes from standing on their own ground. They come into a relationship less empty, less angry, less dependent on women—and with a whole lot more to offer."[16]

Dr. John Guarnaschelli adds, "The men's movement isn't about rejecting women. In fact, it's teaching us how to *connect* with them. What we're saying is, 'We men have to stop plaguing women for the answers to our lives. We're demanding something that can't be supplied. Let's look to ourselves, take care of ourselves, and get the answers from ourselves. To get the information we need as men, we can compare notes with other men. Once we get that information we return to women with a totally different posture.'

"At a men's meeting there's nothing you do except stand there, hold your 'brother,' and witness him in his grief or anger. You provide a channel where he can express his feelings and receive compassion. Once you learn that another man is hurting just like you are, it's a totally different ball game. And what this invites is compassion for women."[17]

As you grow as a man, you find out that it isn't necessary to have a woman nearby when you express your emotions. You learn to give yourself approval and to also get it from other men[18]—instead of desperately seeking it from just your lover.

Becoming Powerful Men

In his essay "The Glory of Manhood," men's movement leader Forrest Craver eloquently sums up how it feels to find one's own identity and strength as a man:

> At some moment, you discover the glory of manhood. It is a time you have longed for, knowingly or unknowingly, your whole life. You move out of the head space and feel the deep, ancient blood pulsing in your heart. You have found *the way in* for you, the way into the labyrinth of the male world. As your being is 're-tuned' by the brotherhood, you become the hunter-warrior, the total creation, the magician of soul energy. . . .
>
> Your emotional thinness falls away. You no longer feel that you are walking the narrow edge of a cliff. You are on firm, wide ground. Male energy is a vast plain on which you can walk with assurance. Your isolation and loneliness are healed within the energy of the brotherhood, the exchange of life-giving male energy. You have come home to your unique identity in the bond of the brotherhood.[19]

Going "within" takes a long time. And it can be slow and painful. But it is rewarding. Christopher Harding, editor of *Wingspan: Inside the Men's Movement*, explains that men often turn to the men's movement when they're out of a relationship with a woman and need emotional support. Once they connect with other men and themselves, they become inwardly strong enough to understand and face women's anger and eventually to negotiate love. They return to women as more sensitive lovers.[20] Empowered men see women neither as powerless nor as overpowering—but as *equals*. They are comfortable riding the seesaw of power with their lover.

Once men heal their self wound, they come to women as whole persons grounded in their masculinity and accepting of their lover's femininity. In short, they are ready to successfully negotiate love.

MEN'S SPECIAL POWERS IN A RELATIONSHIP

Men need to recognize that they have their own relationship powers and shouldn't resign themselves to being "emotionally illiterate." Women aren't the only people who know how to "do" relationships; a caring male lover can discuss feelings as well as sports. Therefore, negotiating love isn't just women's business; it's men's business too. Women have urgent needs that men can meet, and deep feelings that men can hear. Together women and men can make agreements that benefit them *both*.

What are men's relationship powers? Men have the powers of valuing and recognition, of affection and caring, and of sexual acceptance. They also have the power of occupational support and the power of fathering.

THE POWER OF VALUING AND RECOGNITION

When men value women and recognize their worth, they are giving women what they need most. A woman who is requesting your time and attention is really asking you to value her. And you can do that easily. When you tell your lover, "I'll fly back a day early to celebrate your birthday," or "I'll help you with the kids so you can get to your meeting," what you're really saying is *"You're worth it."* When you let your female coworker know that you take her ideas seriously, you help increase her inner power—and her productivity. Just as a woman can be powerful by nurturing men, you, as a man, can nurture the other sex.

THE POWER OF AFFECTION AND CARING

Many men know the power they have when they are affectionate and caring. So do florists, greeting-card vendors, and candy salespersons. But although a dozen roses or a birthday present are excellent ways to express love, caring means more than giving gifts. Above all, what women really need, what they really want, from men is *friendship*. When you listen to what your lover says as you are negotiating your relationship, you become truly powerful; you are healing your lover's date wound. Men who relate to women first as friends and then as sex partners find their relationship thrives.

THE POWER OF SEXUAL ACCEPTANCE

When men and women do make love, men have the unique power of providing their partner with sexual acceptance. What a woman wants to hear—outwardly or inwardly—when you are making love is "Your body is beautiful to me." When she knows you accept her "heavy thighs," "tiny breasts," or whatever real or imagined defect(s) she sees, you emit a special energy. Furthermore, a man who is willing to listen to a woman's prior experience of sexual abuse becomes an enormously powerful lover.

One woman told me how she was unable to be satisfied in her lovemaking until she met her husband. Early in the relationship, he told her that he wanted to know everything about her—both the good and the bad. As a result, she was able to tell him that she had been sexually abused by her father. Afterward their sexual and emotional connection deepened enormously. His total, loving acceptance enabled her to trust him.

THE POWER OF OCCUPATIONAL SUPPORT

Men in relationships with women also have the power of occupational support. Women thirst for a man who will appreciate their talents, give them praise when it is due, and offer help so they can get the job done. Your power to do this is the ointment that will heal even the deepest boss wound (see Chapter 9).

Another way men can provide occupational support is by nurturing a woman financially. A woman told me, "No matter how hard I try, I won't be able to get a high-paying government job like my lover has. He puts up with a tremendous amount of pressure and inconvenience to earn his high salary. I recognize that this is a way that he, as a man, nurtures me, and I let him know that."

THE POWER OF FATHERING

All men have the precious power of fathering. Men care about their offspring. They long not only to co-create but also to co-nurture children.[21] Both women and men need to get in touch with men's latent capacity—and desire—to participate in parenting. The male style of caretaking may be different from the female, but children need both of them to become healthy adults.

Dr. John Guarnaschelli commented: "I have been at meetings where men shared their sadness about wanting children and not being able to have them. You haven't touched grief until you've heard these guys. It's devastating. If we don't perceive that men feel strongly about their children, then we're missing something powerful. All men's hearts are very deeply involved with their kids.

"A lot of 'deadbeat' dads distance themselves because they've been hurt; that's why they get out of the house. If they could express their feelings, they would say, 'Why would I want to be in a place where there's nothing but pain for me?' They're too macho to sit on the steps and cry. They don't know how to say to their wives, 'You don't realize it but you're killing me inside.' "[22]

Undeniably, there are some fathers who abandon their children both emotionally and financially. However, according to U.S. Census figures cited by Stuart A. Miller, senior legislative analyst for the American Fathers Coalition, when fathers have regular access to their children, the percentage of support payments made is high.[23] The father-child connection is vital to men of all ages. Men's issues authority Fred Hayward has discovered, "Teen fathers *want* to participate in childbirth and childrearing. And many of them maintain contact with the mother after the birth."[24]

As Jungian psychoanalyst and author Dr. Robert Moore tells us, we all have an instinctual potential for parenting. The king who fathers is the counterpart to the queen who mothers; the two complement each other.[25] Fathering power means, "Our decision to have a child will be a joint one. After the baby is born, let's raise her/him *together*." Co-nurturing means that *both* parents become free to pursue other occupations as well.

How Men Can Manifest Their Power

When men value themselves as men, they feel truly powerful. As Dr. Roy Schenk, author of *The Other Side of the Coin*, tells us, instead of accepting women's morality, men can create their own.[26] Expert on male leadership Dr. Joseph Palmour gives men this advice: "Be proud of your power. Be strong in the service of justice. Think of yourself as good. Refuse to allow anyone to make you feel bad about yourself."[27] Men must believe they *are* good enough and refuse to be shamed for not measuring up to women's standards.

Powerful men accept their feminine as well as their masculine sides. To get ready to negotiate love, they learn to feel as well as to do. There is nothing unmanly about kindness, compassion, and all those "soft" qualities that are often frowned upon in men. On the contrary, they give men *more* power.

As a man, your challenge is to *heal yourself*. You can identify your own wounds either on your own, with a same- or other-sex friend, with your lover, or with a trained therapist. As a woman your challenge is to realize how we injure and reinjure men. When men's wounds heal, we *all* will be better able to negotiate love.

CHAPTER 11

What Women and Men Need: A New Conversation

When you are ready to negotiate love, your lover may not necessarily welcome you with open arms. If your lover feels powerless, s/he may perceive you as a threat, not as a source of support. If you offer to discuss your feelings and needs honestly, s/he may turn you down at first. You may feel disappointed and hurt, but don't give up.

Your lover is hiding her/his emotions from you—and also from her/himself. The angry, rejecting behavior is a mask. How does your lover really feel deep inside? Wounded—and powerless. Afraid to admit these feelings, s/he withdraws or lashes out. *Your lover is not yet ready to negotiate.*

Female Lovers Who Feel Powerless

If your lover is a woman, she will tend to abuse you with words. She may try to overcontrol you—to boss you around like an overpowering mother. For example, one woman informed me, "If a man doesn't meet me on my ground, forget it. Why should I go halfway?" Another added, "Unless I get one hundred percent of what I ask for, it's totally unsatisfactory." Your lover may even tell you that women's ways are better than yours. She may put men down, criticize you, and call you names. She may reject you when you take initiatives, refuse your support, shame you, or make you feel guilty about your maleness. She even may show contempt for your entire gender by saying, "I don't need a man." Or she may hide her anger until it becomes resentment. She may refuse to make love to you, and deprive you of the emotional nurturing you need. She may subtly manipulate you; as one woman put it, "play to their fantasies, massage their egos, do whatever it takes to get your way." She may act pleasant toward you but be making angry, cutting remarks behind your back.[1]

Why do women act this way? Psychologist and author Dr. Susan Jeffers gives us an honest answer. In *The Journey from Lost to Found*, she writes that she made the following journal entry many years ago: "How do I handle my fear of a man dominating me? I dominate him." During our interview she told me, "If we perceive ourselves to be inferior, self-righteous anger makes us feel big again. It's an 'I'll show you' kind of feeling. We become numb to men's pain; we don't even notice that we might be hurting men deeply. To a certain point, it's okay to feel our anger, but then we have to get beneath it and understand why we're acting this way."[2] As Bill Kauth, cofounder of the New Warrior Training Adventure, points out, women can sabotage themselves: "By screaming and yelling and calling the man who hurts you—and whom you love—names, you're not going to get his attention. He's just going to say, 'I am not' and walk right out of the room."[3]

Acting as if women are morally superior to men *is* a form of hostility. It keeps us from being vulnerable and admitting what we really need. Women in this frame of mind gravitate toward each other. They tell each other, "You're right," and support each other in their victimhood; gradually they develop a common blindness about men. As gender communications workshop leader Alice Forrester reminds us: "There are a lot of men who desperately want to be in a relationship with a woman. But because it's the man who generally takes the initiative, he is set up to get rejected and be hurt. If I were a man, it wouldn't take long before I'd get very angry at women."[4] Men who are repeatedly spurned by the other sex feel wounded and powerless, and fairly soon their pain turns to anger.

Male Lovers Who Feel Powerless

Men are often confused; they don't know why women act the way they do. Having no explanation, they create their own, and they use the vocabulary of sports, which they are familiar with, to describe their dilemma and allay their confusion. As radio talk-show host Paul Cassidy said to me, "A man doesn't know what he's supposed to do. Sometimes I feel as if I'm playing football and the second half has just started. I've still got a football helmet and shoulder pads on, but all of a sudden the other team's out there wearing baseball caps and carrying bats and balls. *Someone's changed the rules without telling me.* And these new rules are not the rules I grew up with. Who's on first, who's on second? *I don't know.*"[5]

Some men ridicule and make sport of the other gender when they can't seem to communicate effectively. We've all seen one version or another of the list that begins something like "The Female Always Makes the Rules. The Rules Are Subject to Change at Any Time Without Prior Notification. No Male Can Possibly Know All the Rules. . . . The Female Is Never Wrong. . . ." This is a form of hostility as well; in reality, it's not funny.

When their feelings of powerlessness and anxiety turn to anger, many men resort to name-calling. When radio talk-show host Rush Limbaugh calls some women "femi-nazis," what he really means is that he sees them as powerful and frightening.[6] Other men who use this term or who call women "witches" and "bitches" are of the same mind.

Most common of all are men who give up completely, hide their anger, and withdraw. A man who feels powerful in the world of work still can be emotionally powerless in the presence of a woman. When he believes that there is no way he can make his lover happy, he feels useless and weak.[7] Saying to himself, "I can't," he loses his self-confidence and simply avoids her and their unresolved issues.

Other men become physically violent. A man who hits is hurting inside. He knows no other way to express his feelings and still "be a man." Typically he'll hide his anger and build up resentment until he explodes.

Why do these men act this way? Because they're embarrassed to admit how vulnerable and weak they feel. Rather than negotiating love, they resort to ridiculing and overpowering women instead.

ENDING THE OLD CONVERSATION

We're all familiar with the old conversation. This is how it starts: A person feels powerless in a relationship and starts thinking, "I don't like myself too much. . . . I'm worthless. . . . I don't know what my life is about. . . . I feel so stupid . . . so inferior. . . . I can't talk about these things to anyone. . . ." This lover's self wound starts to hurt. Instead of swallowing her/his pride and sharing the feelings honestly, s/he acts angry or gets resentful. Or else s/he withdraws. If the other lover retaliates, a vicious cycle begins. *Both* start feeling powerless, and each starts thinking, "What's the use? I'll never understand women [or men] . . . My lover has all the power . . . I'm always wrong . . . I can't win . . . I'll never get my needs met . . . And I can't even talk about them. . . ." As long as they both continue to perceive themselves as powerless, they will stay that way. *Neither one has the energy to turn the relationship around,* and inevitably their powerlessness turns to anger. A chain reaction then starts; they take turns attacking each other and being defensive. *The only way to negotiate love is to start a new conversation.*

What you seek is to make a genuine emotional connection with your lover, and you can do this only by speaking deeply from the heart. One of you *has* to make the first move. Otherwise the two of you will never negotiate the issues that divide you. But first you have to stop pretending that everything's fine when it's not. You also have to refrain from giving mixed messages like "Well, I'd like to talk, but I'm not sure I have the time." And you can't let your mind run on about "worst case" scenarios: "If I do this, then s/he might . . ."

Admittedly it's sometimes hard to recognize that underneath your lover's coldness or rejection or fury is a deeply wounded person. How can you get yourself to reach out to a lover who hurts? By feeling strong enough to face your lover's negative feelings[8] and withstand her/his criticism.[9] If your lover is angry, you must state clearly what behavior is unacceptable to you, and always protect yourself if s/he becomes abusive.

Your lover also has to trust you before s/he can share the pain beneath her/his anger. When s/he does so, you must be ready to forgive. When you create a safe space where your lover feels s/he can be truly heard, you will begin to negotiate love.

Robert Bly told me, "Men and women are each out there wearing a pair of sunglasses that keeps them from seeing each other's reality. Women are looking out through theirs and seeing that they're not being valued. Men are looking out through theirs and seeing that they've lost what they really need. Each is living in a different, but complementary, emotional world. Only if one 'shuts up' can their difference be clear. Otherwise all we do is listen to ourselves talk."[10]

A female therapist shared a dramatic example of what happens when we don't tune in to each other. She was at a male-female gathering where three men who had recently been to a men's weekend asked if they could share their experiences. The spokesperson for the three said that they were scared to speak their minds in front of women because up to that time they had been talking only with other men. To test the women, they went around the room and asked each one what her feelings were about the other sex. All of the women responded with warmth and enthusiasm. "Wow!" exclaimed one of the men. "This really feels good. Since you've created a safe environment, we're willing to explore our feelings with you." His two friends agreed.

As the conversation continued, a fourth man stood up and said to the group, "As a man, I feel very sad that sometimes I can't just take a woman for a walk, hold her hand, and have a sweet experience communicating with her." One of the women immediately snapped back, "You could do that if you didn't always turn it into a sexual encounter." Suddenly there was a dead silence. The female therapist who told me the story commented: "There it was in living color: a woman still believing the old mythology, 'Men are only after our asses.' The whole spirit of the event was shattered, and the woman's bitterness remained with us. Later on one of the men said to the other women there, '*Please* try to think of us males as human beings instead of in our stereotypical roles. Please don't misinterpret our good intentions.' But no reconciliation was achieved. It was sad and discouraging. Hopefully someday we'll be able to talk to each other."[11]

Only when we shed our negative stereotypes can a new conversation begin. Men aren't all "pricks" who are out to get sex from women. Women aren't all "bitches" who use men for their money. Women don't hold all the power in relationships. Neither do men.

As psychologist and historian Jean Houston points out, "Men and women *are* dissatisfied with the old ways. Women are disenchanted with men as they used to be. Men don't want women as they were. We all need to reclaim our deeper power and strip off the old forms of the last three hundred years."[12] What do women and men seek? In Robert Bly's words, "another human being who can stand up to the kind of conflict they have inside themselves. Someone with whom they can fight—in a happy way."[13]

You and your lover each have your own wounds, and each of you gives and receives love in your own different, special styles. If you both take off your "sunglasses," you can see each other's point of view. You will be able to empathize with your lover's feelings—and the perspective of her/his gender. You will be able to find out about your lover's real needs—and the agenda of her/his gender. Then your loving negotiations can begin.

The New Conversation

Between two powerful people, there is a new conversation: The man is full of masculine energy and the woman replete with feminine force. They negotiate love as equals. Conscious of their own wounds, they are able to heal each other's.

How do you start this new way of conversing? Here are three guidelines:

1. Get rid of the old categories
2. Stop using the old conversational phrases
3. Become accustomed to using your little observer

GET RID OF THE OLD CATEGORIES

Get rid of the old negative categories: "Women are helpless; men are the oppressors." "Men are just money machines; women have all the emotional power."

Why are the old categories irrelevant? Because, in truth, *there are no victims, just as there are no victimizers.* Women's wounds are as deep as men's; men's injuries are as painful as women's. *We are all wounded, so we all hurt.*

In *True Love*, Daphne Rose Kingma writes about the "torn-ear theory of love." She tells about her old cat, Max, whose ear was torn in a street fight. Eventually his ear healed, but the scar remained. All of us have been wounded like Max. Sometimes our scars are visible; sometimes they're not. But we all still ache.[14] Once you see the wounded person beneath your lover's angry, resentful, or indifferent façade, you will feel compassion for her/him.

No one is completely good. No one is completely bad. We are all "good enough." A new conversation starts off something like, "I'm good enough and you're good enough. I'm proud of my femininity and you're proud of your masculinity. We both have our faults and virtues. Neither of us is perfect, but we do our best."

When you sit down on the negotiating couch together, remember that you and your lover both have equal power—and that you're friends, not adversaries. Don't take rigid positions; adopt a flexible approach. When the going gets rough, use your sense of humor instead of digging in for battle.

STOP USING THE OLD CONVERSATIONAL PHRASES

Get away from the old stock conversational phrases and try new ones instead:

OLD PHRASE	NEW PHRASE
"Do it my way or else . . ."	"Let's see if we can work out our differences."
"My way is better than your way."	"Both of us have good ideas to contribute."
"I'm innocent"; "It's all your fault."	"Both of us bear responsibility for whatever is happening."
"You're a bad person."	"We're both good, but imperfect, people."
"I don't need you."	"We both need each other. We both strengthen each other."
"All you women are alike." "All you men are the same."	"We're individual human beings, not stereotypes."
"Women are weird." "Men are impossible to understand."	"We can understand each other if we honestly share our feelings and needs."
"I'm powerless." "You have all the power."	"We're both powerful people."

In a new conversation, you'll notice each other saying, "How do you feel?" "What do you need?" "What do you think about this idea?" You use phrases like "I feel," "I need," "What about?" and "We agree." You listen carefully to each other instead of talking on and on and on. . . .

BECOME ACCUSTOMED TO USING YOUR LITTLE OBSERVER

When you negotiate love, be conscious of your wounds. When an issue comes up that touches one of your sensitive spots, be aware of the possibility that you might just go a little ballistic. If this happens, train your little observer to say, "Ouch. S/he must have touched my self/mother/buddy wound." Then you inform your lover, "That was my self/mother/buddy wound you just jabbed." Before this ever happens, take some time to figure out which hotspot issues are associated with your most sensitive wounds. For example, if you have a painful boss wound, it may be activated when you negotiate career issues. If your date wound hurts a lot, be careful when discussing sexual disagreements.

Your lover has her/his own wounds too. Identify them together so you can support your lover if s/he loses control. Then your little observer can say, "Wow. We must have just touched on my lover's spousal/father/boss wound. Time to tread more lightly, give a little more consideration, and back off slightly."

Be aware of what you're saying when you negotiate love. If the two of you get into an argument, call upon your little observer. Say to yourself, "I am blaming my lover." Or "S/he is shaming me." Then deliberately shift the conversation. "How do you feel right now? I feel. . . ." Or "What do you need from me right now? This is what I need from you. . . ."

When Phil and I negotiate love, I frequently find myself shifting from the old conversation to a new one. For example, recently we had a disagreement about time. After Phil had been away on business for a week, he came home and told me, "I'm leaving tomorrow evening for Baltimore, because I have a business meeting there the following morning. Then I'm coming back here to go to my men's group and leaving the next morning to go to Denver." My initial reaction was something like "You never pay any attention to me. You're never home. You don't love me." As bizarre as I sounded, it was better that I was in touch with my feelings and able to share them. At least I didn't ignore them and become resentful.

Inevitably, Phil reacted defensively. "Of course I'm available. It's *you* who're always busy with *your* work." When I realized that we were starting the old conversation, I shifted to a new one. "I feel sad that I'm not seeing you very often. I wish we could be together. I need to spend some time with you." Fortunately, Phil didn't reply "It's ridiculous to feel that way," or else our loving negotiation probably would have ended right there—at least for the time being. Nor did he ignore what I said, which also might have led me to put off discussing the issue. Instead, he answered, "I feel the same way. How about your coming up to Baltimore Sunday evening and staying with me at the hotel? Or else I could leave for Baltimore first thing Monday morning and spend Sunday evening here with you." Had I replied "Absolutely not" to his suggestions, I could have sabotaged our loving negotiation. Instead, I responded, "Either one sounds great," and we were ready to reach agreement.

Another time I shifted the conversation was when we were negotiating a money issue. Phil and I have an agreement that if either of us pays for a household expense out of our own personal funds, s/he gets reimbursed from the household budget. One day Phil said to me, "I never get paid back for all the money I lay out for groceries, restaurant meals, and family trip expenses. But you always do." My initial reaction was, "You're picking on me. You're accusing me of being greedy. Well, I'm not. All I do is ask for my fair share." Suddenly my little observer whispered to me, "You're getting defensive, Riki. Here goes the old conversation again." So I shifted immediately. "How is this making you feel, Phil?" "Unfairly treated," he replied. "I need the money I lay out to be repaid too." So I suggested, "How about you add up all the money you've spent on household items that you haven't gotten reimbursed for? Then we'll budget the money to pay you back." Instead of having an argument, Phil ended up getting what he needed: to have his financial contributions valued the same as mine.

Each of these loving negotiations lasted no more than five minutes—and that's okay. *There is no reason to prolong a conflict.* Nor does anybody benefit from having the same argument over and over again. The benefit of negotiating love, once you know how to do it, is that you get to the root of your disagreement, simplify it, and resolve it. Once you learn how, you and your lover can negotiate love anywhere: at the dinner table, lying in bed together, on the beach, or in the car. (If you get into an argument while you're driving, stop the argument—or the car—immediately!) No matter where you have it, your new conversation is shorter, sweeter, and more productive.

CHAPTER 12

Healing Each Other

Can we heal each other's wounds while we negotiate love? Can we comfort and support each other as we share our feelings and needs? Is it possible for us to "re-parent" each other—to give each other the healthy valuing and nurturing we might not have had as children? The answer to all three questions is *yes*. Although ultimately we are responsible for healing ourselves, women and men can work together to create a safe environment where this healing can occur.

Fifteen Things Women and Men Can Do to Heal Each Other

For women and men to resolve their disagreements with love and compassion, we need to:

1. See each other as allies, not enemies
2. Appreciate each other's power without being threatened by it
3. Value and nurture ourselves and each other
4. Stop seeing each other as stereotypes
5. Accept our need for each other
6. Recognize our common humanness
7. Honor each other's special qualities as men and women
8. Realize we both have our own wounds
9. Be willing to share our unique gifts with each other
10. Communicate our own personal and "gender" agendas honestly
11. Trust ourselves and each other, so it is safe to discuss differences
12. Be there for each other
13. Allow each other on occasion to express anger—without being nasty—so you can get past it
14. Create our own lasting relationship bond
15. Negotiate love

1. SEE EACH OTHER AS ALLIES, NOT AS ENEMIES

Men and women have enormous potential to either destroy or nourish each other. Our fundamental instincts are toward cooperation, friendship, and love, so when your lover lashes out, it's because s/he's hurting inside. Rather than retaliating in kind, you can choose to discover the source of her/his pain.

2. APPRECIATE EACH OTHER'S POWER WITHOUT BEING THREATENED BY IT

A lover who tries to overpower you is feeling empty and powerless inside. Support her/him in becoming genuinely strong within. To resolve conflicts through healthy, loving negotiations, both women and men have to recognize their own power. Your lover's inner strength is an asset, not a threat.

Women have their own unique strengths. Men have theirs. Over the long run our power is equal, as we ride the seesaw together.

3. VALUE AND NURTURE OURSELVES AND EACH OTHER

Women need to have their true worth appreciated. Men need to be loved unconditionally. When your female lover receives your honest praise, she will flourish. Once your male lover realizes that you love him no matter what, he will open his heart to you.

4. STOP SEEING EACH OTHER AS STEREOTYPES

Men are not all "jerks." Neither are they "Prince Charmings," "jocks," or "sex maniacs." Women are not all "bitches." Nor are they "bimbos," "trophies," or "princesses." Judge each woman or man as you yourself would wish to be judged: as a unique and precious human being.

Stereotypes about female-male relationships are equally damaging. Generalizations such as "women should follow men" and "women should be against men" have not served us well. If we accept any relationship stereotype at all, it might as well be "Now is the time for women and men to unite."

5. ACCEPT OUR NEED FOR EACH OTHER

No matter how much some so-called "gender spokespersons" vilify one sex or the other, the majority of us keep falling in love, living together, and getting married. *We need each other.* So let's stop fighting it, and admit it.

6. RECOGNIZE OUR COMMON HUMANNESS

There are a lot more similarities than there are differences between men and women. In the words of writer Harry Stein: "Why not focus on what we all have in common; that we're *all* imperfect, vulnerable, confused?"[1] When you and your lover are arguing over your differences, keep in mind your shared history, common values, and mutual goals.

7. HONOR EACH OTHER'S SPECIAL QUALITIES AS WOMEN AND MEN

Women and men are not totally the same. As Jean Houston, author of *The Possible Human*, points out: "That's what makes relationships so fascinating. The gods must have had some reason for putting two sexes here—for creating the tension of their two energies."[2] Rather than recoiling at our differences, why not enjoy and appreciate them?

8. REALIZE WE BOTH HAVE OUR OWN WOUNDS

Getting into a my-wound-is-bigger-than-your-wound contest is an old conversation. The bottom line is that *women and men both hurt.* The new conversation begins when we stop comparing our wounds and, instead of focusing only on our own pain, realize we might be better off healing each other's.

9. BE WILLING TO SHARE OUR UNIQUE GIFTS WITH EACH OTHER

Each of us has her/his own unique gifts to share. I have learned to appreciate Phil's silence, as he has come to value my skill with words. He has taught me how to work together as a team, as I have shown him how to receive criticism. What does "sharing our unique gifts" mean to you and your lover? It is up to you to decide.

10. COMMUNICATE OUR OWN PERSONAL AND "GENDER" AGENDAS HONESTLY

First of all, you have to know what your needs are—both as a woman or man and as a human being. Then you have to believe that you are entitled to get them met. And you have to speak up. Lovers who say what they need when they negotiate love at least have *a chance* of getting it. Forget what you learned about dissembling, pretending, and playing games. If you don't say "This would make me happy," how can your lover possibly know what is in your mind?

11. TRUST OURSELVES AND EACH OTHER, SO IT IS SAFE TO DISCUSS DIFFERENCES

The foundation for negotiating love is mutual trust. *Without trust, "negotiating love" becomes simply "negotiating."* Before you know it, you're plotting tricks and strategies to get the best of your lover.

To share your feelings and needs, you and your lover must first trust each other. If you don't, your loving negotiation will soon be on quicksand. The time to build trust is *before* the two of you sit down together on the negotiating couch.

12. BE THERE FOR EACH OTHER

Negotiating love takes energy—especially at the beginning. While I don't recommend that your negotiating sessions be marathons, don't count the minutes either. Be willing to listen to each other's expressions of pain and grief until each of you feels heard. If either of you feels tired, stop and set another time to continue your loving negotiations. It may take several half-hour to hour sessions before you reach an understanding. Remember, being there is the most precious gift you can give each other.

13. ALLOW EACH OTHER ON OCCASION TO EXPRESS ANGER—WITHOUT BEING NASTY—SO YOU CAN GET PAST IT

It is painful to listen to the one you love shout or slam the door. But until s/he lets out her/his anger, you won't get to the negotiating couch. As one of my interviewees put it, "The only way out is *through*." Psychologist Dr. Judith Sherven advises us that *both* genders sometimes have to be "fierce."[3] We have to toughen ourselves up so that our lover won't be afraid to express her/his feelings—but this should be done without being physically or emotionally abusive.[4]

In the words of Dr. Robert Moore, professor of psychology and religion at Chicago Theological Seminary, "women and men need to bless each other in their aggression."[5] When we embrace our own—and each other's—angry and competitive feelings,[6] we come to each other as whole people ready to negotiate love.

14. CREATE OUR OWN LASTING RELATIONSHIP BOND

You're not negotiating simply to do your lover a favor. In the long run, the two of you benefit *equally*. Sometimes both of you will agree to meet your needs; other times you'll agree to put your lover's first. You have a "two for two," not a "two for one," relationship. Once you and your lover realize this fundamental truth, your loving negotiations will be more frequent and more productive.

The more love you give, the more you receive. Empathy begets empathy. Generosity begets generosity. Caring begets caring. This is how you create a lasting relationship bond.

15. NEGOTIATE LOVE

Hopefully you're on the right track by now. Remember, as you negotiate love, always keep your "little observer" nearby. When the conversation isn't going the way you'd like it, don't hesitate to speak up. Remember, *50 percent of the responsibility for making the loving negotiation work is yours.* If the two of you get sidetracked from the issue at hand, if you start arguing, or if you're just plain bored, you have the power to say, "Stop. Let's look at what's going on. Is something wrong here?" If you feel this way, chances are your lover feels the same way too.[7]

WHY SHOULD YOU NEGOTIATE LOVE?

One of the most beautiful images in literature, music, and drama is that of the loving couple. Many of us wish for this joy. Indeed, it is the most valuable heritage we can give our children. As Vietnamese monk and poet Thich Nhat Hanh writes, "If Father and Mother themselves are happy, the children will receive seeds of happiness in their consciousness and when they grow up, they will know how to make others happy too."[8] But there are no shortcuts. Until you and your lover know how to handle your disagreements effectively, happiness will elude you.

CAN YOU MAKE A DIFFERENCE?

"Even if my lover and I learn to negotiate love, will it make any difference in the world?" you may ask. "After all, we're just two people."

You can make a big difference. We can't have world peace

until one man and one woman learn to live in peace with each other. Domestic violence diminishes when a couple knows how to negotiate love. Faced with nuclear, environmental, and animal protection emergencies, we must all begin to pool our energies, resolve our conflicts, and work together toward our common goals. Men and women today can't afford *not* to support one another.[9]

By negotiating love, you and your lover have the opportunity to make an important contribution both to your own relationship and to the world. The cooperation, friendship, love, and clear communication you two create will inevitably expand to include the other people around you[10] and, indeed, all of nature. Old stereotypes and negative attitudes don't have to hold you back; you have the power to transform society.

We can heal ourselves, each other, and the world by negotiating love.

Exercises

The following exercises, which incorporate the principles and guidelines of each chapter of this book, will put you on your way to successfully negotiating love.

CHAPTER 1: CAN LOVERS NEGOTIATE?

1. GET COMFORTABLE WITH NEGOTIATING.

Concentrate on the word "negotiate." Now write down or record on tape all the associations that come up. Do you think of negotiating as something you'd like to try with your lover? If not, figure out what your main reservations are.

Ask your partner to do the same thing, either with you or alone. Afterward, share your reservations with each other and discuss how you can support each other in overcoming them.

2. IMPROVE YOUR MINDSET ABOUT THE OTHER SEX.

Sit next to your lover. Each of you has five minutes to tell the other how you see relationships between women and men. Write down or record what you say. Did either of you use stereotypical, negative phrases, like "war between the sexes" or "peaceful coexistence"? Or did you say positive words, like "co-operation," "mutual support," "teamwork," "partnership," "friendship," and "love"?

Now that you've identified the mindsets you both have about relationships with the other sex, see if you can make them more positive. Each of you should take a moment each day to visualize your lover's face while silently repeating words such as "friendship" and "love" at the same time. Or visualize scenes of men and women caring about each other as you say your lover's name to yourself. If you and your lover both do this, you will be preparing yourselves well for the negotiating couch.

CHAPTER 2: GETTING PAST YOUR ANGER SO YOU CAN SIT DOWN AND TALK

1. MAKE AN ANGER AGREEMENT.

Take time with your lover to decide exactly what expressions of toxic rage each of you considers off limits. You may devise your own agreement or use this sample: "Certain ways of showing anger are off limits to us. Together we agree not to do the following . . . We are comfortable with other ways of getting angry. When we get mad it is okay to . . . We will both do our best not to get angry at the same time." If you don't write your limits down, at least have a clear understanding about them.

2. EXPLORE YOUR ANGER.

Most of us feel angry at our lovers sometimes. Make a commitment to find out what you are angry about. Complete these sentences either on paper or on tape: "I am angry at my lover about . . . When my lover does . . . it screws up my life. Her/his . . . has to stop. When I think these thoughts, I feel like . . ." Ask your lover to do the same exercise privately. When you are both ready, read each other your lists. As you discuss them, be sure to respect the limits about expressing anger you have agreed upon.

3. COMMUNICATE POWERFULLY BY ASKING QUESTIONS.

After you've made your agreement about expressing healthy anger, the next time your lover is irritable or out of sorts, start saying, "What's the matter? I care about you." If you get the usual "Nothing. Leave me alone," try again an hour or a day later. Whenever your lover finally decides to tell you what is bothering her/him, stop whatever you're doing. Be prepared to receive her/his healthy anger. Don't interrupt, argue, criticize, or troubleshoot; just listen and be there for your lover. Walk away only if s/he breaks the agreement and starts showing toxic rage. Practice this approach until it becomes comfortable for both of you—part of your daily routine.

Chapter 3: Creating the Right Mindset: Ten Ways to Get to the Negotiating Couch

1. GET PAST THE "I'M RIGHT; YOU'RE WRONG" MINDSET.

When you realize you're starting to play "moral policeman," end the loving negotiation *immediately.* Go off by yourself and complete this sentence: "I need to be right about this issue because . . ." Repeat these words until you've figured out an answer that satisfies you. Once you figure out *why* you're playing this role, you'll be able to discard it.

Then have an imaginary conversation with your lover: "I'm acting like a 'moral policeman' because . . . What I really need now is . . . You are acting this way because you need . . . Another way to resolve this conflict besides my way is . . ." When you are satisfied with your responses, invite your lover to go back to the negotiating couch.

2. SAY "I'M SORRY."

Sit down in a comfortable place next to your lover. Pretend one of you has accidentally hurt the other and is ready to say "I'm sorry." Take turns playing the role of the person making amends and the person who is injured. Each of you has approximately two minutes. Is it difficult for either of you to apologize with words, gestures, or actions? Is it uncomfortable for either of you to accept the other's apology? Can you and your lover each say "You caused me pain" without putting the other on the defensive? If one or both of you feel embarrassed, keep on talking until you figure out why.

3. LEARN ABOUT YOUR PAST WOUNDS.

Find a quiet place and take at least an hour to answer these questions either on paper or on tape: How did your parents get along with each other? How did they handle their anger: Did they avoid expressing it, deal with it directly, or withdraw from their relationship completely? How did they resolve their conflicts, or did they deny any existed at all? Did one of them usually get her/his way, or did they sit down together and discuss their differences? How did you get along with each of your parents?

What kind of lovers have you tended to pick? What kind of things have they done that have made you angry? How have you handled conflicts with your spouse(s) or significant other(s) in the past?

You and your lover may do this activity separately and then compare notes.

4. DISCOVER HOW YOU FEEL RIGHT NOW.

After an argument with your lover, sit quietly by yourself with your eyes closed. Take a few deep breaths. Now say each of these sentences aloud at least five times: "I feel hurt because . . ." "I feel sad because . . ." "I feel afraid because . . ." "I feel angry because . . ." "I feel wounded because . . ." What comes up for you? If you feel comfortable, share your feelings with your lover afterward. When you're both ready, you and your lover may do this exercise together. Remember to honor each other's different ways of self-expression.

Chapter 4: How to Reach an Agreement That Satisfies You Both

1. PREPARE TO NEGOTIATE LOVE.

Together with your lover, pick an issue you disagree about. After you have cleared out your anger, go through the four preparatory steps in phase one. Figure out how you feel and what you need, acknowledge and define the issue, negotiate about how you're going to proceed, and determine your non-negotiable issues. Then create an agenda.

2. DISCUSS THE ISSUE.

Now is the time to negotiate love. Communicate your feelings, state your needs, and figure out how both of your feelings and needs can be honored. Allow yourselves as many negotiating sessions as you need.

3. MAKE AN AGREEMENT.

Continue negotiating until you find a solution that works for both of you. Write it down if you like. Now select another issue, and start with phase one again. When you are ready, expand your discussion to include several issues—even an entire issue area. By this time, you're negotiating love like a pro! Congratulations.

Chapter 5: The Eleven Secrets of Negotiating Love

1. DISCOVER YOUR ASSUMPTIONS.

When you and your lover reach an impasse, the first thing to do is to find out what you're assuming about each other.

Ask yourself these three questions: What am I assuming my lover feels? What am I assuming my lover needs? How am I reacting to these assumptions? Share what you have discovered with your lover, so you can figure out if you've erred in your assumptions. Then ask her/him to check out her/his assumptions about you.

2. MAKE A SUGGESTION.

Identify the biggest unfulfilled need you have in your relationship and how your lover could meet your need. Then think about how you could suggest it. When you are alone, say to yourself, "I feel . . ." and "I need . . ." and "I suggest . . ." as if your lover were right there with you. Imagine how s/he might respond. What might be your lover's countersuggestion? Can you imagine a solution that would meet your lover's needs as well as yours? You may want to write down what you want to say, speak into a tape recorder, or just practice your dialogue silently. When you are ready, make an appointment with your lover to negotiate love.

3. ACCEPT A SUGGESTION.

Figure out how you would react if your lover told you what s/he really needed. Would you resist or welcome your lover's suggestion? Would you state your own needs too, and make a counteroffer? Would you continue to brainstorm until you found a solution that was acceptable to both of you? If you find you are not openminded and willing to compromise, try to figure out what resistances are blocking you.

4. SHARE YOUR COMMUNICATION STYLES.

Do the communication activity with your lover that Robert Bly describes. To keep it interesting, take turns speaking first and vary the amount of time you each have to talk.

CHAPTER 6: THE SEESAW OF POWER: WHO HAS MORE CONTROL?

1. UNCOVER YOUR POWER.

Think of all the different sources of your own inner power. Do you have a lot of energy? Do you value yourself? Do you believe you can get what you need? Are you a person of honesty and integrity? What are your talents? Are you charming? Do you get along well with other people? With this information you can increase your energy and expand your inner power.

2. DETERMINE YOUR ME/YOU POWER BALANCE.

How is power balanced between the two of you? Is it approximately equal? Or does one of you monopolize power? If so, are you comfortable with this imbalance? If not, how could you negotiate love to alter it? For those of you who take turns being on top of the seesaw, what do you do when you're on the bottom? Sulk? Manipulate? Have an honest discussion? Answer these questions by yourself. Then compare your answers with your lover's.

What do you do if you have different perceptions of your balance of power? Talk it out: "Why do you think I'm more powerful than you are? Why do you see yourself as less powerful than I? How can I support your feeling more powerful in this relationship?"

3. DISCOVER YOUR US/THEM POWER BALANCE.

Who are the most important people in your life besides your lover? Think of each of them, one at a time. With whom do you have the strongest alliances? Are any of them stronger than the one you have with your lover? How could you shift your energy so that your alliance with your lover is the strongest? Ask your lover to answer these questions too. The two of you will learn a lot by sharing your answers.

Chapter 7: What to Do When Romance Fades

1. UNDERSTAND YOUR ROMANTIC NEGOTIATIONS.

Think of a romantic relationship you are in or used to have. What were the main emotional issues that provoked conflicts? How did you and your lover negotiate each of them? Did you both get your needs met? Did the two of you get stuck at an impasse? Did one of you refuse to negotiate? Did either of you walk away from the negotiating couch? Did a pattern eventually develop? If you stayed together, did this pattern persist? If you broke up, did your pattern for resolving conflicts contribute to the demise of your relationship? How? Ask your lover to do this activity either by her/himself or together with you.

2. RESOLVE AN EMOTIONAL CONFLICT.

Can you remember any of your dating dilemmas? Perhaps it was about where to go, how much money to spend, or what should happen at the end of the evening. How did you handle it? Did you avoid the issue or did you discuss it? What would you say and do today, now that you know about the importance of negotiating love early in a dating relationship?

3. CREATE THE RELATIONSHIP SPIRIT.

List three activities you can do to support your lover. Start doing one of them. For example, offer to give your lover a mini-massage, make lunch, pay the bills, drive him/her to the dentist, or leave work to take a sick child home from day care or school.

As you continue to support your lover, notice how your relationship benefits. Whenever you're ready, start the other two activities. If you and your lover do this exercise together, you will soon see how your relationship can be transformed through mutual support.

Chapter 8: Handling Relationship Hotspots

1. IDENTIFY YOUR HOTSPOTS.

Go through the list of twelve hotspots with your lover. Which ones do you disagree most about? Which is your hottest hotspot? To negotiate it, start by identifying your own—and your lover's—feelings and needs.

2. ASSESS YOUR BALANCE OF POWER.

Make a list of each of the hotspots where you and your lover conflict frequently. Consider them one at a time. What are your main differences? In each hotspot, who has the most power? When you consider the whole spectrum of hotspots, is your power evenly balanced? If not, what can you do to get the seesaw of power moving in your relationship? You and your lover may make separate lists and then compare your assessments.

3. NEGOTIATE A HOTSPOT ISSUE.

Pick a hotspot issue that you and your lover disagree about. Then, after you clear out your anger, negotiate together until you reach agreement. Next time let your lover have a turn selecting the issue. Or both of you may decide together—if you can agree!

If you have difficulty with this activity, do the following

one first: Go shopping in the supermarket together or make a grocery shopping list. Notice which foods you each select. How do you handle nonnegotiable issues? ("I'm allergic to chocolate." "I won't eat red meat.") How do you reach agreement about what to buy? Then use this knowledge to resolve the hotspot issue you and your lover select.

CHAPTER 9: HOW WOMEN CAN GET READY TO NEGOTIATE LOVE

(FOR WOMEN ONLY)

1. EMPOWER YOURSELF.

Say each of these affirmations aloud at least once a day: I am a worthwhile person. My feelings and needs count. I have the right to ask for what I need. I can do what has to be done. I can take care of myself. I know who I am. I set clear limits as to what is and is not acceptable. No one can take advantage of me.

2. UNDERSTAND YOUR NEEDS.

Complete this sentence with at least twenty-five different endings: "What I need as a woman is . . ." If you feel comfortable doing so, share your answers with your lover. If not, silently analyze your relationship to see which of your needs is being fulfilled. Then try to work on ways of having your unmet needs addressed.

3. DETERMINE YOUR LIMITS.

Imagine you and your lover in each of the following hypothetical situations. Which behaviors would violate your limits—and which would end the relationship?

a. You and your lover are at a party together with several attractive women.

—He stares at another woman longingly.

—He converses with another woman.

—He flirts with another woman.

—He asks another woman for her phone number.

—He asks another woman out.

—He has sex with another woman.

b. You and your lover are angry with each other.

—He shouts at you.

—He calls you names.

—He throws something across the room.

—He throws something *at you.*

—He pushes you.

—He slaps you.

c. You and your lover are having a discussion about money.

—He insists you can't buy something you need.

—He insists that he buy something he needs, in spite of your opposition.

—He tells you that he has spent your entire joint checking account (and not on paying the bills).

—He refuses to share his paycheck.

—He demands that you turn over your paycheck to him.

—He tells you that from now on, he will decide how much money you have to spend.

Once you have defined your limits, share them with your lover.

4. BE A VALUED WOMAN.

Imagine what it would be like to be really valued by your lover. What would you like him to say? What would you want him to do? When you are ready, tell your lover.

Chapter 10: How Men Can Get Ready to Negotiate Love

(FOR MEN ONLY)

1. IDENTIFY YOUR WOUNDS.

Men often carry their emotional wounds in their bodies, because they are unaccustomed to venting their feelings. So lie down by yourself in a quiet, dark place. Close your eyes and loosen your clothing. Breathe deeply, "in . . . out . . . in . . . out . . ." for two minutes. Focus your attention on your body, one part at a time. Start with your forehead, and notice if there's any pain or tension there. Move your attention to your eyes, ears, nose, mouth, and so on. When you have located a body part that hurts, stay with the tension or ache. Let your mind wander; see what comes up for you. Whose face do you see? What incident do you recall?

If your mind is blank, repeat this activity a few days later. Sooner or later you will start to notice your pain. If you want to understand more about your wounds, read pages 127–209 of Louise Hay's book *You Can Heal Your Life* (Santa Monica, California: Hay House, 1987). It will tell you exactly how each part of your body is connected with your feelings—and your spirit.

2. HEAL YOUR WOUNDS—TOGETHER.

When you are ready, invite your lover to join you in this activity. Sit quietly facing each other, in silence, for five minutes. Say to yourself only, "I feel wounded because . . ." "I hurt because . . ."

Now reach out and take your lover's hands. Look directly into each other's eyes. Share with your lover what you have said to yourself, "I feel wounded because . . ." "I hurt because . . ." Give her the time she needs to react to your feelings. Before you end the activity, suggest to her, "You can heal my wounds by . . ."

At a later time do this activity again, and reverse your roles.

3. GET IN TOUCH WITH YOUR FEELINGS.

Find a quiet place where you can sit by yourself. If possible, be outdoors so you can be close to nature—grass, flowers, trees, birds, water. Close your eyes and affirm to yourself, "I feel happy." Repeat this phrase over and over again for at least three minutes. As you say it, recall the happiest moments in your own life and the people with whom you've felt happy. What comes up for you? How does your body feel now? Whenever you get this feeling again, you will recognize that you are happy.

Now repeat the activity, but say to yourself instead, "I feel sad." Again, notice what you experience in your body. Do this activity twice more, once saying to yourself, "I feel angry" and then "I feel afraid." Take a few moments at the end of each time to remember exactly how you feel, and give these feelings a label. How did your body feel different when you focused on happiness, sadness, anger, and fear?

After you've done this exercise a couple of times, perhaps you'll be able to tell your lover how you feel when she asks you "How do you feel?"

4. UNDERSTAND YOUR NEEDS.

Complete this sentence with at least twenty-five different endings, either on paper or on tape: "What I need as a man is . . ." When you feel comfortable, share your insights with your lover.

CHAPTER 11: WHAT WOMEN AND MEN NEED: A NEW CONVERSATION

1. SHARE GENDER PERSPECTIVES.

Sit on the floor across from your lover. Each of you has five minutes to tell each other about what it's like to be a woman—or a man. If anger or pain comes up, describe it.

Now imagine that you are a person of the other sex. Take three minutes to tell your lover about how you would feel. If you experience anger or pain, share it. After you have finished, allow your lover to react to what you have said. Then switch roles.

2. FIGURE OUT HOW YOU "HEAR" EACH OTHER.

After you and your lover have negotiated an issue, ask your lover a few days later to tell you her/his version of the conversation. Then share yours. Compare the two. How are your perceptions different? Can these differences teach you something about yourselves?

3. VALUE AND NURTURE EACH OTHER.

You and your lover are invited to answer your appropriate set of questions separately:

(FOR WOMEN)

a. What could you do to nurture your lover? What could you say?

b. What would it be like to be truly valued by your lover? What would he say? What would he do? How would you feel?

(FOR MEN)

a. What could you say to show your lover how much you value her? What could you do?

b. What would it be like to be truly nurtured by your lover? What would she say? What would she do? How would you feel?

Now compare your answers.

4. ASSESS YOUR RELATIONSHIP.

Now that you're practically a pro at negotiating love, take this quick quiz. Ask your lover to do the same. When you're finished, compare your answers.

a. Do you trust your lover?

b. Do you respect your lover's gender differences?

c. Are you aware of your own special powers?

d. Are you willing to share your powers with your lover?

e. Do you know what your major wounds are?

f. Do you know what your lover's major wounds are?

g. Are you comfortable communicating about your feelings with your lover?

h. Can you honestly tell your lover what you need?

i. Are you willing to explore solutions that meet both your needs?

j. When you and your lover make an agreement, will you keep it?

Now is the time to start working on those questions you and your lover did not say yes to.

CHAPTER 12: HEALING EACH OTHER

SUM IT ALL UP.

Think about how reading this book has helped you. How are you learning to negotiate love? Have you and your lover had a particularly memorable loving negotiation? If you would like to share your thoughts and experiences, find out about my couples mediation services, or sponsor a Negotiating Love™ seminar in your community, you are invited to write to me at P.O. Box 22213, Alexandria, VA 22304.

Good luck and keep on negotiating love!

Annotated Resources

Where do you go from here? Negotiating love takes a lifetime to learn, so start by reading whichever book appeals to you. Then try another one. At some point you may want to subscribe to a men's or women's newsletter. Or you may prefer listening to an audiotape or watching a videotape. You don't have to do these activities alone; you and your lover can do them together and discuss what you have learned.

To share your knowledge with others, take a class, seminar, or workshop. Attend alone at first if you like; when you are ready, go together with your lover. For a memorable experience, invite a speaker to address members of your community.

An ongoing support group will enable you to continue your personal growth for months or even years. Contact a women's or men's center and sign up. Encourage your lover to do the same. Each resource you use is another step toward negotiating love.

Books

FOR WOMEN:

Borensky, Joan. *Fire in the Soul.* Boston: Little, Brown, 1993.

Offers a wide-ranging list of tools and approaches a woman can use for her own personal healing.

Hancock, Emily. *The Girl Within.* New York: Fawcett Columbine, 1989.

A sensitive treatment of a woman's quest to find her "self."

Jeffers, Susan, Ph.D. *Opening Our Hearts to Men.* New York: Fawcett Columbine, 1989.

A must-read guidebook for women who want to love themselves and men.

Jones, Riki Robbins, Ph.D. *The Empowered Woman.* New York: SPI Books, 1992.

Women who yearn to discover their own inner power should read this book.

Kingma, Daphne Rose. *The Men We Never Knew: Women's Role in the Evolution of a Gender.* Berkeley, California: Conari Press, 1993.

A caring therapist empowers women to support men emotionally.

Leonard, Linda. *On the Way to the Wedding.* New York: Random House, 1987.

Insights about the personal development a woman must undergo before entering a permanent relationship.

Secunda, Victoria. *When You and Your Mother Can't Be Friends: Resolving the Most Complicated Relationship of Your Life.* New

York: Delacorte Press, 1990; and *Women and Their Fathers: The Sexual and Romantic Impact of the First Man in Your Life.* New York: Delacorte Press, 1992.

Two books that enable women to explore their mother and father wounds respectively.

Woodman, Marion, with Kate Danson, Mary Hamilton, and Rita Greer Allen. *Leaving My Father's House: A Journey to Conscious Femininity.* Boston: Shambhala Publications, 1993.

A Jungian analyst explores the spiritual and emotional side of womanhood.

FOR MEN:

Bly, Robert. *Iron John: A Book About Men.* New York: Vintage Books, 1992.

Using a fairy tale as his motif, this famous poet writes eloquently about how it feels to be a man.

Farrell, Warren, Ph.D. *The Myth of Male Power: Why Men Are the Disposable Sex.* New York: Simon & Schuster, 1993.

The most courageous and honest discussion of men's wounds I have ever read.

Gerzon, Mark. *A Choice of Heroes: The Changing Faces of American Manhood.* Boston: Houghton Mifflin Company, 1992.

A well-written treatment of male role models and how they have evolved since the sixties.

Gurian, Michael. *Mothers, Sons and Lovers: How a Man's Relationship with His Mother Affects the Rest of His Life.* Boston: Shambhala Publications, 1994.

For men who want to heal their mother wound, this is the *book to read.*

Harding, Christopher, Ph.D., ed. *Wingspan: Inside the Men's Movement.* New York: St. Martin's Press, 1992.

The best selection of essays about the men's movement available anywhere.

Kauth, Bill, M.S. *A Circle of Men: The Original Manual for Men's Support Groups.* New York: St. Martin's Press, 1992.

An invaluable guide for any man who wants to start or join a men's group.

Lee, John. *The Flying Boy: Healing the Wounded Man.* Deerfield Beach, Florida: Health Communications, Inc., 1987.

The eloquent story of the author's struggle to reach out to the woman he loved.

Kipnis, Aaron R., Ph.D. *Knights Without Armor: A Practical Guide for Men in Quest of Masculine Soul.* New York: William Morrow, 1992.

A thoughtful psychologist explores contemporary men's dilemmas and shares his ideas for resolving them.

Moore, Robert, Ph.D., and Douglas Gillette. *The King Within.* New York: Avon Books, 1992; *The Warrior Within.* New York: William Morrow and Company, 1992; *The Magician Within* and *The Lover Within.* New York: William Morrow, 1993.

A series of four excellent books by Jungian psychoanalyst Robert Moore and men's therapist Douglas Gillette about their vision of masculine power.

Osherson, Samuel. *Finding Our Fathers: How a Man's Life Is Shaped by His Relationship with His Father.* New York: Fawcett Columbine, 1986.

The definitive work on the origins of a man's father wound—and how to heal it.

Schenk, Roy, Ph.D. *The Other Side of the Coin: Causes and Consequences of Men's Oppression.* Madison, Wisconsin: Bioenergetics Press, 1982.

Don't let the militant subtitle deter you from reading this important book. The author's honest discussion of men's shame is outstanding and still pertinent.

Thompson, Keith, ed. *To Be a Man.* New York: Putnam, 1991.

Wonderful short essays about manhood written by male poets, artists, scientists, and political leaders.

FOR WOMEN AND MEN:

Baber, Asa. *Naked at Gender Gap: A Man's View of the War Between the Sexes.* New York: Birch Lane Press, 1992.

A humorous, penetrating look at the issues that divide women and men.

Baldwin, Martha, M.S.S.W. *Beyond Victim: You Can Overcome Childhood Abuse—Even Sexual Abuse.* Moore Haven, Florida: Rainbow Books, 1988.

Helpful information about dealing with our childhood wounds.

Blanton, Brad, Ph.D. *Radical Honesty: How to Transform Your Life by Telling the Truth.* Stanley, Virginia: Sparrowhawk Publications, 1993.

A powerful work about honesty in personal relationships. Necessary reading for couples who are committed to negotiating love.

Blumstein, Philip, Ph.D., and Pepper Schwartz, Ph.D. *American Couples: Money, Work, Sex.* New York: William Morrow, 1983.

A splendid source of material on the most difficult hotspots.

Bradshaw, John. *Healing the Shame That Binds You.* Deerfield Beach, Florida: Health Communications, Inc., 1988.

If toxic shame is keeping you from negotiating love, read this superb handbook.

Branden, Nathaniel, Ph.D. *The Psychology of Romantic Love: What Love Is; Why Love Is Born; Why It Sometimes Grows; Why It Sometimes Dies.* New York: Bantam Books, 1981.

Tells you exactly what the romantic tie is and how to move beyond it.

Burnell, Ivan, Ph.D. *The Power of Positive Doing.* Center Ossipee, New Hampshire: International Personal Development, 1994.

An easy-to-read book that will help you get in touch with your own power.

Campbell, Susan M., Ph.D. The Couples Journey: Intimacy As a Path to Wholeness. San Luis Obispo, California: Impact Publishers, 1988.

A knowledgeable therapist's view about how relationships evolve over time.

DeAngelis, Barbara, Ph.D. *How to Make Love All the Time.* New York: Rawson Associates, 1987.

This book delivers what it promises: to teach you how to make love a part of your everyday life.

Dym, Barry, Ph.D., and Michael L. Glenn, M.D. *Couples: Exploring and Understanding the Cycles of Intimate Relationships.* New York: HarperCollins, 1993.

An excellent complement to Negotiating Love, *especially on the dynamics of balancing power.*

Farrell, Warren, Ph.D. *Why Men Are the Way They Are: The Male-Female Dynamic.* New York: McGraw-Hill, 1986.

Why do women and men see each other as objects? To find out, read this milestone book.

Gerzon, Mark. *Coming into Our Own.* New York: Bantam, 1992.

Wisely and compassionately discusses the issues women and men face during midlife transition.

Gordon, Lori H., Ph.D. *Passage to Intimacy: Key Concepts and Skills from the Pairs Program Which Has Helped Thousands of Couples Rekindle Their Love.* New York: Simon & Schuster, 1993.

The subtitle speaks for itself.

Gray, John. *Men Are from Mars; Women Are from Venus: A Practical Guide for Improving Communication and Getting What You Want in Your Relationships.* New York: HarperCollins, 1992.

An enjoyable and practical guide to communicating better with your lover.

Gray, John. *What Your Mother Couldn't Tell You and Your Father Didn't Know.* New York: HarperCollins, 1994.

Fundamental relationship skills that prepare you to negotiate love. Chapter 13, "Dance Steps for Lasting Intimacy," is a must-read.

Hay, Louise L. *You Can Heal Your Life.* Santa Monica, California: Hay House, 1987.

Tells how to gain self-knowledge, self-confidence, and self-respect. Written by a woman who has all three.

Houston, Jean. *The Search for the Beloved: Journeys in Mythology and Sacred Psychology.* Los Angeles, California: Jeremy Tarcher, 1987.

Presents original, imaginative processes and methods you can use for self-transformation.

Jeffers, Susan, Ph.D. *Feel the Fear and Do It Anyway.* New York: Fawcett Columbine, 1987.

Helps you fight fear and create trust—the foundation of negotiating love.

Kammer, Jack. *Good Will Toward Men.* New York: St. Martin's Press, 1994.

Thought-provoking conversations with powerful women who like men.

Kingma, Daphne Rose. *True Love: How to Make Your Relationships Sweeter, Deeper and More Passionate.* Berkeley, California: Conari Press, 1991.

My favorite "relationships book." Daphne Rose is both a therapist and a poet.

Kipnis, Aaron, Ph.D., and Liz Herron, M.A. *Gender War, Gender Peace.* New York: William Morrow and Company, 1994.

Two well-known experts share how women and men can stop being at odds and create lasting peace together instead.

Krantzler, Mel, Ph.D., and Patricia B. Krantzler, M.A. *The Seven Marriages of Your Marriage.* San Francisco, California: HarperSanFrancisco, 1992.

Every married couple should read this valuable work together.

McCallum, Patricia. *Stepping Free of Limiting Patterns.* Chevy Chase, Maryland: Source Unlimited, 1992.

Describes Essence Repatterning, a brand-new way to catalyze your inner growth.

Rhodes, Carol L., Ph.D., and Norman S. Goldner, Ph.D. *Why Women and Men Don't Get Along.* Troy, Michigan: Somerset Publishing Company, 1992.

Contains a wealth of useful information that can enable women and men to understand each other better.

Scarf, Maggie. *Intimate Partners: Patterns in Love and Marriage.* New York: Ballantine Books, 1988.

Use this book to explore your family background and discover your wounds.

Tannen, Deborah, Ph.D. *You Just Don't Understand: Women and Men in Conversation.* New York: William Morrow and Company, 1990.

If you want to know why women and men have difficulties communicating, read this bestseller.

AUDIOTAPES

FOR WOMEN:

Sherven, Judith. *Womanhood, Power, and Identity.* Los Angeles, California: Judith Sherven and Jim Sniechowski, 1950 Sawtelle Boulevard, Suite 340, Los Angeles, CA 90025, 1994.

For women who want to increase their self-confidence, self-reliance, and self-respect, this is the *tape to listen to.*

Woodman, Marion. *The Emergence of Consciousness Femininity and Consciousness Masculinity.* Berkeley, California: New Medicine Tapes, 1992.

Marion Woodman is one of the visionaries of our time. She reminds us how self-awareness is the first step toward self-knowledge—and toward negotiating love.

FOR MEN:

Diggs, Lawrence. *Introduction to Men's Issues.* Roslyn, South Dakota: Quiet Storm Trading Company, 1991.

Lawrence Diggs blends his powerful voice with delightful music to make a dramatic statement of the problems men face today.

Hillman, James, Michael Meade, and Malidoma Somé. *Images of Initiation.* Pacific Grove, California: Oral Tradition Archives, 1992.

Three outstanding leaders share their ideas about why male initiation is crucial to the survival of our society. Their discussion is enlivened with stories, poems, and songs.

Moore, Robert, and Forrest Craver. *Dancing the Four Quarters: Visions of Grassroots Masculine Leadership in the 1990's.* Arlington, Virginia: North American Mysteries School, 1991.

For any man who is concerned about the future of the men's movement and how he can empower himself as a man.

Somé, Malidoma. *Creating a New Sense of Home.* Boulder, Colorado: Sounds True Recordings, 1993.

This inspiring leader shows men how to find their true selves by supporting each other, creating communities, and developing a spirit of brotherhood.

FOR WOMEN AND MEN:

Arrien, Angeles, Ph.D. *Change, Conflict and Resolution from a Cross-Cultural Perspective.* Berkeley, California: New Medicine Tapes, 1991.

What can we learn from other cultures about negotiating love? Listen to these valuable tapes and find out.

Arrien, Angeles, Ph.D. *Power and Love in Relationships.* Boulder, Colorado: Sounds True Recordings, 1991.

Dr. Arrien illustrates her discussion of this challenging topic with two ancient folktales.

Bly, Robert. *Iron John and the Male Mode of Feeling.* Pacific Grove, California: Oral Tradition Archives, 1992.

Side one of this tape is a dramatization and interpretation of the "Iron John" fairytale. Side two contains the most important information on female-male differences you'll ever have. Listen and decide for yourself.

Farrell, Warren. *Men Only—A Hero's Journey.* Boulder, Colorado: Sounds True Recordings, 1992.

I may be violating a rule here, but this outstanding two-tape series is for women too. In fact, it's for anyone who wants to learn how to receive criticism, which is vital when you're negotiating love.

Farrell, Warren, Ph.D. *Understanding Each Other.* Boulder, Colorado: Sounds True Recordings, 1993.

Want to walk in your lover's moccasins for a while? Then listen to these splendid tapes. By the time you finish, you'll feel the pain of being a member of the other sex—and understand your lover much better.

Jeffers, Susan, Ph.D. *Inner Talk for a Confident Day.* Carson, California: Hay House, 1990.

A magical tape that nourishes your self-esteem and gets you ready to negotiate love.

Jeffers, Susan, Ph.D. *Inner Talk for a Love That Works.* Carson, California: Hay House, 1993.

Enables you to get beyond the fears that keep you from enjoying your relationships. Dr. Jeffers's combination of affirmations, positive-self talk, and music is truly inspiring.

Meade, Michael. *The Dance of Gender: When the Women Went One Way and the Men Went the Other.* Pacific Grove, California: Oral Tradition Archives, 1992.

This is a tape of a presentation by master storyteller Michael Meade that was given to five hundred people in California. Through drumming, reciting poetry, and sharing myths he awakens us to who we really are as women and men.

Sherven, Judith, Ph.D. *Breaking Through Resistance to Reclaim Your Life.* Los Angeles, California: "Reclaiming the Self" Series, 1989.

For those of you who are resisting knowing your true self, here is a tape you should listen to attentively.

Sniechowski, Jim, Ph.D., and Judith Sherven, Ph.D. *Practical Spirituality.* Los Angeles, California: Judith Sherven and Jim

Sniechowski, 1950 Sawtelle Boulevard, Suite 340, Los Angeles, California 90025, 1989.

Jim and Judith are a dynamic team who share themselves openly and allow their audience to participate in the dialogue. Now you can listen to one of their remarkable workshops.

Tannen, Deborah, and Robert Bly. *Men and Women Talking Together.* New York: Sound Horizons, 1992.

These audiotapes made me laugh so much that I actually had to stop my car until I could drive it safely. To listen to these two renowned figures speak to an overflow crowd in New York Open Center is an unforgettable experience.

VIDEOTAPES

FOR WOMEN:

The Empowered Woman: A Leadership Style That Works. Alexandria, Virginia: Creative Relationships, Inc., 1994.

After you smash the glass ceiling, what do you do next? Do women have their own leadership style? If so, what is it? This tape of a workshop I did in 1993 answers these questions—and more.

FOR MEN:

The New Locker Room™ Project, c/o Manquest Productions, 73 Belleau Avenue, Atherton, CA 94973.

According to Sanford Anderson, its creator, the purpose of The New Locker Room™ Project is to promote a healthy nationwide dialogue about the roles of men. On these videotapes, men talk heart to heart about what really matters to them.

FOR WOMEN AND MEN:

Bly, Robert, and Marion Woodman. *Bly and Woodman on Men and Women.* Belleville, Ontario: Applewood Communications, 1992.

This six-tape video series is an awesome contribution to the literature of gender reconciliation.

NEWSLETTERS AND MAGAZINES

FOR WOMEN:

The Alexandra. The Alexandra Women's Services Association, International, 4220 Rossiter Drive, Victoria, B.C., Canada V8N 457 (604) 721-5065.

Rhona Hume Konnelly's inspirational publication is of interest to both Canadian and American women.

NEWsletter. The Network for Empowering Women, P.O. Box 22213, Alexandra, VA 22304 (703) 212-8111.

NEW is dedicated to enabling women to value themselves, realize their own power, support each other, and create caring relationships with men. Its mission is to provide a space where a healthy dialogue between women and men can occur through networking, conferences, seminars, and other educational opportunities. The quarterly NEWsletter contains a summary of these events, reviews of gender books, and opportunities for member networking.

FOR MEN:

MenStuff. The National Men's Resource, P.O. Box 800-R, San Anselmo, CA 94979 (415) 453-2839.

Gordon Clay, who is an expert on men's issues, edits this detailed newsletter full of news tidbits and commentary. There is also a complete listing of men's events both in California and across the country.

MR (Men's Rights), Inc., P.O. Box 163180, Sacramento, CA 95816 (916) 484-7333.

Fredric Hayward, the founder of M.R., Inc., publishes valuable literature for men who want to raise their consciousness on a variety of contemporary issues.

Wingspan: Journal of the Male Spirit. Christopher Harding, Editor, 8 Mount Vernon Street, Dorchester, MA 02125 (617) 282-3379.

This groundbreaking magazine covers a wide scope of men's work, including interviews, workshop profiles, and reviews of men's books and tapes.

FOR WOMEN AND MEN:

Balance: The Inclusive Version of Gender Equality, 10011-116th Street, #501, Edmonton, Alberta, Canada T5K IV4.

An innovative, attractive magazine featuring both Canadian and American writers and edited by gender issues authority Ferrel Christiansen.

The Egalitarian, P.O. Box 70524, Bellevue, WA 98007.

Edited by author Rod Van Mechelen, this magazine is full of articles on male-female issues, gender book reviews, and interviews with relationship experts.

CLASSES, SEMINARS, AND WORKSHOPS

FOR WOMEN:

Healing the Father Wound™, P.O. Box 800-B, San Anselmo, CA 94979 (415) 457-3389.

Gordon Clay and his daughter Natalie have been co-leading this workshop since 1986. It is a moving experience for both the fathers and the daughters who attend. In a safe and loving atmosphere, fathers learn to teach their daughters how to accept their own masculine side—and to trust men.

Woman Within International, 7186 Driftwood Drive, Fenton, MI 48430 (810) 750-7227.

The female counterpart to the male New Warrior Training, Woman Within has a flavor all its own. It is psychologically rigorous but physically gentle. Women nurture each other with loving kindness as they probe their emotional depths. While painful at times, it is well worth the rewards.

FOR MEN:

Ally Press Center, 524 Orleans Street, Saint Paul, MN 55107 (612) 291-2652.

Founded by Robert Bly and Paul Feroe, the center publishes a newsletter, Dragonsmoke, *which lists the speaking engagements of Bly, James Hillman, Michael Meade, and Robert Moore. It also offers important books and tapes by Bly and other experts in men's work.*

Archon Institute for Leadership Development, 3700 Massachusetts Avenue, N.W., Suite #121, Washington, DC 20016 (202) 342-7710.

Dr. Joseph Palmour, the institute's director, gives seminars on how men can mentor each other. His presentations are extremely valuable, especially to male secondary school students and their parents.

The Men's Room, P.O. Box 603, Evanston, IL 60204 (708) 492-0335.

The Men's Room experience encourages each man who participates to become more effectively involved in his relationships. Bob Mark, Ph.D., and Buddy Portugal, L.C.S.W., are among the experienced therapists who lead this deeply meaningful weekend.

The New Warrior Training Adventure™, 61 Bullard Pasture Road, Wendell, MA 03179 (800) 870-4611.

This is a unique experience of initiation and self-examination that enables a man to develop a healthy, mature self. It consists of a rigorous weekend followed by an optional series of support groups that continue the unfolding. The New Warrior Training is the best way I know for a man to get ready to access his feelings and negotiate love.

On the Common Ground, 250 West 57 Street, Suite 1527, New York, NY 10107 (212) 265-0584.

Founded by historian and men's issues expert Dr. John Guarnaschelli, On the Common Ground is an exciting "nonorganization" for men in New York City. Its goals are to make men's work widely available, to help men form communities with each other, and to enable men to build bridges with women. On the Common Ground sponsors highly regarded men's groups, retreats, and events that foster a healthy dialogue among men.

Opening to Feelings, P.O. Box 5244, Santa Barbara, CA 93150.

Gifted therapist Daphne Rose Kingma conducts these workshops for men. She is the only woman I know who has the courage to attempt such a difficult task. If you're a man who feels "blocked," taking this workshop may be the answer to your prayers.

FOR WOMEN AND MEN:

Office of Angeles Arrien, Ph.D., P.O. Box 2077, Sausalito, CA 94966 (415) 331-5050.

You can receive a calendar of Dr. Arrien's events across the country, plus a list of her current books and tapes.

Bioenergetics Press, P.O. Box 9141, Madison, WS 53715 (608) 255-4028.

Dr. Roy Schenk will send you a catalogue not only of his own books and tapes but also of the ones he distributes. He also conducts the seminar "Building Better Bonding Between Men and Women" for businesses and universities.

The Center for Well-Being, Sparrowhawk Farm, Rt. 1, Box 291, Stanley, VA 22851 (202) 537-1875 and 1-800-EL-TRUTH.

In addition to seeing patients, Dr. Brad Blanton gives courses for couples. Together with his wife, Amy Silverman, he leads "The Nine-Day Workshop: Telling the Truth," which is conducted at Sparrowhawk Farm in Stanley, Virginia.

Creative Relationships, Inc., P.O. Box 22213, Alexandra, VA 22304.

CRI offers "Negotiating Love" three-hour classes, one-day seminars, and weekend workshops to large and small groups throughout the world. Together with other women and men, you and your lover have the opportunity to master the skills described in this book. For a free brochure, send a SASE.

Warren Farrell, Ph.D., P.O. Box 220, Encinitas, San Diego, CA 92024.

Dr. Farrell is available for speaking engagements and for his workshops where men and women switch gender roles. From personal experience I can testify that he transforms your view of the other sex and gets you ready to negotiate love.

International Personal Development, P.O. Box 277, Center Ossipee, NH 03814 (603) 539-4975.

Dr. Ivan Burnell speaks to groups and corporations about maximizing personal potential. He and his wife, Dahny, also conduct seminars for couples.

Susan Jeffers, Ph.D., P.O. Box 663, Tesukue, NM 87574.

Dr. Jeffers accepts speaking engagements and does healing workshops for women and men throughout the world. She's a dynamic speaker who has the power to inspire and motivate you.

The La Jolla Program, Center for Studies of the Person, 1125 Torrey Pines Road, La Jolla, CA 92037 (619) 459-3861.

After I attended this powerful program, my communication skills vastly improved. Write to Dr. Bruce Meador, the director, for more information.

The Living Arts Foundation, P.O. Box 17341, Boulder, CO 80301 (303) 530-3337 or 530-1896.

Dr. Tom Daly and Jude Blitz use their many talents—dance, art, and soul work—to offer outstanding leadership training and initiation programs. They have worked together for over ten years to foster partnership between women and men. Invite them to do a workshop in your city.

The Loving Relationships Training Center, P.O. Box 1465, Washington, CT 06793 (203) 927-1349.

If you're interested in "rebirthing" (reenacting your birth), the Loving Relationships Training may be what you're looking for. The center also has a list of rebirthers in your local community.

Mediation: Creative Mediation Services, P.O. Box 22213, Alexandria, VA 22304.

As a female-male team, Riki Robbins Jones and her husband Phil, both qualified mediators, can effectively help you reach agreement on whatever issues you and your partner face.

Mediation: Donald Greenstein, Esq., 218 Midvale Street, Falls Church, VA 22046.

A skilled and sensitive mediator, Donald Greenstein offers his services to couples at reasonable rates. For further information, drop him a note at the above address and write "personal and confidential" on the envelope.

Mediation: Nancy Richardson, Counseling and Mediation Services, Alexandria, VA 22304 (703) 751-6433.

Nancy is an experienced therapist who also mediates disputes between couples.

The Mystery School, Box 4400, Pomona, NY 10970 (914) 354-4965.

Call or write for a schedule of the presentations of Jean Houston, the founder of this Mystery School. Her unique cross-cultural perspective will broaden your perspective and enrich your life.

The New Field Group, 149 Natoma, Third Floor, San Francisco, CA 94105 (415) 512-8282.

Offers innovative, practical courses based on recent advances in communication and the philosophy of language. Their Relationship Course, an in-depth personal educational experience facilitated by communications expert Julio Olalla, M.A., and therapist Annie Brown, M.S., is definitely helpful.

PAIRS (Practical Application of Intimate Relationship Skills), 3705 S. George Mason Drive, Falls Church, VA 22041 (703) 998-5550.

Created by Lori H. Gordon, Ph.D., PAIRS is a six-month course that has helped thousands of couples prepare themselves for negotiating love. Although PAIRS is time-consuming, it is worth taking.

The Gender Relations Institute, P.O. Box 4782, Santa Barbara, CA 93140 (805) 963-8285.

Co-founders Dr. Aaron Kipnis and Liz Herron, M.A., offer valuable trainings nationwide for men and women. Their topics include empowerment for women, men's health, and "gender diplomacy" training for professionals.

"Small Kindnesses," 1950 Sawtelle Boulevard, Suite 340, Los Angeles, CA 90025 (310) 829-3353.

Judith Sherven, Ph.D., a practicing psychologist, does workshops with her husband, men's issues expert Jim Sniechowski, Ph.D., around the country for both singles and couples. They are stimulating, skilled leaders well worth inviting to your community.

Source Unlimited, P.O. Box 15826, Chevy Chase, MD 20815 (301) 951-3308.

Patricia McCallum will travel to your area to consult or give a seminar on her cutting-edge concept, Essence Repatterning.

"Venturing Out of the Lodges: Creating Safe and Meaningful Connecting Space for Men and Women," presented by Karen Kahn Wilson, Ed.D., and Joseph Mancini, Ph.D., L.C.S.W., 9215 Quintana Drive, Bethesda, MD 20817.

Karen and Joseph, who are partners in "real life," give this seminar. Since women and men work separately during the day-long session, you don't have to be part of a couple to attend. Send a SASE for a brochure.

SUPPORT GROUPS

FOR WOMEN:

Contact your local women's center, church, or synagogue to find a support group near you. Your hospital, health food store, or college or university bulletin board may also have an announcement posted. When you go to the first meeting, check that the members don't have an obvious antimale bias. If they do, try another support group—or else form your own.

FOR MEN:

Many local communities now have a men's center that sponsors ongoing support groups. Check the directory at the back of *Wingspan: Inside the Men's Movement*, edited by Christopher

Harding, to find a men's center in your area. If you've checked local bulletin boards and the Yellow Pages and still can't find one, write to *MenStuff* or M.R., Inc. (both listed above). Or read Bill Kauth's book *A Circle of Men* and create a support group yourself.

Here are three outstanding men's centers that offer support groups:

Austin Men's Center, 1611 West Sixth Street, Austin, TX 78703 (512) 477-9595.

Recovery expert John Lee has founded this holistic, family-oriented facility. It is a focal point for ongoing support groups in the area.

On the Common Ground/Pathways for a Man, 250 West 57 Street, Suite 1527, New York, NY 10107 (212) 265-0584.

Founded by men's issues expert Dr. John Guarnaschelli, Pathways for a Man has over forty support groups for working-class men in New York City. Spread the word. You may want to contact Dr. Guarnaschelli and bring his program to your city.

Men's Work, P.O. Box 603, Woodstock, NY 12498-0603 (914) 246-3316.

Directed by men's issues expert Onaje Benjamin, this center offers men in the New York area counseling and support groups as well as seminars, workshops, and trainings for men across the nation.

FOR WOMEN AND MEN:

Movement for the Establishment of Real Gender Equality (M.E.R.G.E.), Paul Shaner, Chair, 19502 61st Street, N.E., Seattle, WA 91855 (206) 486-4966.

M.E.R.G.E. holds monthly forums in which women and men practice communication skills as equals. M.E.R.G.E. also has branches in Calgary and Edmonton, Canada, where its founder, Ferrel Christiansen, resides.

Stepfamily Association of America, Inc., 215 Centennial Mall South, Suite #212, Lincoln, NE 68508 (800) 735-0329.

This nonprofit association helps individual members start local chapters with support groups for stepparents and their children.

Where do you go from here? The next step is up to you!

Notes

CHAPTER 1: CAN LOVERS NEGOTIATE?

[1]William Ury, *Getting Past No* (New York: Bantam Books, 1991), p. 3.

[2]Roger Fisher and William Ury, *Getting to Yes* (Boston: Houghton Mifflin, 1991), pp. xi–xii.

[3]*The American Heritage Dictionary of the English Language* New College Edition (Boston: Houghton Mifflin, 1976), p. 1378.

[4]For example, see the popular book by Roger Dawson, *You Can Get Anything You Want: Secrets of Power Negotiating* (New York: Simon & Schuster, 1985), pp. 24–89. This information is also on audiotape: Roger Dawson, *The Secrets of Power Negotiating* (Chicago, Illinois: Nightingale Conant, 1987), sides 3–6.

[5]Roger Fisher and William Ury, *Getting to Yes, op. cit.*, pp. 101–11.

CHAPTER 2: GETTING PAST YOUR ANGER SO YOU CAN SIT DOWN AND TALK

[1]Daniel Henderson, M.Div., D.P.C., interview with author, January 27, 1993.

[2]A handful of us were raised in homes where the grown-ups were always polite.

[3]Onaje Benjamin, interview with author, June 6, 1993; Forrest Craver, interview with author, October 30, 1992.

[4]My colleague Jim Bridy, who facilitates workshops for people in recovery, has assisted me in clarifying the difference between toxic rage and healthy anger.

[5]Tom Daly, Ph.D., and Jude Blitz, interview with author, February 15, 1993.

[6]Irene Gad, Ph.D., interview with author, November 30, 1992.

[7]John Lee, interview with author, January 29, 1994. For additional information about the Woman Within weekend (which I highly recommend), please see the Annotated Resources.

[8]I prefer to use this term, instead of emotional abuse, to emphasize its seriousness.

[9]Brad Blanton, Ph.D., interview with author, December 15, 1992.

[10]Ibid.

[11]Warren Farrell, Ph.D., interview with author, June 10, 1993. Also listen to his audiotape series, *Men Only—A Hero's Journey* (Boulder, Colorado: Sounds True Recordings, 1992), tape 2, side 1.

[12]Tom Daly, Ph.D., and Jude Blitz, interview with author, February 15, 1993.

[13]Susan Jeffers, Ph.D., interview with author, February 24, 1993.

[14]*20/20*, "The Secrets of Staying Together," February 12, 1993, Journal Graphics Transcript #1307.

CHAPTER 3: CREATING THE RIGHT MINDSET: TEN WAYS TO GET TO THE NEGOTIATING COUCH

[1]Judith Sherven, Ph.D., and Jim Sniechowski, Ph.D., interview with author, February 4, 1993.

[2]Tom Daly, Ph.D., and Jude Blitz, interview with author, February 15, 1993.

[3]Jim Sniechowski, Ph.D., and Judith Sherven, Ph.D., *The Healing Power of Relationships* (Boulder, Colorado: Sounds True Cassettes, 1992), tape 1, side A.

[4]Aaron Kipnis, Ph.D., and Liz Herron, M.A., interview with author,

July 22, 1993; Julio Olalla, M.A., interview with author, February 17, 1993.

[5]Joe Smith, talk-show host, WTMJ Radio, Milwaukee, Wisconsin, interview with author, September 5, 1992.

[6]Joseph Palmour, Ph.D., interview with author, December 2, 1993.

[7]Jean Houston, interview with author, August 1, 1993; Marion Woodman, interview with author, January 23, 1993.

[8]Jean Houston, interview with author, August 1, 1993.

[9]See Kare Anderson, *Getting What You Want* (New York: Dutton, 1993), pp. 165–168.

[10]Warren Farrell, Ph.D., *Men Only—A Hero's Journey* (Boulder, Colorado: Sounds True Recordings, 1992), tape 3, side 1.

[11]Roy Schenk, Ph.D., *Let's End the War Between the Sexes* (Boulder, Colorado: Sounds True Recordings, 1992).

[12]See Roberta M. Gilbert, M.D., *Extraordinary Relationships* (Minneapolis, Minnesota: Chronimed Publishing, 1992), pp. 48–49.

[13]See Jeff Wagenheim, "M. Scott Peck's New Road," *New Age Journal*, May/June 1991, pp. 102–105, and M. Scott Peck, *The Different Drum* (New York: Simon & Schuster, 1987), *passim*.

[14]Susan M. Campbell, Ph.D., *The Couples Journey* (San Luis Obispo, California: Impact Publishers, 1980), pp. 148–149.

[15]Ivan Burnell, Ph.D., interview with author, January 29, 1993.

[16]Bill Thompson, Sky Radio talk-show host, and Nancy Thompson, interview with author, February 12, 1993.

[17]See Mel Krantzler, Ph.D., and Patricia B. Krantzler, *The Seven Marriages of Your Marriage* (San Francisco, California: HarperSanFrancisco, 1992), p. 63.

[18]See "Is There Love After Baby?" *Psychology Today*, July/August 1992, p. 78.

[19]*A Course in Miracles* (Glen Ellen, California: Foundation for Inner Peace, 1992), Workbook for Students, lesson 134, p. 249.

[20]Judith Sherven, Ph.D., interview with author, February 4, 1993.

[21]Susan Jeffers, Ph.D., interview with author, February 24, 1993.

[22]Or a neutral third party has to intervene. See Chapter 5, Secret 9. John Murray, Esq., and Jane Juliano, Esq., make this point in a workshop they have given to lawyers, "Representing Your Client in Mediation," Fairfax, Virginia, 1993.

CHAPTER 4: HOW TO REACH AN AGREEMENT THAT SATISFIES YOU BOTH

[1]Aaron Kipnis, Ph.D., interview with author, July 22, 1993.

[2]After each New Warrior Training Adventure weekend, there are follow-up groups that meet weekly. For more information, see Annotated Resources.

[3]The Woman Within, the women's counterpart to the New Warrior Training Adventure, is a good place to start getting in touch with your needs. Further details about this weekend are in Annotated Resources.

[4]Irene Gad, Ph.D., interview with author, November 30, 1992. Your "inner child" is your childhood self that remains within you even when you become an adult. See John Bradshaw, *Homecoming: Reclaiming and Championing Your Inner Child* (New York: Bantam, 1990).

[5]Asa Baber, interview with author, June 15, 1993.

[6]To understand how businesspersons and lawyers negotiate about procedures, see William Ury, *Getting Past No,* pp. 98–102.

[7]Carolyn Pape Cowan, Ph.D., and Philip A. Cowan, Ph.D., "Love After Baby," *Psychology Today*, July/August 1992, p. 78.

[8]For a useful but brief discussion of this topic, see Lori H. Gordon, Ph.D., *Passage to Intimacy* (New York: Simon & Schuster, 1993), pp. 128–129.

[9]Roger Dawson, *You Can Get Anything You Want*, p. 226.

[10]Aaron Kipnis, Ph.D., and Liz Herron, Seminar, Carmel, New York, April 22, 1993.

[11]John Guarnaschelli, Ph.D., interview with author, August 4, 1993.

[12]Bill Kauth, interview with author, February 19, 1993.

[13]William Ury, *Getting Past No*, pp. 128–129.

[14]Julio Olalla, M.A., interview with author, February 17, 1993.

CHAPTER 5: THE ELEVEN SECRETS OF NEGOTIATING LOVE

[1]Judith Sherven, Ph.D., interview with author, February 4, 1993.

[2]Ibid.

[3]See Kare Anderson, *Getting What You Want*, p. 65.
[4]Karen Kahn Wilson, Ed.D., interview with author, November 30, 1992.
[5]Robert Bly makes this point in his excellent tape, *The Male Mode of Feeling* (Pacific Grove, California: Oral Tradition Archives, 1991).
[6]Karen Kahn Wilson, Ed.D., interview with author, November 30, 1992.
[7]Joe Smith, interview with author, September 5, 1992.
[8]Shepherd Bliss, D. Min., interview with author, May 11, 1993.
[9]Ibid.
[10]Ibid.
[11]Robert Bly, interview with author, May 26, 1993.
[12]Ibid. Men's issues expert John Lee also believes that women and men have "different rhythms." To communicate well, both sexes have to give up their longing to have the other absolutely in sync with their own. John Lee, interview with author, January 29, 1994.
[13]Robert Bly, interview with author, May 26, 1993. This exercise is from Maggie Scarf, *Intimate Partners*, New York, Ballantine Books, 1987, pp. 205–9.
[14]John Bradshaw, television special, Channel 19, Jones InterCable Television, December 11, 1992.
[15]Tamiko, interview with author, May 20, 1993.
[16]Forrest Craver, interview with author, October 30, 1992.
[17]Brad Blanton, Ph.D., and Amy Silverman, interview with author, December 5, 1992.
[18]Brad Blanton, Ph.D., interview with author, December 5, 1992.
[19]Susan Jeffers, Ph.D., interview with author, February 24, 1993. Also Brad Blanton, Ph.D., interview with author, December 5, 1992.
[20]Susan Jeffers, Ph.D., interview with author, February 24, 1993.
[21]Brad Blanton, Ph.D., and Amy Silverman, interview with author, December 5, 1992.
[22]Angeles Arrien, Ph.D., interview with author, June 9, 1993. According to Dr. Arrien, Africans, Latinos, and many Europeans are also accustomed to having a third party come in and mediate a dispute.
[23]Donald Greenstein, Esq., interview with author, November 19, 1992, and letter to author, October 31, 1993. Also Angeles Arrien, Ph.D., interview with author, June 9, 1993.

[24]Angeles Arrien, Ph.D., *Change, Conflict and Resolution from a Cross-Cultural Perspective* (Petaluma, California: Angeles Arrien, 1991).

CHAPTER 6: THE SEESAW OF POWER: WHO HAS MORE CONTROL?

[1]See Bill Kauth, M.S., *A Circle of Men* (New York: St. Martin's Press, 1992), pp. 123–24.

[2]See Robert Moore, Ph.D., and Douglas Gillette, *The King Within* (New York: Avon Books, 1992), p. 25.

[3]See Roger Dawson, *The Secrets of Power Negotiating* (Chicago: Nightingale Conant, 1987), tape 7, and Marilyn Loden, *Feminine Leadership* (New York: Times Books, 1985). Dawson and Loden both distinguish between position (external) power and personal (inner) power. Their books are written for businesspersons, not lovers, however.

[4]See Chapter 8 for a complete discussion of the needs lovers have in their relationships.

[5]Jude Blitz, interview with author, February 20, 1993.

[6]William Ury, *Getting Past No*, pp. 144–45.

[7]This concept has been consistently validated both in my own life and in the experiences of my interviewees.

[8]Warren Farrell, Ph.D., refers to this as the "worst infidelity" in *Why Men Are the Way They Are* (New York: McGraw-Hill, 1986), p. 341.

[9]Jim Sniechowski, Ph.D., and Judith Sherven, Ph.D., interview with author, February 4, 1993.

[10]Laurie Ingraham, M.S.W., interview with author, June 28, 1993.

[11]See Samuel Osherson, *Finding Our Fathers* (New York: Fawcett Columbine, 1986), pp. 167–70.

[12]Emily Hancock, *The Girl Within* (New York: Fawcett Columbine, 1989), p. 163.

CHAPTER 7: WHAT TO DO WHEN ROMANCE FADES

[1]Laurie Ingraham, M.S.W., interview with author, June 28, 1993.

[2]Anecdote recounted by Jane Blanchard, reporter, *The Journal and Express*, Alexandria, Virginia, May 9, 1991.

[3]Irene Gad, Ph.D., interview with author, November 30, 1992.
[4]Daphne Rose Kingma, *True Love* (Berkeley, California: Conari Press, 1991), pp. 16–17.
[5]Warren Farrell, Ph.D., *The Myth of Male Power* (New York: Simon & Schuster, 1993), pp. 17–18.
[6]Irene Gad, Ph.D., interview with author, November 30, 1992.
[7]Warren Farrell, Ph.D., interview with author, June 10, 1993.
[8]Liz Mitchell, conversation with author, November 22, 1991.
[9]Ann McGill, speech to the National Council of Career Women, Northern Virginia Branch, July 15, 1992.

CHAPTER 8: HANDLING RELATIONSHIP HOTSPOTS

[1]The Sally Jessy Raphael show, "My Husband's Middle Name Is Cheap," March 8, 1993.
[2]Ivan Burnell, Ph.D., and Dahny Burnell, interview with author, January 29, 1993.
[3]See "Women—a Progress Report: Couples—the Silverbergs Believe in Sharing Family Finances," *Daily Breeze* (Los Angeles), October 8, 1991, p. C-2.
[4]This anecdote was told to me by Daniel Henderson, M. Div., D.P.C., during our interview, January 27, 1993.
[5]Ibid.

CHAPTER 9: HOW WOMEN CAN GET READY TO NEGOTIATE LOVE

[1]Liz Herron, M.A., interview with author, July 22, 1993. Liz is the coauthor (together with Aaron Kipnis, Ph.D.) of *Gender War; Gender Peace* (New York: William Morrow, 1994).
[2]Marion Woodman, interview with author, January 23, 1993.
[3]Jude Blitz, interview with author, February 15, 1993.
[4]James C. Dobson, Ph.D., *What Wives Wish Their Husbands Knew About Women* (Colorado Springs, Colorado: Focus on the Family, 1992), side 1.
[5]Angeles Arrien, Ph.D. *Change, Conflict, and Resolution from a Cross-*

Cultural Perspective (Petaluma, California: Angeles Arrien, 1992), tape 3, side 2. Also Roy Schenk, Ph.D., interview with author, March 11, 1993.

[6]Angeles Arrien, Ph.D., *Change, Conflict, and Resolution from a Cross-Cultural Perspective*, tape 1, side 1.

[7]Ivan Burnell, Ph.D., interview with author, January 29, 1993.

[8]Irene Gad, Ph.D., interview with author, November 30, 1992.

[9]Roy Schenk, Ph.D., interview with author, March 11, 1993.

[10]Marion Woodman, interview with author, January 23, 1993.

[11]Robert Bly, interview with author, May 26, 1993.

[12]For more information, write Woman Within International, 7186 Driftwood Drive, Fenton, MI 48430, or call (810) 750-7227.

[13]Gordon Clay, interview with author, July 17, 1993. See also Victoria Secunda, *Women and Their Fathers* (New York: Delacorte Press, 1992).

[14]For techniques that can be applied to the father-daughter as well as the mother-son relationship, see Michael Gurian, *Mothers, Sons, and Lovers: How a Man's Relationship with His Mother Affects the Rest of His Life* (Boston: Shambhala Publications, 1994), pp. 223–247.

[15]Betty Friedan, *The Feminine Mystique* (Middlesex, England: Penguin Books, 1963).

[16]Liz Herron, M.A., seminar given with Aaron Kipnis, Ph.D., at Arms Acres, Carmel, New York, April 22, 1993.

[17]Daphne Rose Kingma, *The Men We Never Knew* (Berkeley, California: Conari Press, 1993).

[18]Aaron Kipnis, Ph.D., interview with author, July 22, 1993.

[19]Joseph Palmour, Ph.D., interview with author, December 2, 1992.

[20]Warren Farrell, Ph.D., *Men Only—A Hero's Journey* (Boulder, Colorado: Sounds True Audiotapes, 1992), tape 1, side A.

[21]Gordon Clay, interview with author, July 17, 1993.

[22]Asa Baber, interview with author, June 15, 1993.

[23]Ibid.

[24]Onaje Benjamin, interview with author, June 6, 1993.

[25]Alice Forrester, interview with author, July 7, 1992.

[26]If this man had initially taken responsibility for birth control, he probably wouldn't have been in this predicament.

[27]These women have been labeled "difference feminists." See Katha Pollitt, "Are Women Morally Superior to Men?" *Utne Reader*, September/October 1993 (reprinted from *The Nation*, December 28, 1992).

CHAPTER 10: HOW MEN CAN GET READY TO NEGOTIATE LOVE

[1]I am indebted to Robert Bly for making this important distinction in his audiotape *The Male Mode of Feeling*. Robert Bly, *Iron John and the Male Mode of Feeling* (Pacific Grove, California: Oral Tradition Archives, 1989), side 2.

As a result, men's wounds differ from women's. Certain wounds are more common among men—for example, the buddy wound. Others, such as the boss wound, are more prevalent among women. A wound that women and men both have, such as the self wound, is generally deeper in women, according to my experience. This is why my descriptions of women's and men's wounds are not identical.

[2]Robert Bly, interview with author, May 26, 1993.

[3]Samuel Osherson, *Finding Our Fathers* (New York: Fawcett Columbine, 1986), p. 9; Willard Gaylin, M.D., *The Male Ego* (New York: Viking, 1992), p. 170.

[4]Robert Bly, interview with author, May 26, 1993.

[5]Asa Baber, interview with author, June 15, 1993; Robert Bly, interview with author, May 26, 1993.

[6]Asa Baber, interview with author, June 15, 1993; Michael Gurian, interview with author, January 24, 1994. See Robert Moore and Douglas Gillette, *The Warrior Within* (New York: William Morrow and Company, 1992), pp. 102–103.

[7]Gordon Clay, interview with author, July 17, 1993.

[8]For more information about the New Warrior Training Adventure, write the New Warrior Network, National Headquarters, 61 Bullard Pasture Road, Wendell, MA 01379, or call (800) 870-4611.

[9]Gordon Clay, interview with author, July 17, 1993.

[10]Aaron Kipnis, Ph.D., interview with author, July 22, 1993. See

Aaron Kipnis, Ph.D., *Knights Without Armor* (Los Angeles, California: Jeremy P. Tarcher, 1991).

[11]John Lee, interview with author, January 29, 1994. See his book, *At My Father's Wedding: Men Coming to Terms with Their Fathers and Themselves* (New York: Bantam Books, 1991), pp. 45–46 for a poignant description of how the numbing process begins.

[12]John Guarnaschelli, Ph.D., interview with author, August 4, 1993.

[13]Daniel Henderson, M. Div., D.P.C., and David Ebaugh, M.A., C.P.C., interview with author, January 27, 1993.

[14]Gordon Clay, interview with author, July 17, 1993.

[15]Char Tosi in *Good Will Toward Men* by Jack Kammer (New York: St. Martin's Press, 1994).

[16]Aaron Kipnis, Ph.D., interview with author, July 22, 1993.

[17]John Guarnaschelli, Ph.D., interview with author, August 4, 1993.

[18]"What Do Men Really Want?" *Time*, Fall 1990, p. 82.

[19]Forrest Craver, "The Glory of Manhood," *Chesapeake Men's Exchange*, March 1993, pp. 1, 4.

[20]Christopher Harding, Ph.D., conversation with author, January 20, 1993.

[21]See Mark Gerzon, *A Choice of Heroes* (Boston: Houghton Mifflin Company, 1992), pp. 259–61.

[22]John Guarnaschelli, Ph.D., interview with author, August 4, 1993.

[23]Stuart A. Miller, Senior Legislative Analyst, American Fathers Coalition, Washington, D.C., conversation with author, July 12, 1994. According to the U.S. Census Bureau, 79 percent of fathers with visitation privileges pay their child support, while 90.2 percent of fathers with joint custody pay. U.S. Census Bureau, "Child Support and Alimony," 1989, Series P-6, #173, pp. 6–7.

[24]Fred Hayward, interview with author, July 16, 1992. Fred Hayward's source is an article by Bryan E. Robinson, Ph.D., in the *American Journal of Orthopsychiatry*, January 1988, quoted in *Behavior Today*, February 8, 1988.

[25]Robert Moore, Ph.D., interview with author, August 17, 1993. See Robert Moore, Ph.D., and Douglas Gillette, *The King Within* (New York: Avon Books, 1992).

[26]Roy Schenk, Ph.D., interview with author, March 11, 1993. See Roy Schenk, Ph.D., *The Other Side of the Coin* (Madison, Wisconsin: Bioenergetics Press, 1992).

[27]Joseph Palmour, Ph.D., interview with author, December 2, 1992.

CHAPTER 11: WHAT WOMEN AND MEN NEED: A NEW CONVERSATION

[1]Laurie Ingraham, M.S.W., interview with author, June 28, 1993.

[2]Susan Jeffers, *The Journey from Lost to Found* (New York: Ballantine Books, 1993), p. 87; Susan Jeffers, Ph.D., interview with author, February 24, 1993.

[3]Bill Kauth, interview with author, February 19, 1993.

[4]Alice Forrester, interview with author, July 7, 1992.

[5]Paul Cassidy, talk-show host, WGY Radio, Schenectady, New York, August 16, 1992.

[6]See Rush H. Limbaugh, III, *The Way Things Ought to Be* (New York: Pocket Books, 1992), pp. 193–194.

[7]Daphne Rose Kingma, interview with author, February 15, 1993.

[8]Forrest Craver, interview with author, October 30, 1992. Forrest made this statement with regard to men receiving women's anger, but the reverse is also true.

[9]In *Men Only—A Hero's Journey* (Boulder, Colorado: Sounds True Recordings, 1992), Warren Farrell, Ph.D., presents a superb workshop about how to give and receive criticism which I highly recommend to *both* women and men.

[10]Robert Bly, interview with author, May 26, 1993.

[11]The expert who told me this story asked not to be identified.

[12]Jean Houston, interview with author, August 1, 1993.

[13]Robert Bly, *Men and Women Talking Together*, audiotape together with Deborah Tannen (New York: Sound Horizons, 1992), tape 2, side B.

[14]Daphne Rose Kingma, *True Love* (Berkeley, California: Conari Press, 1991), pp. 10–11.

CHAPTER 12: HEALING EACH OTHER

[1]Harry Stein, "Pigs 'R Us," *Psychology Today*, July/August, 1992, p. 87.

[2]Jean Houston, interview with author, August 1, 1993.

[3]Judith Sherven, Ph.D., in *Good Will Toward Men* by Jack Kammer (New York: St. Martin's Press, 1994), p. 21.

[4]Fighting fairly without nastiness is actually good for your health, according to Timothy Smith, Ph.D., quoted in "Love and Longevity" by Linda Murray, *Longevity*, October, 1993, p. 84.

[5]Robert Moore, Ph.D., interview with author, August 17, 1993.

[6]Karen Kahn Wilson, Ed.D., interview with author, November 30, 1992. Dr. Wilson referred to these feelings as "our shadow."

[7]How do you know if your "little observer" is correct? Usually it is, if you feel its message deep within. If you have doubts, check with your lover and see if her/his assessment is similar. Even if it isn't, in the last analysis you have to trust yourself.

[8]Thich Nhat Hanh, "The Roots of War," *Common Ground*, Autumn, 1993, p. 157.

[9]Jerry Kiwala, talk-show host, WMT, Cedar Rapids, Iowa, August 13, 1992.

[10]I believe that lesbian and gay couples can negotiate love with each other and that parents can negotiate love with their children. Because there are different power dynamics and cultural factors in gay, lesbian, and parent-child loving negotiations, they are all subjects for future research.

Index

INDEX

INDEX

INDEX

INDEX

BACHRACH

ABOUT THE AUTHOR

RIKI ROBBINS JONES, Ph.D., is a Phi Beta Kappa graduate of Wellesley College and holds a Ph.D. in political science from Harvard University. She is the author of *The Empowered Woman*, the founder of the Network for Empowering Women (NEW), the creator of the International Gender Reconciliation Conference, and a frequent guest on radio and television shows. An expert in gender issues, Dr. Jones conducts "Negotiating Love" seminars throughout the United States and around the world.